Personal Effectiveness

Third edition

Alex Murdock and Carol N. Scutt

chartered
management
institute

OXFORD AMSTERDAM BOSTON LONDON NEW YORK PARIS
SAN DIEGO SAN FRANCISCO SINGAPORE SYDNEY TOKYO

Butterworth-Heinemann
An imprint of Elsevier Science
Linacre House, Jordan Hill, Oxford OX2 8DP
200 Wheeler Road, Burlington MA 01803

First published 1993
Reprinted 1994, 1995
Second edition 1997
Third edition 2003

British Library Cataloguing in Publication Data
A catalogue record for this book is available from the British Library

ISBN 0 7506 5622 0

For information on all Butterworth-Heinemann publications
visit our website at www.bh.com

Typeset by Keyword Typesetting Services Ltd, Wallington, Surrey
Printed and bound in Great Britain

For Zöe, Lauren and Molly

Contents

CONTENTS

Series adviser's preface

This book is one of a series designed for people wanting to develop their capabilities as managers. You might think that there isn't anything very new in that. In one way you would be right. The fact that very many people want to learn to become better managers is not new, and for many years a wide range of approaches to such learning and development has been available. These have included courses leading to formal qualifications, organizationally-based management development programmes and a whole variety of self-study materials. A copious literature, extending from academic textbooks to sometimes idiosyncratic prescriptions from successful managers and consultants, has existed to aid – or perhaps confuse – the potential seeker after managerial truth and enlightenment.

So what is new about this series? In fact, a great deal – marking in some ways a revolution in our thinking both about the art of managing and also the process of developing managers.

Where did it all begin? Like most revolutions, although there may be a single, identifiable act that precipitated the uprising, the roots of discontent are many and long-established. The debate about the performance of British managers, the way managers are educated and trained, and the extent to which shortcomings in both these areas have contributed to our economic decline, has been running for several decades.

Until recently, this debate had been marked by periods of frenetic activity – stimulated by some report or enquiry and perhaps ending in some new initiatives or policy changes – followed by relatively long periods of comparative calm. But the underlying causes for concern persisted. Basically, the majority of managers in the UK appeared to have little or no training for their role, certainly far less than their counterparts in our major competitor nations. And there was concern about the nature, style and appropriateness of the management education and training that was available.

- British managers are undertrained by comparison with their counterparts internationally.
- The majority of employers invest far too little in training and developing their managers.
- Many employers find it difficult to specify with any degree of detail just what it was that they required successful managers to be able to do.

Under the umbrella of the National Forum for Management Education and Development (NFMED) a series of employer-led working parties tackled the problem of defining what it was that managers should be able to do, and how this differed for people at different levels in their organizations; how this satisfactory ability to perform might be verified; and how an appropriate structure of management qualifications could be put in place. This work drew upon the methods used to specify vocational standards in industry and commerce, and led to the development and introduction of competence-based management standards and qualifications. In this context, competence is defined as the ability to perform the activities within an occupation or function to the standards expected in employment.

The series was originally commissioned to support the Chartered Management Institute's Diploma and Executive Diploma qualifications, which were one of the first to be based on the vocational standards. However, these books are equally appropriate to any university, college or indeed company course leading to a certificate in management or diploma in management studies.

The standards were specified through an extensive process of consultation with a large number of managers in organizations of many different typcs and sizes. They are therefore employment based and employer-supported. And they fill the gap that Mangham and Silver identified – now we do have a language to describe what it is employers want their managers to be able to do – at least in part.

If you are engaged in any form of management development leading to a certificate or diploma qualification conforming to the national management standards, then you are probably already familiar with most of the key ideas on which the standards are based. To achieve their key purpose, which is defined as achieving the organization's objectives and continuously improving its performance, managers need to perform four key roles: managing operations, managing finance, managing people and managing information. Each of these key roles has a sub-structure of units and elements, each with associated performance and assessment criteria.

The reason for the qualification 'in part' is that organizations are different, and jobs within them are different. Thus the generic management standards probably do not cover all the management competencies that you may need to possess in your job. There are almost certainly additional things, specific to your own situation in your own organization, that you need to be able to do. The standards are necessary, but almost certainly not sufficient. Only you, in discussion with your boss, will be able to decide what other capabilities you need to possess. But the standards are a place to start, a basis on which to build. Once you have demonstrated your proficiency against the standards, it will stand you in good stead as you progress through your organization, or change jobs.

So how do the standards change the process by which you develop yourself as a manger? They change the process of development, or of gaining a management qualification, quite a lot. It is no longer a question of acquiring information and facts, perhaps by being 'taught' in some classroom environment, and then being tested to see what you can recall. It involves demonstrating, in a quite specific way, that you can do certain things to a particular standard of performance. And because of this, it puts a much greater onus on you to manage your own development, to decide how you can demonstrate any particular competence, what evidence you need to present, and how you can collect it. Of course, there will always be people to advise and guide you in this, if you need help.

But there is another dimension, and it is to this that this series of books is addressed. While the standards stress ability to perform, they do not ignore the traditional knowledge base that has been associated with management studies. Rather, they set this in a different context. The standards are supported by 'underpinning knowledge and understanding' which has three components:

- Purpose and context, which is knowledge and understanding of the manager's objectives, and of the relevant organizational and environmental influences, opportunities and values.
- Principles and methods, which is knowledge and understanding of the theories, models, principles, methods and techniques that provide the basis of competent managerial performance.

■ Data, which is knowledge and understanding of specific facts likely to be important to meeting the standards.

Possession of the relevant knowledge and understanding underpinning the standards is needed to support competent mangerial performance as specified in the standards. It also has an important role in supporting the transferability of management capabilities. It helps to ensure that you have done more than learned 'the way we do things around here' in your own organization. It indicates a recognition of the wider things which underpin competence, and that you will be able to change jobs or organizations and still be able to perform effectively.

These books cover the knowledge and understanding underpinning the management standards, most specifically in the category of principles and methods. But their coverage is not limited to the minimum required by the standards, and extends in both depth and breadth in many areas. The authors have tried to approach these underlying principles and methods in a practical way. They use many short cases and examples which we hope will demonstrate how, in practice, the principles and methods, and knowledge of purpose and context plus data, support the ability to perform as required by the management standards. In particular we hope that this type of presentation will enable you to identify and learn from similar examples in your own managerial work.

You will already have noticed that one consequence of this focus on the standards is that the traditional 'functional' packages of knowledge and theory do not appear. The standard textbook titles such as 'quantitative methods', 'production management', 'organizational behaviour' etc. disappear. Instead, principles and methods have been collected together in clusters that more closely match the key roles within the standards. You will also find a small degree of overlap in some of the volumes, because some principles and methods support several of the individual units within the standards. We hope you will find this useful reinforcement.

There is still some debate about the way competencies are defined, and whether those in the standards are the most appropriate on which to base assessment of managerial performance. There are other models of management competencies than those in the standards. We should also be careful not to see the standards as set in stone. They determine what today's managers need to be able to do. As the arena in which managers operate changes, then so will the standards. The lesson for all of us as managers is that we need to go on learning and developing, acquiring new skills or refining existing ones. Obtaining your certificate or diploma is like passing a mile post, not crossing the finishing line.

All the changes and developments of recent years have brought management qualifications, and the processes by which they are gained, much closer to your job as a manager. We hope these books support this process by providing bridges between your own experience and the underlying principles and methods which will help you to demonstrate your competence. Already, there is a lot of evidence that managers enjoy the challenge of demonstrating competence, and find immediate benefits in their jobs from the programmes based on these new-style qualifications. We hope you do too. Good luck in your career development.

From 2nd Edition
Paul Jervis

Foreword to the third edition

Since the publication of the second edition of *Personal Effectiveness* in 1997, many changes have come about.

Like any area of management in these times of constant change, the National Standards for Management (management competences— the processes/function of management) have also changed, from the Management Charter Initiative (MCI)—originally their 'caretakers' (from 1991 to 2000)—to the Chartered Management Institute (was the Institute of Management) by whom they will be revised during the next two years in the continuous process of improving the management of people, processes, information and physical resources. It is likely that the Personal Competency Model (PCM)—the individual competencies or behavioural underpinnings of these processes or functions—will also be further developed.

Whilst this book follows the PCM currently in favour, it also anticipates some developments, which are vital to all managers/professionals' continuing professional development. It is with this in mind that the chapters as detailed in the table of contents have evolved from the two previous editions.

We have endeavoured to retain the simplicity of our approach whilst developing the effectiveness behind contemporary leadership and team-building which makes full use, as well as to promote the development, of all individuals comprising those teams. All the competencies defined and promoted are essentially what you need to become effective leaders of high-performing work teams. Such teams may be relatively constant in your working environment, or they emerge periodically in order to undertake *specific* projects for *specified* periods to meet *specific* objectives.

We hope you enjoy this book and are able to apply and develop further the concepts and models identified within it. You will see that a number of contributions of varying experience have been made to the book by managers and professionals carrying out roles similar to your own. These key contributions come from those from a wide range of organizational backgrounds and cultures. But please remember, they are 'snapshots' taken at specific times, during periods of (sometimes major) change and development, and the organizations concerned may already have moved on significantly.

Learning can be negative (how *not* to do something in certain situations or circumstances) as well as positive, so you may identify approaches and concepts that are not appropriate to you, or to your organization, or to its stage of development, as well as those that are.

Best wishes and happy learning.

Alexander Murdock
Carol N. Scutt
August 2002

Glossary of terms

Adviser In the context of NVQ, SVQ, or crediting occupational competence purposes, an adviser is a person specially trained and accredited to help in the process of development and in the compilation of evidence for assessment.

Approved centre An organization that has been approved by an awarding body to deliver assessment to NVQs/SVQs.

Assessment The process by which a manager is judged as competent (or not yet competent) against the Management Standards.

Assessment contract This is a document summarizing the units and elements for which a manager will be seeking credit and the date by which they undertake to present their completed portfolio (or sections of it). It is signed by the manager and the crediting competence adviser.

Assessor The person who undertakes the formal evaluation and assessment of a manager's evidence for the purpose of judging whether he/she is competent. The assessor requires EOSC units D32 and D33 and be able to accurately interpret the Management Standards, against the manager's job, to the level being assessed.

Authenticity Concerns whether evidence in your portfolio is genuinely the result of your own work (if it is the result of group work you will need to directly identify your role).

Award In the N/SVQ context, an award is another name for a qualification.

Awarding body A body that develops and awards the qualifications based on Occupational Standards.

Business links Business links are contracted to Training and Enterprise Councils (TECs) to provide business support services in a local area. There could be a number of outlets working to the hub of the business link. Formed from partnerships often involving services from local enterprise agencies, chambers of commerce, local authorities and transferred activities from TECs.

Continuing professional development (CPD) CPD can be used in association with any Management Standard to help managers take responsibility for their own learning and continue their development through planned activities (real and simulated) which are clearly defined and have measurable outcomes.

Career profile The career profile enables you to list your experiences, responsibilities, accomplishments, training, education and voluntary activities, which will help you identify your competences.

Competence The ability to perform in the workplace to the standards required in employment.

Competency The personal behaviour (note: *competency* applies to behavioural skills, whereas *competence* applies to functional performance) required in order to achieve competence. The Personal Competency Model defines this behaviour under various categories.

Context Another word for situation. A competent manager or supervisor must be able to show that they are competent in a variety of contexts (see Transferability.)

Credit It is possible for individuals to gain one credit per unit of competence towards a full qualification. For management, there are between 8 and 10 units per level of qualification.

Element of competence Describes what a manager is expected to be able to do within one aspect of his/her role.

Evidence Material that directly or indirectly proves individuals' competence. This material might include documents, video recordings, audio recordings, photographs, published material, etc.

External verifier A person appointed by the awarding body to provide independent verification on the quality of assessments and internal quality assurance arrangements at centres. The external verifier requires EOSC units D35, D32 and D33.

Generic This is a term used for all MCI Standards, meaning that they apply to all managers, or potential managers, from any sector or industry.

Internal verifier A person within the approved centre with responsibility for ensuring quality of assessment within a centre. The internal verifier requires EOSC units D34, D32 and D33.

Key roles Different areas in which a manager operates within their role.

Key purpose (of management) To achieve the organization's objectives and continuously improve its performance.

Knowledge and understanding The knowledge and understanding which underpins competent performance.

Management Standards The National Standards of performance for managers and supervisors, developed by the MCI under contract from the DfEE as part of the National Standards programme.

Mentor A person who assists a manager to develop and grow personally, often a more experienced manager.

National Standard Statement of what is expected in terms of competent performance in employment.

QCA (Qualifications and Curriculum Authority) The accrediting body for all NVQs and GNVQs in England, Wales and Northern Ireland.

NVQ National Vocational Qualification

Performance criteria The outcomes that a manager has to achieve in order to demonstrate competent performance.

Personal competency The Personal Competency Model (PCM) serves to identify the personal qualities, skills and attributes which are associated with effective management behaviour.

Portfolio An individual manager's package of information and evidence necessary to support his/her claim to competence. A portfolio may contain, as well as documentary evidence, photographs, video recordings, audio recordings, published material, etc.

SQA (Scottish Qualifications Authority) Scottish accrediting body for VQS. SCOTVEC is also the Awarding Body for SVQs in Scotland. There are some UK-based awarding bodies who also award SVQs.

SVQ Scottish Vocational Qualification.

Total quality management Provides internal and external customers with products and services that fully satisfy mutually agreed requirements, at the lowest cost.

Transferability The ability to perform competently in various contexts/situations.

Unit of competence A grouping of elements of competence, covering part of a manager's role. This is the level at which assessment for NVQs/SVQs takes place and is the smallest part of a set of standards which can be awarded separate certification.

Introduction

THE AIMS OF THIS BOOK

This book aims at introducing the manager to the *idea* of managerial *competence* (effective performance) and the underlying *techniques and approaches* required in personal *competency* (behaviour and skills) in order to achieve effective performance. In particular:

- It identifies the personal effectiveness skills involved in the gaining of competence.
- It identifies the central role of communication in all aspects of personal effectiveness.
- It shows the relationship to the national units of managerial *competence* and personal *competency* required to perform at management level 4 (National Qualifications Framework—academic and NVQ level), including those managers who, for example, may also be studying for the Advanced Certificate or Diploma in Management (Chartered Management Institute new courses) based on the national Units of Competence, as well as the continuing development of experienced managers.

Whilst the book introduces you to certain theoretical concepts and models throughout the chapters, it is not the authors' intention to provide the background and history for each. This is adequately explored by other authors and the recommendations for further reading will provide this for you, as well as the specialist thinking behind each topic area.

LINKS TO THE CHARTERED MANAGEMENT INSTITUTE'S MODULE 'UNDERSTANDING YOURSELF'

With the exception of Chapters 3, 6, 9 and 10, the chapters relate directly to the Chartered Management Institute's Certificate level module 'Understanding Yourself'. All chapters, however, have significance for 'Personal Development Planning'. Thus, for those who are participating in the Institute's Advanced Certificate in Management programme, the aims of this particular module and where they link to this text are given in Figure I.1.

BACKGROUND TO THE UNITS OF COMPETENCE

As the result of various research carried out in the 1980s by such leading authorities in the field of managerial competence as Charles B. Handy, The National Forum for Management Education and Development was established to identify the competences required by British managers and to obtain employer commitment to the development of their managers. The National Forum, of which the Management Charter Initiative (MCI) was the operating arm, was the industry-lead body recognized by the Department for Education and Employment for the development of competence-based standards in the area of management from 1991 to 2000.

Recruitment of employers, academic institutions and private agencies was achieved through approaches by, and public relations exer-

Module aims & learning outcomes At the end of the module, participants should be able to:	Linked to chapters:
Evaluate their use of time and resources at work and identify strategies for improvement	1, 4 and 8
Understand the impact of their behaviour on other people in a range of management situations (performance management, conflict situations, team-working, deadline delivery)	1, 2, 4, 5, 8 and 10
Demonstrate how they can gain more flexibility in their style and approach to others, to enhance the delivery of the above objective	1, 2, 5, and 7
Construct a short-term, one-year, (SMART) Personal Development Plan based on an awareness of their strengths as a manager and their development needs	7, 8 (and all chapters as regarding 'action planning')

Figure I.1
Extract from 'Understanding Yourself' module, Chartered Management Institute (1995).

cises launched through, the Confederation of British Industry (CBI), the British Institute of Management (BIM) (now the Chartered Management Institute) and other National Forum members and founder members of the MCI.

The Chartered Management Institute became the caretaker of the national standards of competence and related materials in 2000 and is currently charged with the further review of the standards to meet the managerial challenges of the new millennium. These are due to be completed in 2004 and will be the third version of the national standards of competence across the four main key roles, which in general cover: A, managing activities; B, managing physical and financial resources; C, managing self and others; and D, managing information and methods of communication. There are a number of specialist standards in current use—for example, managing projects, management consultancy, managing energy, senior management—and these are likely to be added to.

WHAT IS PERSONAL EFFECTIVENESS?

Personal effectiveness is herein defined as a distinct set of behavioural competencies (as opposed to competences that define the performance of functions) that are a group of skills embedded within all work-related activities. Personal effectiveness relates to the behavioural aspects of the *national standards of managerial competence* as identified holistically in the *integrated model of personal competency* (Figure I.2).

Each *unit of managerial competence* (which includes the relevant standard to be achieved in the form of a specific set of performance criteria and the knowledge specification against which individuals can develop) also provides the performance and knowledge evidence requirements and guidance for individual assessment for the award of National or Scottish Vocational Qualifications (N/SVQs). Every unit has an identified set of *key behaviours* without which a manager will not be able to achieve competence.

Key behaviours *are* the personal competencies needed by managers in order to develop effective performance. It is these key behaviours which this book attempts to help managers build and apply appropriately.

THE IMPORTANCE OF DEVELOPING SELF-KNOWLEDGE

In order to achieve personal competency, it is necessary for you, as the manager (or potential manager), to understand your own strengths, to maximize them as well as to identify your own weaknesses and learn how to overcome them. By taking responsibility for your own learning through self-development, you will be able to improve your own opportunities and prospects, as well as build the ability to facilitate the identification of the strengths and weaknesses of others. This, in turn, will provide you with the opportunity to agree with others how to address their own self-development needs, through formal reviews, daily interaction and informal feedback, advice and guidance.

This book's ethos is therefore about managers developing self-knowledge and applying it to their behaviour, both in relation to their own job performance and in the role of leading and managing others. By *managing others*, the authors are referring both to those managers who have direct line responsibility for their own staff and those *working with and through people* who are not necessarily their direct responsibility. Each chapter makes its own contribution to this self-knowledge ethos, and readers are invited to approach any of them, in any order, according to their immediate needs, as well as for their future development plans.

FURTHER READING

At the end of each chapter, you will be given suggestions for further reading, several of which will be repeated in other chapters. If your access to further texts is limited for any reason, the following titles should provide you with sufficient information and ideas to further your own development:

Hannagan, T. (1995) *Management Concepts and Practices*. London: Pitman Publishing

Honey, P. and Mumford, A. (1988) *Learning Styles*. Maidenhead: Peter Honey

Honey, P. and Mumford, A. (1990) *The Manual of Learning Opportunities*. Maidenhead: Peter Honey

Howell, J. P. and Costley, D.L. (2001) *Understanding Behaviours for Effective Leadership*. New Jersey: Prentice Hall

Morris, M. (2001) *The First-time Manager* (revised 2nd edition). London: Kogan Page

Pedler, M. and Boydell, T. (1985) *Managing Yourself.* London: Fontana

Pedler, M., Burgoyne, J. and Boydell, T. (1986) *A Manager's Guide to Self-Development.* Maidenhead: McGraw-Hill

Whetton, D., Cameron, K. and Woods, M. (2000) *Developing Management Skills for Europe* (2nd edition). Harlow: Pearson Education

THE UNITS OF COMPETENCE AND THE PERSONAL COMPETENCY MODEL

The overview of the standards of competence and their groupings (Appendix 2) identifies how they fit into the N/SVQ structure. The standards themselves can be obtained directly from the Chartered Management Institute at their HQ in Corby.

The Personal Competency Model (PCM) (Figure I.2; full version in Appendix 3) identifies the behaviours and skills necessary for you to develop before you are able to prove competence in the functions as identified in each of the units identified (Appendix 2). Whilst each chapter attempts to separate out the various behaviours and skills for ease of learning and development, it must be understood that all these behaviours and skills are necessary for managers to apply across

Behavioural indicator	Subindicators
Acting assertively	—
Acting strategically	—
Behaving ethically	—
Building teams	Managing others Relating to others
Communicating	—
Focusing on results	Planning and prioritizing Striving for excellence
Influencing others	—
Managing self	Controlling emotions and stress Managing personal learning and development
Searching for information	—
Thinking and decision-making	Analysing Conceptualizing Taking decisions

Figure I.2
Overview of the Personal Competency Model (Crown Copyright, 1997).

all the units of competence, at different times and under varying circumstances.

CHAPTER OVERVIEW

The chapters in this book address each of these ten areas of personal competency, although not necessarily in the same order. More recent developments have also been incorporated into this edition of the book. The titles and detailed behavioural *outcomes* within each of the personal competencies, as shown above, do not always reflect those used in the chapters, although the relationship should be easily identifiable from the chapter descriptions below. The *outcomes* used in each of the chapters are there for learning and development purposes and can been seen as *objectives* to be achieved following input received, exercises undertaken, case studies followed or on-the-job learning and observational outputs obtained, and so forth.

Chapter 1

Chapter 1 looks at the need for managers to develop their ability in *building teams.*

> Managers who build effective teams encourage team effort, build cohesion and maintain motivation.

There are two major behaviours addressed in this chapter. The first looks at competency needed in *relating and showing sensitivity to others.* This involves the manager developing skills and behaviour so that she/he:

- Actively builds effective working relationships with others.
- Makes time available to support others in assuming responsibility in and for their work.
- Encourages and stimulates others to make the best use of their abilities.
- Evaluates and enhances people's capability to do the job, taking the necessary action to ensure they receive the appropriate training and development as needed.
- Provides constructive feedback that is designed to improve people's future performance.
- Shows respect for the views and actions of others.

- Shows sensitivity to the needs and feelings of others.
- Uses power and authority in a fair and equitable manner.

The second set of behaviours addresses the important competency of *managing and obtaining the commitment of others.* This involves the manager developing behaviours that guarantees that she/he:

- Keeps others informed about plans and progress.
- Clearly identifies what is required of, and by, others.
- Invites others to contribute to the planning and organizing of work.
- Agrees and sets objectives that are both achievable and challenging.
- Checks individuals' understanding and commitment to a specific course of action.
- Uses a variety of techniques to promote good morale and individuals' productivity.
- Protects others and their work against negative impacts.
- Identifies and resolves causes of conflict or resistance between individuals, within groups, or those between individuals or groups and the organization.
- Communicates a vision that generates excitement, enthusiasm and commitment.

Chapter 2

Chapter 2 helps individual managers to develop their *communication and presentation* skills.

> *Managers with skills in communication and presentation are able to share information, ideas and arguments with a variety of audiences.*

This involves the manager in performing in such a way that she/he:

- Listens actively, asks questions, clarifies points and rephrases others' statements to check mutual understanding.
- Adopts personal communication and presentation styles appropriate to listeners and situations, including selecting an appropriate time and place for the event.
- Uses a variety of media and communication aids to reinforce points and maintain interest.

- Presents difficult ideas, concepts and problems in a way that promotes understanding.
- Confirms listeners' understanding through questioning and interpretation of non-verbal signals.
- Encourages listeners to ask questions or rephrase statements to clarify their understanding.
- Modifies communication and presentation in response to expectations, responses and feedback from listeners as necessary.

Chapter 3

Chapter 3 addresses the more controversial topic of *ethical perspective*.

Managers with an ethical perspective identify concerns and resolve complex dilemmas in an open reasoned manner.

This chapter invites the manager to develop behaviours that demonstrate that she/he:

- Complies with legislation, industry regulation, professional and organizational codes.
- Shows integrity and fairness in decision-making.
- Sets objectives and creates cultures that are ethical.
- Identifies the interests of stakeholders and their implications for the organization and individuals.
- Clearly identifies and raises ethical concerns relevant to the organization.
- Works towards resolution of ethical dilemmas based on reasoned approaches.
- Understands and resists personal pressures that encourage non-ethical behaviour.
- Understands and resists apparent pressures from organizational systems to achieve results by any means.

Chapter 4

Chapter 4 identifies the need for all managers to *focus on results*.

Managers who focus on results are proactive and take responsibility for getting things done.

There are two major sets of behaviour addressed in this chapter. The first identifies that, when a manager is *planning and prioritizing objectives*, behaviour is developed which shows that she/he:

- Maintains a focus on objectives.
- Tackles problems or takes advantage of opportunities as they arise.
- Prioritizes objectives and schedules work to make best use of time and resources.
- Sets objectives in uncertain and complex situations.
- Focuses personal attention on specific details that are critical to the success of a key event.

The second set of behaviours contained in this chapter concentrates on the manager *showing commitment to excellence*. In showing such concern, it is believed by management gurus that the individual manager:

- Actively seeks to do things better.
- Uses change as an opportunity for improvement.
- Establishes and communicates high expectations of performance, including setting an example to others.
- Sets goals that are demanding of self and others.
- Monitors quality of work and progress against plans.
- Continually strives to identify and minimize barriers to excellence.

Chapter 5

Chapter 5 focuses on the need for the manager to develop skills in *influencing others*.

> Managers who are able to influence the behaviour of others plan their approaches and communicate clearly using a variety of techniques.

This requires development of behaviour by the manager (keeping ethical considerations in mind at all times) whereby she/he:

- Develops and uses contacts to trade information and obtain support and the necessary resources.
- Creates and prepares strategies for influencing others.
- Presents herself or himself positively to others.

- Uses a variety of techniques, as appropriate to the audience and circumstances, to influence others.
- Understands the culture of the organization and acts to work within it or influence its change or development.

Chapter 6

Chapter 6 is about *information search*. This is a skill that is often underestimated by managers and left to others to perform, but is, nonetheless, an exceptionally important managerial skill.

> *Managers with information search skills gather many different kinds of information, using a variety of means, develop important working relationships and produce better decisions as a result.*

In developing this skill, the manager:

- Establishes information networks to search for and gather relevant information.
- Actively encourages the free exchange of information.
- Makes best use of existing sources of information.
- Seeks information from multiple sources.
- Challenges the validity and reliability of sources of information.
- Pushes for concrete information in ambiguous situations.

Chapter 7

Chapter 7 highlights the need for the manager to develop *self-confidence and personal drive*.

> *Managers with self-confidence and personal drive, show resilience and determination to succeed in the face of pressure and difficulties.*

In demonstrating this behaviour, the manager:

- Takes a leading role in initiating action and making decisions.
- Takes personal responsibility for making things happen.
- Takes control of situations and events.
- Acts in an assured and unhesitating manner when faced with a challenge.

- Says no to unreasonable requests.
- States her/his own position and views clearly in conflict situations.
- Maintains beliefs, commitment and effort in spite of setbacks or opposition.

Chapter 8

Chapter 8 is about *self-management* and the belief that, in order to manage others and/or tasks, a manager must first manage him/herself.

> *Managers skilled in managing themselves show adaptability to the changing world, taking advantage of new ways of doing things.*

Again, there are two major sets of behaviour highlighted in this chapter. The first concentrates on the importance of the individual manager's *self-control*, whereby she/he focuses on her/his own stress management and:

- Gives a consistent and stable performance.
- Takes action to reduce the causes of stress.
- Accepts personal comments or criticism without becoming defensive or offensive.
- Remains calm in difficult or uncertain situations.
- Handles others' emotions without becoming personally involved in them.

The second behavioural set focuses on *managing personal learning and development.* In this situation, the manager:

- Takes responsibility for meeting her/his own learning and development needs.
- Seeks feedback on performance to identify his/her own strengths and weaknesses (*and, in addition, carries out self-administered diagnostic exercises*—authors' italics).
- Learns from her/his own mistakes and those of others.
- Changes behaviour where needed as a result of feedback.
- Reflects systematically on own performance and modifies behaviour accordingly.
- Develops self to meet the competence demand of changing situations.
- Transfers learning from one situation to another.

Chapter 9

Chapter 9 is about the manager's *strategic perspective*.

> *Managers with a strategic perspective identify the way forward in a complex environment, referring constantly to a longer-term vision for the organization.*

In order to demonstrate effective behaviour here, the manager:

- Displays understanding of how the different parts of the organization and its environment fit together.
- Works towards a clearly defined vision of the future.
- Clearly relates goals and actions to the strategic aims of the business.
- Takes opportunities when they arise to achieve longer-term aims or needs of the organization.

Chapter 10

Chapter 10 focuses on the largest responsibility of managers and the most difficult managerial behaviour to assess as a process: *thinking and decision-making.* It is only possible to assess the process in terms of the outcomes achieved.

> *Managers displaying thinking and decision-making skills analyse and make deductions from information in order to form judgements and take decisions.*

There are three major sets of behaviour to this chapter. The first is the manager's ability in *analysing* situations. When analysing, the manager:

- Breaks situations down into simple tasks and activities.
- Identifies a range of elements in and perspectives on a situation.
- Identifies implications, consequences or causal relationships in a situation.
- Uses a range of ideas to explain the actions, needs and motives of others.

The second behavioural set focuses on the manager's need for *conceptualizing* in order to make decisions. In this process, the manager:

- Uses her/his own experience and evidence from others to identify problems and understand situations.
- Identifies patterns or meaning from events and data that are not obviously related.
- Builds a total and valid picture (or concept) from restricted or incomplete data (which happens to be most of the time).

The third behavioural set addresses a manager's *judgement and decision-making* abilities. When forming judgements and making decisions, the manager:

- Produces a variety of solutions before taking a decision.
- Balances intuition with logic in decision-making.
- Reconciles and makes use of a variety of perspectives when making sense of a situation.
- Produces his/her own ideas from experience and practice.
- Takes the experience and practice of others into account.
- Takes decisions that are realistic for the situation.
- Focuses on facts, problems and solutions when handling an emotional situation (not personalities).
- Takes decisions in uncertain situations, or based on restricted information when necessary.

ACTION PLANNING

A book of this nature can only get you started on the way to being more effective as a manager. If you are using it as part of a distance learning or taught course, then you will have undertaken a range of assessed tasks. It is helpful to review your progress by considering what is involved in and learned through doing those tasks. This section will help you to:

- Identify aspects of ongoing learning.
- Learn how to learn from non-success and its importance (as well as to evaluate your successes for future use).
- Review the competences in the PCM and furnish yourself with specially developed questions to review your own situation.
- Develop a model to plan for your development of increased effectiveness in areas of managerial and personal effectiveness.

- Understand the sort of managerial competency questions used by trained assessors and advisers by providing you with a typical checklist (Appendix 1).
- Plan your personal development and change requirements.

USE OF INFORMATION AND COMMUNICATION TECHNOLOGY

An essential skill for managers to develop is the relevant and practical application of information and communication technology. A good place to start if the approach is completely new to you is with your personal development planning. If you are well practised in this art, you will have automatically developed your own files and spreadsheets.

It is recommended, therefore, that you develop a word-processing file for your narrative and examples, together with an electronic spreadsheet of objectives and timescales for your personal development planning. Your learning and development objectives can be drawn directly from the management standards, the PCM and/or the various questions that appear throughout this text to help your understanding of your own personal development needs.

THE IMPORTANCE OF ONGOING LEARNING

The learning cycle (Figure I.3) is a critical concept for people who wish to continue to make progress in their managerial development.

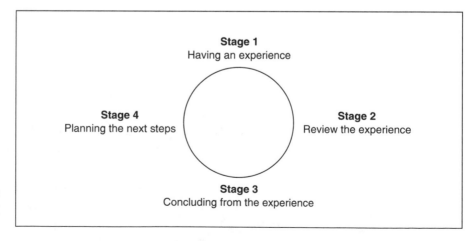

Stage 1
Having an experience

Stage 4
Planning the next steps

Stage 2
Review the experience

Stage 3
Concluding from the experience

Figure I.3
The Kolb learning cycle.

This learning cycle represents an ongoing process of learning and development. Our experience forms the basis for reviewing, drawing conclusions and planning future learning. Learning can arise just as easily from lack of success as from succeeding in activities.

Failure is a word that has an unfortunate negative meaning associated with it. Who would wish to have the word applied to them? However, failure nearly always brings with it the opportunity to learn. It is only when failure is not used for learning that there is really true failure.

Roget's Thesaurus offers the words 'cessation', 'discontinuance' or 'stall' as alternatives to 'failure'. These words imply that some expected event or progress has not taken place. If a domestic appliance such as a vacuum cleaner stops working, then most intelligent people would consider some obvious reasons before calling in an expensive technician or throwing the appliance away. By finding out why the cleaner did not work you would gain knowledge that you could apply to other appliances in your house.

Similarly, when, as a manager, you find that something you set out to accomplish does not work out as planned, you have an opportunity to learn why this should be. The opportunity is to learn, not only how you might have set about it differently, but also how you might act in future situations. It is called learning from experience.

There is a perception of experience that is familiar to all who have to plough through piles of curricula vitae or application forms. The phrase 'I have X years of experience' often appears. The question that might go through the reader's mind is: 'X years of experience, or one year's experience repeated X times?' How much has the person learned from that experience?

Personal effectiveness is not simply acquired from reading a book or carrying out book-based activities. It is something derived from the thoughtful and informed *application* of learning and experience, in the workplace.

THE APPLICATION OF LEARNING

The national standards of competence, and the personal competencies identified within them, will have considerable relevance for you as a manager. Furthermore, these competences and competencies, respectively, have acquired wide acceptance as a basis for many academic as well as occupational management qualifications.

We would suggest that you take the standards of competence as a basis and add or amend them as necessary. You will need to plan how you can put into practice the knowledge base that this book offers in the area of personal effectiveness, and the development of the personal competencies. The opportunities to do this are probably far greater than you might think. For example:

- The obvious opportunities of your current job that you are currently making use of.
- The obvious opportunities of your current job that you are *not* currently using but which you could use if, for example, you managed your time better.
- Whatever aspects of your manager's job that he/she may be persuaded to let you undertake.
- The opportunities presented by jobs that colleagues undertake for which you may be able to negotiate time to spend learning yourself.
- The opportunities offered by your workplace to become involved in the organization and management of social, sports, trade union and welfare activities.
- The range of non-work involvements and activities that you are currently undertaking (e.g. sports, leisure, religious interests, etc.).
- The range of non-work involvements and activities that you are *not* currently undertaking (as above for example), but which you could undertake if, for instance, you managed your time better.
- The family-based activities, that you are currently undertaking (problem-solving, planning, organizing. etc.).
- The family-based activities that you are *not* currently undertaking (as above, for example) but which you could undertake if, for example, you managed your time better.

A PRACTICAL EXAMPLE

One of the units of managerial competence is unit C12: Lead the work of teams and individuals to achieve their objectives (an *optional* unit for those managers interested in achieving a Level 4 management Vocational Qualification (VQ).

You will see from the overview in Appendix 2 that the unit has three elements, each of which may need separate development planning in order for you to achieve competence. Against each element are identified the *key behaviours* of *acting assertively*, *building teams*, *communicating* and *thinking and taking decisions*, broken down as shown in Figure I.4.

It is these key behaviours or *personal competencies* which this book seeks to help you develop or improve.

It is possible that some readers may not have the opportunity to do all of the elements in their current job role. Perhaps you do not manage a team of staff with whom you can plan work, assess performance and provide feedback. This difficulty has been identified and incorporated into the Vocational Qualification framework; however, it is recommended that managers, or potential managers, take all the

Personal competency	In performing effectively in this unit, you will show that you:
Acting assertively	• Take a leading role in initiating action and making decisions • Take personal responsibility for making things happen • Take control of situations and events
Building teams	• Actively build relationships with others • Make time available to support others • Encourage and stimulate others to make the best use of their abilities • Evaluate and enhance people's capability to do their jobs • Provide feedback designed to improve people's future performance • Show respect for the views and actions of others • Show sensitivity to the needs and feelings of others • Use power and authority in a fair and equitable manner • Keep others informed about plans and progress • Clearly identify what is required of others • Invite others to contribute to planning and organizing work • Set objectives that are both achievable and challenging • Check individuals' commitment to a specific course of action • Use a variety of techniques to promote morale and productivity • Identify and resolve conflict or resistance
Communicating	• Listen actively, ask questions, clarify points and rephrase others' statements to check mutual understanding • Adopt communication styles appropriate to listeners and situations, including selecting an appropriate time and place • Confirm listeners' understanding through questioning and interpretation of non-verbal signals • Modify communication in response to feedback from listeners
Thinking and taking decisions	• Break processes down into tasks and activities • Take decisions that are realistic for the situation

Figure I.4
Extract from the management standards 'Managing People: Key Role C' (Crown Copyright, 1997).

opportunities they can to develop as many of the competences, and thereby the competencies, as possible.

The first question(s) you should ask yourself is:

'Is it a part of my job?'

or, more broadly,

'Is it conceivable that I should do it at some point in my job?'

Although you may not manage staff as part of your normal activities, perhaps the opportunity arises to take the responsibility from time to time. Most organizations involve staff in project teams or working parties. Co-ordination of such activities is not automatically associated with seniority. Sometimes it rests with the person who shows willingness to do it.

Management skills are acquired through practice and the application of learning. Taking advantage of suitable opportunities is crucial. A person who does not reach beyond proficiency in their current job is saying that they do not seek to progress further.

Let us suppose that the particular competence is not one that is currently part of your job—taking a fairly broad definition. The next question you might put to yourself is:

'Is it likely to become a part of my job (in the future)?'

This might involve a bit of crystal ball gazing. Many organizations have 'downsized' in recent years, which is *management speak* for reducing staff and layers of management. This exercise almost inevitably brings new responsibilities to bear on the remaining staff. There is an awareness that the environment is constantly changing for many organizations. Their employees need to be focused on innovation and develop new skills. So it is quite possible that the skills your job does not require now may be essential for your job next year—if your job is to remain yours!

Let us assume that the particular managerial competence or personal competency is one that you cannot see as applicable for your job now or in the foreseeable future. The next question to ask yourself, then, is:

'Does it represent a skill that I might need for my own future career development?'

Before answering that question it may be worth pausing and considering the views of Charles Handy, a respected management writer who spends a lot of his time analysing what the future might hold for the world of work and organizations. He believes that, in the future, it is not employment that will be important but rather *employability*. This could be as: an established manager; an interim, or fixed-term manager—of a project for example; a consultant; or Charles Handy's 'portfolio' manager (simply taking around your 'portfolio' much as an artist might in order to 'sell' your experiences to employers). The possession of a job will not count for much unless the person has *saleable* skills, since security of employment for life has become a thing of the past for most people.

So the question revolves around whether possessing the competence is something that improves your attractiveness to employers. The question thus becomes:

'How can I develop the skill or competence?'

The help list is a simple list for you to use and adapt (Figure I.5). It sets out a number of possible sources for the development of a desired skill or competence. Some of these are related to work activities (section A). These are ongoing activities that you may be doing that enable you to practise the particular skill within the work setting itself. The list allows you to add to it where you feel appropriate.

Often there is a need to acquire more information, either to establish what the desired skill is or where it might be found within the organization. We have listed some information sources that are available within most organizations.

In some cases you may desire to develop a competence but you cannot locate any possibility to do it within your current work situation. Perhaps you do not have the necessary responsibility and your own manager is unable or unwilling to delegate to you. How do you seek and use the opportunity to experience and develop the competence?

There are essentially three areas of possibility:

1 You may find the opportunity within your actual or potential leisure pursuits. Many candidates and students have found that the experience of organizing and managing a sports or social club at work, school or college has made a major positive impression on employers.

A Work-related	D Home/family
1 Subordinate feedback 2 Colleague feedback 3 Line manager feedback 4 Customer feedback 5 Team meetings 6 Liaison work 7 Staff supervision 8 Report writing 9 Verbal reports 10 Interviewing 11 Progress chasing 12 Planning 13 Negotiating 14 Quality checking 15 Standard checking 16 Advice provision 17 Using resources 18 Decision-making 19 Problem-solving 20 Evaluation Others...	1 Decision-making 2 Problem-solving 3 Negotiating 4 Obtaining resources 5 Using resources Others...
B Work information sources	**E Self-help and learning**
1 Staff manuals 2 Annual reports 3 Business plans 4 Job descriptions/specifications 5 Finance procedures 6 Personnel procedures 7 Review documents 8 Meeting minutes 9 Computer databases 10 Information leaflets 11 Working party reports 12 Company newsletters etc. Others...	1 Coach/mentor 2 Management course material 3 Fellow course participants 4 Short courses 5 Management tutors 6 Library resources Others..........
C Leisure activities	**F Other category(ies)**
1 Team memberships 2 Committee involvements 3 Obtaining resources 4 Using resources 5 Decision-making 6 Problem-solving 7 Evaluation Others...	

Figure I.5
Help list (based on a model provided by Richard Hooper of the London Borough of Enfield).

2 In your home life you may find that you can develop and practise competence. 'Sound management of the economy', as Margaret (now Baroness) Thatcher used to say, 'is all about good housekeeping'. Time management, priority-setting, problem-solving and decision-making are all activities that most people have to handle in everyday life.

3 Finally, there is the possibility of self-help and learning through study. Some skills can be acquired through 'simulation'. That is how people learn First Aid. Handling disciplinary situations is best practised in the classroom before trying it out in the *real world*. However, well-planned training courses can often provide a realistic experience for candidates and students.

YOUR FIRST ACTION PLAN

1 Determine whether each of the managerial competences and the related personal competencies are relevant to your present job; refer to Appendix 1 (checklist of questions) and Appendix 2 (examples of units of competence) to help you with this.

2 If they are not relevant now, how might they become relevant in the future?

3 Are there any competences not encapsulated by the national standards of competence or personal competencies that you believe should be included?

4 Make notes regarding your own learning preferences (private study, trial and error, practice, reflecting on events, etc.; or, better still, complete the Honey and Mumford Learning Styles Questionnaire (1988)—see suggested reading for this chapter) and the opportunities you have taken in the past. How might you improve them/develop them in the future?

5 Discuss your skills and behaviour with others who are internal and external to the organization as appropriate. How effective are you now? How might you improve them, in general terms, in the future?

CHAPTER 1

Building teams

Managers who build effective teams encourage team effort, build cohesion and maintain motivation.

LINKS TO THE CHARTERED MANAGEMENT INSTITUTE'S MODULE

This chapter aims to address the aims and learning outcomes as identified in the Introduction under the heading *Links to the Chartered Management Institute's module 'Understanding Yourself'* so that, in conjunction with Chapters 2, 4, 5, 8 and 10, participants should be able to:

- Evaluate their use of time and resources at work and identify strategies for improvement.
- Understand the impact of their behaviour on other people in a range of management situations (e.g. through team-working).
- Demonstrate how they can gain more flexibility in their style and approach to others, to enhance the delivery of the above objective.

INTRODUCING THE RELATIONSHIP BETWEEN THE PERSONAL COMPETENCY MODEL AND BUILDING TEAMS

The Personal Competency Model (PCM), as already discussed, identifies the behaviours and skills that are necessary for you to develop before you are able to prove competence in any managerial function. This chapter attempts to deal with the various behaviours and skills necessary for you to apply across all managerial functions when building teams, transferring your learning to different occasions, at different times and under varying circumstances (contexts), consistently.

The outcomes below, as identified within this section of the model, should be borne in mind while you work through this chapter.

Learning outcomes required in building teams

There are two major areas of behaviour required of managers when building teams. The first looks at the competency needed in *relating and showing sensitivity to others*, the outcomes of which are that the manager:

- Actively builds effective working relationships with others.
- Makes time available to support others in assuming responsibility in and for their work.
- Encourages and stimulates others to make the best use of their abilities.
- Evaluates and enhances people's capability to do the job, taking the necessary action to ensure they receive the appropriate training and development as needed.
- Provides constructive feedback that is designed to improve people's future performance.
- Shows respect for the views and actions of others.
- Shows sensitivity to the needs and feelings of others.
- Uses power and authority in a fair and equitable manner.

The second set of behaviours addresses the important competency of managing and obtaining the commitment of others. This involves the manager developing behaviours that guarantee that she/he:

- Keeps others informed about plans and progress.
- Clearly identifies what is required of and by others.
- Invites others to contribute to the planning and organizing of work.
- Agrees and sets objectives that are both achievable and challenging.
- Checks individuals' understanding and commitment to a specific course of action.

- Uses a variety of techniques to promote good morale and individuals' productivity.
- Protects others and their work against negative impacts.
- Identifies and resolves causes of conflict or resistance, between individuals, between teams, or causes of conflict between individuals or teams and the organization.
- Communicates a vision that generates excitement, enthusiasm and commitment.

INTRODUCTION AND OBJECTIVES

The objectives of this chapter are to:

- Define leadership and introduce various concepts and models to the developing manager.
- Identify the nature and sources of power and influence available to the manager and introduce positive approaches to their application.
- Highlight ways in which teams can become effective.
- Discuss motivation and delegation in developing team members.
- Show how participation in the decision-making process can develop commitment.

You might well have heard the phrase: 'One can choose one's friends, but not one's relatives'. We have all had experiences in private life surrounding the issues of developing relationships with parents, grandparents, siblings, our own children and so on. These relationships develop informally and are more or less effective depending upon how the individuals within the *role set* behave towards each other. Interrelationships within any team may vary between being positive and constructive and being negative and destructive, depending upon situations, circumstances and the predominant motivation and interests within the team.

Each individual within the role set has a contribution to make towards the overall culture of the team, which may, of itself, be positive or negative. If the contribution is unacceptable to the team, and unless the individual is especially *powerful and influential*, the prevailing culture will override any apparent opposition to the *health* of the team. In some cases, if an individual is perceived by the other members of a team as being too different to anyone else, the prevailing culture will be used to override his/her ideas and opinions and even destroy that person's individuality if he/she is not prepared to conform. In the extreme, the individual may even need to leave the team altogether. This can happen in private life, of course, during adolescence when young people attempt to establish their individuality and sometimes demonstrate their opposition to the prevailing family culture. The family may tolerate this period of maturation, occasionally it will not; note the increasing incidence of teenage homelessness.

The workplace is the same. Here again we are unable to choose those with whom we *work*. Sometimes, as managers, we have some control over whom we recruit for particular jobs, but our effectiveness as interviewers and ultimate selectors of personnel will determine how appropriate these final choices will be. We are, whatever these choices, presented with a team of people with whom we must interrelate, with each one of us attempting to influence *positive* interrelationships between all of us.

Once more, the effectiveness of these interrelationships begins with us as individuals relating to other individuals within a working team, all of whom require mutual trust, support, respect and co-operation in order to achieve the team's objectives. The effectiveness of any individual under these circumstances can be seen as a role of informal leadership, which can be held by different people at different times, depending upon the circumstances, or formal leadership, where a named person assumes the responsibility and is usually given a title such as manager or team leader.

LEADERSHIP

As a definition for leadership, one could state that it is a dynamic process whereby one individual provides the *wherewithal* for those she/he is leading to influence each other to contribute voluntarily to the achievement of team tasks in a given situation. The overriding skill that is demonstrated by the person *officially* seen as the *leader* under these circumstances is to be able to 'let go' rather than to 'hold on' whilst retaining the necessary authority and personal credibility within and towards the team. No easy matter.

An ongoing debate between management practitioners has been whether leadership can be separated from the role of management. Specifically, can a manager manage without leading? Can a leader lead without being recognized as a manager? It is obvious that there are effective leaders who do not necessarily have the authority of management; it may therefore not be possible for them to implement certain activities without referring to the relevant authority. The question then becomes: 'Can a manager be effective without also being effective as a *leader*?' It may be possible for a manager to *delegate* certain aspects of the leadership role, but does this not still require the manager to *lead* those to whom he or she delegates?

To meet the objectives of *relating and showing sensitivity to others* and *managing and obtaining the commitment of others*, leaders must first endow trust, support, respect and co-operation onto others within the role set in order to fulfil the team objectives; this will then provide a *mutually enabling* culture. People who feel trusted will then trust in return. It is sometimes difficult for managers to see how they can *release control* in this way and maintain what they perceive to be the vital prerogative of management—to manage.

The role of leaders

John Adair, as long ago as 1985, saw the necessity to separate the needs that leaders should address when developing a team of people into three common *organizational* needs (Figure 1.1):

1 Those of the individual.
2 Those of the team.
3 Those of the task.

It is important to acknowledge that people join a team with expectations for themselves as individuals (personal and professional), concerns about how they will fit into pre-existing teams as regards the skills and abilities they have to offer, as well as how they will be accepted into that team by the other members, regardless of how essential their skills and abilities are to the functioning of that team.

It is then necessary to appreciate that the team's needs, whilst possibly known and understood by everyone before any new members

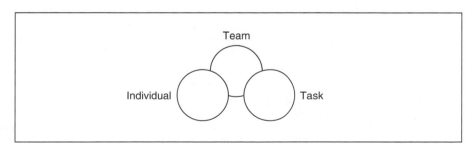

Figure 1.1
Action-centred leadership model (Adair, 1985).

are introduced, could very well change as a result of their joining. New team members will bring new beliefs and values to the team (different culture), which may pose a threat, or at the very least be a cause for consternation within the pre-existing team. The needs of the team are bound to change, but the question is, how and in what way might they change now that the composition of the team is different? Will the original members allow such change, or will they resist it?

Effective teams will understand and welcome such changes and will also provide the wherewithal for the integration of new members. Ineffective teams, on the other hand, are more likely to be defensive of any differences entering their sphere of influence and react negatively, resisting all change however positive and necessary such changes may be to the ultimate success of the team (see Figure 1.2).

Adair's model can then be developed to show that a leader's *function* is to provide the key role in facilitating the *interpretation* of orga-

Figure 1.2
Guide to the development of effective teams (adapted from the National Standards of Management; Crown Copyright, 1997).

Context	Effective teams	Ineffective teams
Atmosphere	Informal, relaxed, congenial, unthreatening	Tense and threatening, boring and dreaded
Discussion	Participative, open, non-judgemental, empathic	Dominated by one or a few, wider discussion not encouraged, often resented
Team objectives	Understood and accepted through discussion of organizational needs and contribution to methods of team achievement	No clarity of overall objectives and individuals'/teams' contribution towards their achievement
Listening	Active listening (encouraging and developmental)	Linked to discussion above, with one or a few *pushing* their ideas
Disagreements	Openly expressed, discussed and resolved	Unresolved, swept aside, not taken on board
Decision making	Decisions reached by consensus—agreed and accepted following full discussion	Often premature because of limited discussion and active listening
Criticism	Open, objective, non-personal, constructive	Embarrassing, personal and destructive
Thoughts and feelings	Openly expressed and empathically received	Hidden, feared, made to believe irrelevant and destructive to team objectives
Activities	Clearly allocated, understood by everyone (individual roles and contributions to overall needs)	No clear allocation, no commitment, limited effort because of all of the above
Leadership	Not dominated (by applying all of the above)	Dominated by one of the few by not attending to issues in column 2.
Performance reviews	Regular (formal), frequent (informal), developmental and beneficial	No discussion, enforced formal reviews threatening and *disciplinary* rather than developmental

nizational objectives by the team, which defines the needs of the task(s) to be performed.

It is unfortunate but true that, due to the time and energy that some teams spend in addressing their individual and team needs, they never fully reach the stage of acknowledging and attending to the needs of the tasks to be performed. The completion, or otherwise, of the tasks will then become a hit or miss affair. It could also be argued that, because of this, many leaders have resorted to the traditional authoritarian approach to leadership: maintaining a close watch on everyone, supervising the detail and trusting very few people, if any, to get the job done without their constant interference. Such leadership styles can be de-motivating, soul-destroying and offensive to many seeking responsibility and professional independence, which in turn will lead to high membership turnover and the ultimate erosion of good working practice (see Figure 1.2, column 2).

Further difficulties can arise for the leader if the individual and team needs conflict with organizational objectives. It is inevitable that these needs and objectives will clash if, for instance, the organization itself is attempting to change. As previously discussed, because individuals and teams bring their own particular beliefs, values, interests and therefore needs to the workplace, a particular *culture* has formed and where these accepted beliefs, values and interests reflect the organization overall any changes enforced from above (or outside) can be seen as threatening by the team who may then close ranks and resist such changes.

The leader then has the task of balancing all these needs, creating mutual support and again helping the team interpret and analyse the implications of such changes and prepare ways of dealing with them as positively and constructively as possible, from the team's point of view. The leader needs to seek the synergy that exists between the varying needs (where measured outcomes are more than the sum of all the parts) so that the members of the team can contribute to the change itself, as well as manage the change process, as effectively as possible, in order to optimize the outcomes. Recruitment of the most effective team members is therefore crucial before the team can *develop* into an effective performance- and results-focused entity.

Types of leadership

There are various views of what constitutes *type* in terms of leadership. *Types* of leadership are a separate category to *styles* of leadership, which will be discussed separately. Individual styles may be applied within any of the following examples of *types* of leadership:

- *Charismatic*—based upon the personality of a leader. Such a leader would be trusted, respected, seen as someone with power based on the effects of achievements gained through their style, knowledge, influence and so on. Examples of charismatic leaders might include Mahatma Gandhi and, more recently, Richard Branson.
- *Traditional*—based upon birthright. Such a leader might, for instance, have inherited a business or title from his/her family. Robert Maxwell's sons, and indeed the Queen herself, may be seen as traditional leaders.
- *Situational*—based on being in the right place at the right time. Such leaders may acquire their position through, for example, the death of the current leader; their deputy would naturally pick up the title as, for instance, Vice President Ford, following the death of President John F. Kennedy.
- *Appointed*—based on bureaucratic authority. Such leaders are appointed after climbing through the ranks and achieving higher authority. This approach can be particularly witnessed in the public domain, where public appointments are based on bureaucratic progression.
- *Functional*—based on behaviour or actions expected. These leaders are only appointed on the basis of the needs of the function itself. For example, an individual who may have all the leadership skills required to perform the job are unlikely to be appointed unless they also have had extensive experience in the function itself (e.g. accounts, sales, personnel, operations, etc.).

What makes you a leader?

Anyone can become a leader if she/he can persuade others to follow. People follow for a variety of reasons, including:

- The fear of criticism and/or punishment.
- The need to obey rules and procedures.
- Respect for a leader because he/she happens to be the leader.
- The leader has gained credibility over time.

These reasons for *following* a leader are not mutually exclusive. For example, followers may both respect their leader and fear the consequences of disobedience. Where respect for a leader exists because he/she happens to be the leader, the continuation of such respect is likely to be more reliant upon effective systems and procedures. Where a leader is followed for fear of their criticism and/or punishment, flexible approaches, creative thinking and effective interpersonal communication are required in order to overcome such fear. Current researchers in organizational behaviour identify a preference among managers and staff alike for the *respect and trust model of leadership*.

Leadership of working teams

If the formally recognized leader is to become the genuinely accepted leader of his/her working team, that *acceptance* must be earned. Leaders constantly find themselves in competition with informal leaders who can exercise certain powers, such as:

- Length of service.
- The ear of a director.
- Champion of the workers.
- Technical expertise.

It would, therefore, be unwise for the formal leader to rely on the negative forces of fear and convention. In the long run, a team's respect and trust are likely to produce more effective results.

The formal leader's aim should not be to depose the informal leaders, but more positively to gain the support of the informal workings of the team in order to meet organizational objectives. Informal leaders will cause fewer problems if the leader shows that she/he merits respect and proves capable of being trusted. The leader must be prepared to commit time and personal effort in achieving satisfactory results from this approach.

Leadership styles

When a problem or demand occurs upon which teams or individuals have to act, the leader is often presented with the dilemma of the choice of leadership style. Should the approach be authoritarian (at one extreme) or would the democratic involvement of the team be more appropriate (at the other)? The choice is not simple; in any given situation, a wide range of approaches present themselves. According to Tannenbaum and Schmidt (1958), these include (see also Figure 1.3):

- The leader gives the orders: the feelings and opinions of the team may or may not be taken into consideration, but they are expected to obey.
- The leader 'sells' his/her decisions: as well as giving the orders, the team is persuaded to accept them and the leader recognizes that there may be resistance.
- The leader explains his/her decisions: the team is given the opportunity to discuss the leader's intentions and thinking, allowing the exploration of the implications of decisions and to develop the instructions for implementation more fully.
- The leader's decisions are open to change: still taking the initial decision, the leader is prepared to hear other ideas and modify/change the decision before taking further action.
- The leader chooses between the ideas of individuals within the team(s): having defined the problem or need, the leader allows team members to suggest ways of tackling it, providing the leader with a range of alternatives, who then selects the most promising.
- The leader states the problem and the team decides: the leader still defines the problem and then states parameters

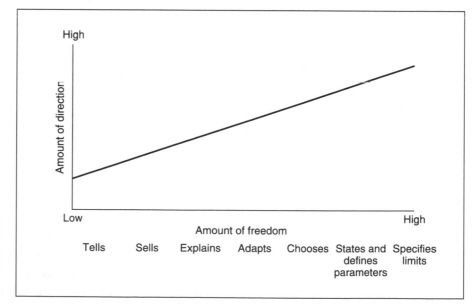

Figure 1.3
Leadership styles (derived from the Tannenbaum and Schmidt model, 1958).

within which the decisions must be made, but the team decides what should be done.

■ The leader defines the limits within which the team has total
freedom: within the specified limits, the team defines and
analyses problems as the individuals perceive them and
decide together what should be done. The leader commits
in advance to help implement whatever the team decides.

The forces behind leaders making the choice

■ Forces within the leader—the leader's own beliefs and incli-
nations. Some people are more comfortable as directive leaders. They may argue that they are paid to take responsibility
for taking decisions and producing results.

■ The leader's confidence in the work-team—a leader's view of
the individuals in their work-team is coloured by the amount
of trust endowed upon people in general. This varies considerably between leaders, which, in turn, affects their willingness to accept people's competence and good intentions.

■ The leader's tolerance of uncertainty—where leaders
involve others, it is implicit that outcomes are less predictable than their own decision-taking. Where some leaders
have low tolerance of such uncertainty, others thrive on it
as a challenge.

Forces within work-teams

■ The strength of their need for independence: where some
individuals want to take responsibility for their own behaviour, seeing it as a challenge and a tribute to their competence, the self-confidence of others may not yet be
sufficiently developed to accept responsibility; they may
need to know that someone else is accountable. Their
defence may be that they see delegation as *buck-passing*.

■ Tolerance of uncertainty: whilst some people prefer clear-cut
directives, others prefer to accept the risks of greater self-
direction.

■ Expectations about leadership style: those used to strong
directives may perceive involvement as a threat; those used
to involvement will resent authoritarian decision-takers.

■ Pressure of time: whilst often less a pressure than perceived
by either leaders or their followers, the idea of time pressure

is perhaps the greatest pressure of all. The more urgent the need for action, the more difficult it is for leaders to involve others and for others to accept involvement.

Situational leadership

Lucy Fry, an experienced manager and company director of ABC Consultancy (a small government-funded training consultancy—the names have been changed on request), who has recently completed a certificate programme, related an incident to the authors, whereby having practised a democratic style of leadership for some years was confronted with a new team member (a newly appointed manager) who strongly objected to her style of leadership. It was several months before Lucy learned this.

After a very difficult period with the manager objecting to her style to everyone else, at all levels of the organization except herself, Lucy discovered that the manager's past experience had only ever involved a 'directive' style of leadership—a senior managers' style towards herself as well as hers towards others. Her view was that Lucy was an ineffectual manager and should not be doing the job.

When Lucy was finally able to persuade the manager to discuss her views openly, they agreed that Lucy would take a different approach, for a period of time, reviewing progress and development needs at very regular intervals. Although Lucy had lost credibility with this manger, who also did her best to influence the views of others, eventually the situation resolved itself with both people realizing that they were jointly both correct and incorrect in their views. Finally, after almost a year of the manager being in post and when her confidence had grown, Lucy was able gradually to revert to a more democratic style, in line with her leadership of the rest of the team.

Making the right choices

There is no one best style for all situations and the able leader is not likely to be consistently autocratic or consistently democratic. Style will depend upon the situation, the problem and the individuals involved. Based upon each issue or situation, an able leader accurately assesses his/her own needs, as well as those of others in the organization likely to be affected by his/her methods of leadership: senior management, colleagues, own staff, as well as people in other departments. An able leader also takes into account individuals' readiness for growth and development. If direction is appropriate, the leader directs; if involvement is relevant, the leader involves.

When assessing and measuring the effectiveness of decisions made by individuals, it is important to remember that it is not the number of decisions they help make, but the significance of each decision made! It is also necessary to remember that, whatever the level of involvement of individuals in the decision-making process, the leader must accept the positive and negative outcomes of all decisions made. Delegation is not passing on the responsibility and accountability of achieving the organization's/department's objectives, but sharing responsibility for the actions employed in attaining them.

In these days of reduced managerial layers, leading to flatter organizational structures, leadership and managerial approaches are likely to have changed (or are changing) to a more self-managed, self-directed culture within project- and/or activity-based teams. Emergent and incremental organizational changes of this kind should be studied to enable an understanding of, as well as in anticipation for, what is likely to be needed in the medium to longer term to achieve effective performance and team development. As an aid to the following exercise, you might like to consider the following actions taken by self-managed teams:

- Plan, control and improve their own work processes.
- Share leadership and management functions.
- Set their own goals.
- Inspect their own work.
- Create their own schedules.
- Review their own performance and plan development as required.
- Prepare their own budget.
- Co-ordinate with other units/departments.
- Order their own supplies.
- Manage their own inventories.
- Negotiate and contract with suppliers.
- Acquire training when needed.
- Discipline their own members.
- Take responsibility for rewarding and recognizing members.
- Lead by coaching and facilitating rather than controlling and directing.
- Reward based on team not individual performance.

- Rely on fewer management layers and fewer functions to accomplish work.
- Encourage individual initiative and accountability.

To reiterate the question posed at the beginning of this section: 'Can leadership be divorced from the role of management?' What do you think?

EXERCISE

One does not necessarily require the title of *manager* in order to manage, and the less obvious the process of management is, the more effective it appears be—a debate that is likely to continue between practitioners for some time yet.

An interesting exercise might be for you and a team of your colleagues to discuss this issue along with the implications for the varying styles of leadership in different organizations in general, focusing on your own organization's overall leadership style in particular.

In discussion, you might consider aspects of:

- Building relationships.
- Time needed to support others.
- Making use of others' abilities.
- Evaluating and enhancing others' abilities.
- Providing feedback.
- Showing respect and sensitivity to others' needs, feelings, views and actions.

THE NATURE OF POWER

This section is based upon the concepts developed by Charles B. Handy in his book *Understanding Organisations* (3rd edition, 1985).

In defining power, it can be said that it relates to the capacity to affect the behaviour of others or the actual ability to do something.

In defining authority in relation to power, it can be termed the 'status' that legitimizes the use of power.

Influence is the application and the effect of power and authority (see also Chapter 5).

Power/authority does not only apply in hierarchies, but also in different ways in all work and social environments. Everyone is influenced by external power sources in some way. For example:

- When a baby cries, it may be *demanding* its food.
- Governments *demand* taxes.
- The organization *demands* that work be done.
- A friend *seeking* a favour.

All four instances exert some kind of power over the individual. Charles Handy distinguishes between power and influence. He says that the difference lies in the fact that *influence is an active process* and that *power is a resource providing the ability to influence*. Recourse to any source of power is likely to provoke different kinds of response in those over whom it is exercised.

Power as a source of influence

This element links to Chapter 5.

Sources of power

Physical power This is a superior physical force using coercion to *make* people work: e.g. the bully, a tyrant or even a commander in the armed forces (threats are often sufficient). In managerial terms this is seen as the power of last resort.

Resource power Possession of a valued reward is often a useful basis for influence. It is calculating, and in order to be effective:

- There must be control of the resources.
- The potential recipient must desire those resources (links to the *expectancy* theory of motivation).

Conflicts of power occur. For example, physical power in the form of, for instance, laws affecting picketing, industrial action etc. resulting in imprisonment for those convicted of infringement of these laws, versus resource power in the form of trades unions' ability to withdraw labour.

Bureaucratization of power reduces individual power. For example, in the public sector, the individual power of a manager to reward by increasing pay or promotion etc. is reduced by corporate procedures and equal opportunities policies.

Position power This is present as the result of legal or legitimate power that comes as a result of the role or position of the individual in the organization. For example, the role of manager allows him/her to give orders to staff. Power tends to reside in the position rather than in the individual. This normally has to be supported by physical and/or resource power; in other words, the organization must back the manager or control the resources otherwise the manager's influence will fail.

Position power gives the occupant potential control over some invisible assets:

- Information.
- Right of access to a variety of networks.
- The right to organize.

Expert power This form of power is vested in someone because of her/his knowledge and expertise. In meritocratic tradition, people do not resent being influenced by *experts*. It is often linked to occupations such as doctors, lawyers, economists, etc.

As a power base, expert power requires no sanctions, but, if expertise is questioned, it may be necessary for the holder to fall back onto other sources of power.

Personal power This is also known as referent or charismatic power, and resides in the person and his/her personality. It can be enhanced by position or expert power, success and self-confidence, but it can be seen to fade when an individual leaves a particular post, leaves a team or suffers defeat or failure. It is less resented than other power sources and comes from those over whom it is exercised. It is tied to the individual rather than to the position. It operates mostly in informal power structures.

Negative or reflective power If power is used in the agreed constituency—i.e. in the appropriate domain—it can be regarded as legitimate. If used contrary to accepted practice or outside the appropriate domain, power is regarded as disruptive and illegitimate—i.e. negative. Managers and all employees have the latent power to disrupt or stop work, distort, filter and confuse information. It is often practised at times of low morale, irritation or stress and major organizational change.

Relativity of power

The power of person 'A' must have salience for person 'B' or it is ineffective. Bribes may sway some people but repulse others; prestige and threats may bring about similar reactions. The effective amount of power possessed by a person will constantly ebb and flow as the constituency in which it is exercised changes its membership.

Balance of power

There is a power equation: power is seldom one-sided—even a prisoner can *hit back*. Negative power is often practised at work—e.g. the power to disrupt production. One type of power can offset another—e.g. money can overrule loyalty.

Domain of power

Few sources of power are universally valid over all constituencies. Some people wish to extend their domain, or scope of power, and diminish the domain of others. For example, one manager may wish to exert control and influence over a particular department or project at the expense of another manager's control and influence. Legitimate power or influence means that managers' domains of power are prescribed and recognized by others; the conditions under which and over whom it can be exercised have been laid down.

It is not always necessary to officially sanction such power; custom is a strong legitimizer, since power is often regarded as legitimate until challenged. Once challenged, the power may not necessarily be destroyed but simply restricted. For example, the computer expert, once an unquestioned organizational genius, has seen his/her domain progressively restricted over recent years, although their expertise is seldom called into question.

The power to influence

A discussion between one of the authors of this book and a residential care manager identified a member of staff in his home, having been in post for 20 years, as having 'more power over some individuals' than the manager herself. This is a kind of 'time served' legitimized power where an individual literally overpowers younger and perceived weaker staff members. The manager was presented with some difficulty over this situation, because it had been allowed to grow over the years and made it impossible to implement any sanctions. The woman's power and influence had become the custom, which met the expectations of the wider team. It was believed that this power would be eroded by the different expectations of new staff members.

CREATING EFFECTIVE WORK-TEAMS

Effective team-working

In order to create effective team-working (refer again to Figure 1.2), individuals should be encouraged to:

- Be open and honest in their dealings with others in the team.
- Use mistakes; eliminate fear of punishment, rejection, etc.
- Use competition and conflict to reach agreements and avoid the unhealthy aspects of extreme competition and conflict.
- Use relationships to build support and trust; no-one should feel isolated or threatened by their choice of behaviour, etc.
- Ensure activities are productive and stimulating; sessions without objectives will be frustrating and time-wasting.
- Provide the wherewithal for all to own the team's decisions; everyone must be involved in the processes, contributing to them in their own unique ways.
- Enable the team to take risks, depending upon circumstances and situations.
- Recognize, acknowledge and compliment personal development.
- Have clear and agreed objectives and roles.

Key factors in team behaviour

Development

Team development is concerned with the processes it undergoes. In general, when a team *forms*, it is concerned with establishing the tasks it needs to perform, the rules associated with the individual activities and so on. Unfortunately, very few teams concentrate on the processes they go through at this early stage, which means that much is left unsaid and unresolved until issues and/or personality difficulties emerge at a later date.

The next stage in the development cycle is where individuals explore the possibilities between them—generally known as *storming*—where conflict occurs, including the struggle for *power* between individual members, followed by establishing the *norms* relevant to the activities of the team, where individuals agree the way in which they will make and implement decisions. The team then begins to *perform* and get things done.

Size and cohesiveness

The size of the team influences its behaviour; a team with more that 12 members will lose cohesiveness and subteams will begin to form in order to develop closer working relationships. As implied, the cohesiveness of teams (or the attractiveness of the team to individual members) is inversely correlated to the size of the team.

Team norms

As norms are established for the overall behaviour of the team, any deviance, or the joining of a new member, will result in team pressures affecting performance and behaviour, with the expectation that individuals will conform. Leaders are likely to bring relevant individuals to the team in order to optimize the team's effectiveness and limit unhealthy conflicts and competition.

However, if the leader is looking for changes or to break up any 'group think' (Janis, 1972) that may have developed (the denial of important or essential information or evidence that threatens the normal thinking and behaviour of the team and which is therefore manipulated or ignored), the leader may wish to bring in someone who is able to resist the pressures to conform. Such individuals will gradually gain credibility through whatever strengths they happen to possess and will eventually influence the original team away from the accepted norms.

Leadership

Leadership is discussed elsewhere in this chapter in some detail, but it must be remembered that, without effective leadership, which adopts the styles necessary to facilitate the motivation and development of the team, the team is unlikely ever to become effective.

Individual role identity

Every member of a work-team has something specific to offer: some will co-ordinate the activities and ideas of others; some prefer to come up with all the ideas, but have little patience for honing them to implementation; some will reflect on their own and others' actions and decisions and analyse their usefulness, etc. Others will analyse current situations and determine the logic of plans and ideas; others have contacts outside the immediate team and are good at finding out things and obtaining information and additional resources. Still others like to get jobs completed and move onto the next challenge and so on.

Meredith Belbin has conducted research into individual team roles over a number of years and as a result he considers that the 'perfect team'—one that demonstrates effective interaction, performance and outcomes—is one that includes people who are able to undertake certain crucial roles. Before studying the characteristics of these individual roles, it should be understood that each individual can, and is likely to, exhibit more than one of these role characteristics at any one time. Thus, a small team of, say, four individuals can prove equally as effective as a team of nine individuals, as long as all roles are covered.

The main point is that, in some way or another, Belbin believes that all role characteristics should be present within any one team. Although they may not be present among individuals, understanding of the roles will allow development of the missing characteristics.

Belbin's nine team roles

1 *The 'plant'* Unlike the 'shaper', the 'plant' is introverted but is intellectually dominant. She/he is the *source of original ideas and proposals*, being the most imaginative member of the team. She/he can, however, be careless of details and may resent criticism. She/he needs to be drawn out or she/he will switch off.

2 *The 'resource investigator'* This is the popular member of the team—extrovert, sociable and relaxed. She/he brings new contacts, ideas and developments to the group—the *salesperson, diplomat or liaison officer*. She/he is not especially original or a driver and needs the team to pick up on their contribution.

3 *The 'co-ordinator'* This is the *chairperson* or enabler. She/he need not be brilliant or creative, but would rather be called

disciplined, focused and balanced. She/he talks and listens well, is a good judge of people and things—a person who works through others.

4 *The 'shaper'* Highly strung, outgoing and dominant. She/he is the *task leader* and in the absence of the chairperson would leap into that role even though she/he might not do it very well. His/her strength lies in the drive and passion for the task, but she/he can be oversensitive, irritable and impatient. She/he is needed as a spur to action.

5 *The 'monitor/evaluator'* She/he has an *analytical* intellect. His/her contribution is the careful dissection of ideas and the ability to see the flaw in an argument. She/he is often less involved than the others, tucked away with the data, aloof from the team, but always necessary as a quality check. She/he is dependable but can be tactless and cold.

6 *The 'team worker'* She/he holds the team together by being *supportive of others*, by listening, encouraging, harmonizing and developing an understanding of individuals, the team and the task needs. Likeable, popular and non-competitive, she/he is the sort of person you do not necessarily notice when there, but miss when absent.

7 *The 'implementer'* She/he is an effective organizer and is disciplined, reliable, conservative and efficient. He/she *turns ideas into practical actions*. The 'implementer' can be inflexible and is slow to respond to new possibilities. He/she tends to adhere to the orthodox and proven. Can obstruct change.

8 *The 'completer/finisher'* Without the 'completer/finisher' the team might never meet its deadline. This is the person who *checks the details, worries about schedules and chivvies the others with a sense of urgency*. His/her relentless follow-through is important but not always popular.

9 *The 'specialist'* This is the person who possesses the *particular knowledge or skill* necessary for the project or task to be completed—often a solitary boffin type who functions best alone. Contributions made often represent the necessary breakthrough to overcome an obstacle that has been holding the team up.

As already discussed, one person may perform more than one role in a team. It should be further understood that the full set of roles is especially important when rapid change is involved. More-stable teams may get by without the full set of roles. Good leaders will anticipate and understand the value of these individual roles, not expecting to carry them out him/herself alone, and especially not expecting to retain the most prized roles at all times (e.g. chairperson and/or 'plant'). When managed effectively, the recognized or official leader may be best as the expert contributor under certain circumstances, the team worker under other conditions, the resource investigator in yet others, perhaps only chairing the team on rare occasions!

All team membership has its purpose; each individual will exhibit mixtures of introversion and extroversion in varying degrees according to the occasion, circumstance and need. Each individual requires the appropriate conditions for them to be motivated—according to their various needs and expectations—through encouragement, recognition, trust and respect, without the fear of threat or recrimination, having the right to be dealt with sensitively by leaders who are aware.

EXERCISE

If you would like to determine your dominant team strengths in more detail and identify how you might improve in your less dominant 'team roles', complete Belbin's 'Self Assessment Inventory' (see Belbin, 2002). Note that this inventory focuses on Belbin's original eight roles devised in the early 1980s.

HOW MOTIVATION AND DELEGATION AFFECT TEAM-BUILDING

Motivation

It is essential to recognize the importance of purpose, self-management and challenge for other people. If viewed as a means of communicating shared interests and needs, identification of individual and organizational motivation/needs can be seen as an effective means of expressing the objectives, targets and plans of all concerned. It is only when there is *congruence* or complementarity between these organizational and individual needs that team members feel motivated.

There are numerous ways in which individuals are motivated to achieve organizational objectives. There are *extrinsic* needs—the obvious, more tangible, rewards for working—associated with pay and conditions and many leaders believed, and still do believe, that people are only motivated by appropriate rewards and sanctions: competitive pay for *a good day's work*, maybe additional bonuses for above-average performance, together with the threat of no bonuses or even disciplinary action for less than a good day's work. There are also *intrinsic* needs that, when satisfied, result in job satisfaction and highly motivated team members. Intrinsic needs are associated with the job itself: recognition, independence, freedom of thought and contribution towards the determination of the team's objectives as well as the manner in which they will be achieved.

Several theories have been formulated from various researches carried out during the 20th century.

Content theories

Content theories emphasize what motivates people:

- Maslow's (1943) hierarchy of needs, in which it was thought that higher-level needs (e.g. recognition and self-fulfilment) would not be sought until lower-level, more fundamental needs related to life itself (e.g. enough money to pay the mortgage or friendship at work) were achieved, can be expressed as shown in Figure 1.4.
- Alderfer (1972) eventually turned this hierarchy on its side—forming a continuum (Figure 1.5)—whereby he showed that individuals flowed backwards and forwards on the motivational continuum depending upon situations, circumstances and changing personal needs, etc.:
- Hertzberg's (1959) two-factor theory of hygiene and motivational needs differentiated between factors, in that, while

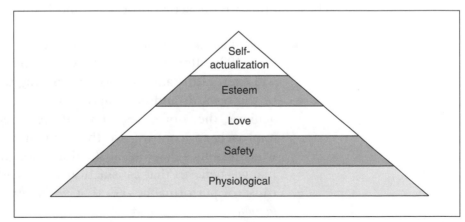

Figure 1.4
Maslow's hierarchy of needs (Maslow, 1943).

Figure 1.5
Alderfer's
continuum of
needs (Alderfer,
1972).

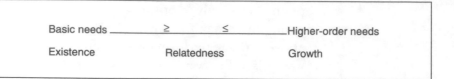

certain things can be de-motivational (e.g. the loss of privileges associated with a job), they are unlikely to motivate people to make extra effort in order to be given them in the first place (hygiene factors), whereas status, security, responsibility and recognition would be motivational (for certain people at certain times).

- Alderfer's (1972) ERG (existence, relatedness and growth) theory, summarizing the Maslow factors into three levels, assumes that people are motivated in three major ways, which are not necessarily separated and hierarchical but can co-exist (see his continuum of needs). In other words, people will be motivated by money (to pay the mortgage, etc.—existence), will seek friendships at work (relatedness) and wish to develop within the job role (growth) all at the same time.
- McClelland (1988) identified four main arousal-based, socially developed, motives:
  - The achievement motive.
  - The power motive.
  - Affiliative motives.
  - Avoidance motives.

Process theories of motivation

These emphasize the actual process of motivation:

- *Expectancy-based theories* Vroom's (1964) expectancy theory (and 1996 after Porter and Lawler) believed that individuals will exert effort and perform, according to their expectation of the rewards and how highly they value them, in order to achieve the outcomes. The Porter and Lawler (1968) approach—in contrast to the human relations approach, which assumes that job satisfaction leads to improved performance—believes that satisfaction is the *effect* rather than the cause of performance—i.e. that *performance* leads to *job satisfaction*.

- *Equity theory* Adams' (1965) theory focuses on people's *feelings* of how well they have been treated compared with others.
- *Goal theory* Locke's (1968) theory assumes that people's *goals or intentions* play an important part in determining behaviour. It is the striving to achieve these goals in order to satisfy emotions and desires that motivates individuals to perform.
- *Attribution theory* Heider (1958) and Kelley (1973) suggest that behaviour is a combination of *perceived* internal and external forces, where internal forces relate to the individual's personal attributes such as skills and abilities and the amount of effort and fatigue and external forces relate to the environmental factors such as the organization's rules and policies, the leadership styles employed, organizational economic situation and state of change, etc.

It is clear that people are motivated in various ways and by various means, including financial gain, status, recognition, achievement and responsibility, as well as freedom and interest. We can also make certain general points about characteristics that are positively associated with people who are highly motivated. These would include:

- *Purpose*: people who are highly motivated tend to be results- or goal-oriented. This would involve a large amount of commitment, which then increases work performance.
- *Self-management*: people seek to have a level of control over their own lives. Highly motivated people seem to desire, and to have a large measure of, self-determination over their lives. This includes the ability to make their own decisions and possessing a certain level of autonomy.
- *Challenge*: highly motivated people have a desire to improve and test themselves against the highest possible standards.

It can be added that people are also seen as 'social animals' who voluntarily *integrate* their own goals with those of teams/organizations within which they work (or move on if they cannot) so that, as a collective, individuals may feel more likely to achieve their needs.

It is interesting to note that externally imposed incentives and controls, favoured by the 'rule them with fear' school, are inefficient, as well as undesirable. This is why organizational development theory now favours moves in management style to provide the wherewithal for people to become motivated from:

- Individual to *shared* responsibility.
- Autocratic to *collaborative* approaches.
- Power relationships to the *empowerment* of others.

In order to look at the question of how we can better facilitate the motivation of others (we cannot directly motivate them, only provide the wherewithal), we need to bear in mind, not only these general points, but also the extremely important principle of being able to identify the needs and goals of those we seek to be motivated. In order to do this, we need to become good listeners. This is where our active listening skills begin to pay off. To facilitate the translation of these ideas into action, the model shown in Figure 1.6 is helpful.

What has been discovered from what the wealth of motivation theory tells us is that, if we increase effort by facilitating the motivation of others, we raise performance levels. From an individual's standpoint, of course, if they perceive that the outcomes are worthy of their effort, they will be willing to make the effort in order to perform and achieve the desired outcomes. The performance has to be focused, however, and must satisfy both organizational and personal needs. How do we do this? We could:

- Tie effort to performance.
- Link performance to desired outcomes.
- Look at the value of the work: i.e. we must assess how much this goal is valued by the person(s) we are trying to motivate.

The needs of individuals may be developmental—starting with small gains or focused rewards, progressing to the higher needs (to use Maslow's terminology) of recognition and self-actualization (fulfilment)—or move backwards and forwards along a continuum of needs depending upon occasions and circumstances. Managers need to keep up-to-date with their team members' changing needs

Figure 1.6
A perception-based model of motivation (similar to Vroom's 1964 model).

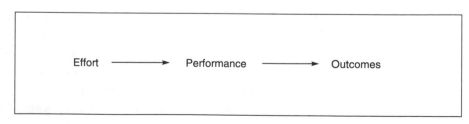

Effort ⟶ Performance ⟶ Outcomes

and circumstances. Personal situations also affect individuals' motivation and their needs of the time. Factors such as moving house, divorce, death in the family, birth of children, marriage of children, etc. can have a bearing on individual motivation, especially as regards the degree of stress they may be undergoing.

Where individuals carry out limited duties, regardless of how intellectually demanding they may be, if they operate in isolation and with little support, they are likely to become tired and bored and feel undervalued. Such individuals can become more insular over time and keep all forms of communication with others to the barest minimum. Thus emerges a vicious cycle of non-motivated people negatively influencing the motivation of others.

Personal effectiveness skills required in facilitating the motivation of others

- Be an active listener.
- Applaud, compliment and reward.
- Give considered answers.
- Consult and take account of what people say.
- Seek out their needs.
- Give responsibility and the necessary authority.
- Offer challenge.

Showing *appreciation* for work done by others is key to the development of good working relationships as well as building assertive behaviour. Some managers appear to think it is *soft* and non-assertive to thank others for what they have done. This is simply not so. This approach will build self-confidence, trust and mutual support between team members.

Likewise, *apologizing* when you are wrong will gain credibility and support from others. False apologies and empty promises will have the reverse effect, but to admit mistakes takes courage initially, which will be eventually rewarded by positive responses from others.

Delegation

It is necessary to identify appropriate reasons for delegating tasks and to match the skills involved in performing tasks with those assuming responsibility.

If managing is about 'achieving results through people', then all managers should delegate. We know that managers in successful companies delegate tasks and responsibilities right down the line—yet delegation is often dealt with badly, if at all!

Some people may see delegation more as a job task than a personal skill, yet there is a personal effectiveness dimension to delegating. Many of the problems associated with poor delegation are either failure to communicate, or inability to do it properly. The following attitudes are all too typical of some managers:

'I would rather do it myself.'
'They'll only do it all wrong.'
'I'll have to watch them like a hawk.'
'I tried delegating once; it was more trouble than it was worth!'
'I don't want them to do my job for me!'

There are three major reasons *for* delegating work to others:

- To free time for yourself.
- As a training or development exercise.
- For motivational purposes.

Delegated tasks usually fail for one of the following reasons:

- Wrong reason for delegating.
- Wrong task(s) delegated.
- Task(s) delegated to the wrong person.
- Factor 'X'.

Delegation works in a management context that is increasingly emphasizing the notions of empowerment and shared responsibility. So sharing and delegating both tasks and responsibility, with the necessary authority, is becoming the norm. However, the three reasons are very different and, when a task is delegated, one should be clear about the motives for doing so:

- *Freeing time for yourself* For a manager, this is a perfectly legitimate reason to delegate. However, it is worth asking yourself if you always delegate only menial tasks, tricky assignments and whether you keep certain tasks for yourself as 'hobbies'. This is ineffective delegation or even buck- passing.
- *Training and development exercises* This is an excellent way to develop skills and confidence in your staff. However, if it is a training exercise, the skills to be learned and practised

should be clearly spelled out with appropriate feedback of individuals' performance for further development.

■ *Motivation* The importance of self-management and challenge in this context has already been discussed.

Delegating the wrong task and/or to the wrong person

Many more delegation exercises would be more successful if the tasks were matched more carefully to the person. The following six rules should be followed for successful delegation:

■ *Clarity*: the purpose should be spelled out.
■ *Matching delegatee to task*: the skills required should be carefully considered. The level of the task should be challenging, but appropriate and within the person's reach.
■ *Discussion*: the task, from the purpose through to the fulfilment, should be talked through.
■ *Resources*: sufficient resources, particularly time, should be made available.
■ *Monitoring*: the rewards should be discussed and progress should be regularly checked.
■ *Review*: achievement should be checked against objectives.

Factor 'X'—the unpredictable element

Little control is possible over factor 'X'. This means that, even when we have been careful to identify our purpose in delegating tasks and responsibility, and even when we have followed the six rules, things can still go wrong. However, a crucial issue is to determine what should be done to be realistic and accept that sometimes things do go wrong—the element of risk!

It is important to allow failure; progress can only be made if we accept occasional failures. It should be a part of the review process to try to identify why things may have gone wrong and to learn the lessons without blaming anyone.

EXERCISE

From the previous discussions relating to team-building—including leadership, motivation and delegation—determine from your own team interaction at work whether improvements can be made in the commitment to achieve organizational outcomes.

PARTICIPATIVE DECISION-MAKING

This section concentrates on the human side of decision-making: the participation of team members in the decision-making process in the course of developing effective performance (reference is made to participating in decision-making in the section on delegation above). For the various approaches, techniques and theories that have been developed for effective decision-making purposes, please refer to Chapter 10.

In general, one can relate approaches to involving others in the process of decision-making to Simon's (1960) concept of a continuum of *programmed to non-programmed* decision-making in order to determine the appropriateness or otherwise of participative decision-making (Figure 1.7).

This approach identifies how *fully programmed* decisions are made based on known and understood knowledge and/or experience that is not likely to require in-depth discussion as to what should be done, by whom and when. For example, if a problem occurs within an organization's IT system and if the in-house experts cannot find the fault, it would be obvious that the system supplier would need to be contacted to help resolve the problem.

By contrast, however, the need to make a thoroughly *non-programmed* decision would require a very different approach because the issue is novel, often involving major change. Approaches and methods to resolving the problem cannot be anticipated because there is no previous experience upon which team members can draw in the process of resolving issues that are completely new to the organization. The reasons for limiting the number of people involved in this kind of decision-making would include:

- Time and cost involved in meetings and activities associated with involving too many people.
- No risk would be involved; therefore decisions of this kind are not likely to threaten anyone.

Figure 1.7
Continuum of programmed to non-programmed decision-making (Simon, 1960).

- Frustration of those requiring a speedy response, including customers as well as organization members; extreme bureaucracy sometimes causes this.
- The problem worsening because of the time taken in reaching a decision.

As the *continuum* would suggest, there are any number of stages between programmed and non-programmed decision-making—depending upon the nature of the issues concerned as well as on the culture and structure of the organization—that would require an initial decision as to how much of the required overall decision is able to draw on previous organizational experience. It would also need to be decided as to how *appropriate* this previous experience is to the current situation.

It would be wise, in all but the most obvious programmed decision-making cases, or one-right-answer decisions as per the above example (see Chapter 10), to involve the team(s) that will be affected by the process and the outcomes of such decision-making.

Participative decision-making by teams leads to the *empowerment* of individual members, which in turn leads to their *buying-in* and *internalizing* the decisions made (being owned by them), as well as their commitment to and acceptance of outcomes achieved through the experience of, for example:

- Delegation of decision-making to those most affected/relevant.
- Delegation of activities to those most appropriate, with the organization/leader providing support, guidance, resources, training and development as needed.
- Acceptance of the risk involved by team members planning and executing the activities required.
- Drawing on team members' experiences (often gained outside the organization itself), ideas and suggestions.
- Wider job satisfaction.

As identified by Guirdham (2002, p. 551), the advantages to leaders in encouraging participative decision-making would include:

- Increases the range of inputs, knowledge and skills.
- Provides the ability to opt for solutions that might have been rejected due to doubt of their acceptance.

- Discussion across a wide range of ideas will provide a clearer idea of the limits that will be accepted.
- Team members are often better able and more willing to take over each other's work if needed, thus providing more flexibility and improving coverage
- Reduces leader's workload by training and developing team members.
- More commitment, mutual encouragement and higher morale of team members.
- Develops members as judges of others' contributions, thereby gaining insights into the competence of each other, under different circumstances, following the training and development identified.
- Members gain first-hand insight into the possible solutions of the problem facing the team.
- Relieves the problem of control, where the adopted solution—based on shared information and frame of reference—is more likely to be one to which team members are committed, leading to less need for monitoring than when a solution is imposed.

Whetton, Cameron and Woods (2000, p. 452) help us to identify some tips for leaders in their approach to the encouragement and effectiveness of participative decision-making:

- Identify the stages teams go through until they are fully able to contribute to the decision-making process (have patience and don't despair!).
- Ensure all team members have been introduced to each other/already know each other.
- Provide initial direction and then gradually *let go* as team members' confidence begins to grow.
- Facilitate the development of mutual trust and support.
- Discourage the belittlement of ideas and thoughts; allow all contributions to be recognized as valuable overall, only eliminating in agreement with others as the issue becomes more focused.
- Encourage synergy—the balance of independence of thought and the interdependence needed between team members.
- Facilitate the notion that individual success is also team success.
- Promote a strong vision of what the team can achieve.

- Facilitate the development of and commitment to a *team vision*.
- Encourage excellence, or the most people can achieve rather than just the *acceptable*.
- Encourage commitment to mutual (team) success as well as individual successes.
- Ensure that Janis's 'group think' is avoided—that survival is more important than achieving group goals.
- Provide constructive and valuable feedback or individual performance, both formally and informally (leaving nothing to the formal occasion that will come as a surprise to those concerned).
- Assist the team in accomplishing its tasks as well as building strong interpersonal relationships.
- Help the team to present the team's vision, goals and accomplishments outside the team.
- Understand, use and develop the team's core competencies.
- Encourage dramatic break-though innovations as well as small continuous improvements.
- Help team to work towards *preventing and learning from mistakes*, not just correcting them later.

SUMMARY OF ISSUES

In working through this chapter, you will have encountered a number of issues and perhaps some ideas that are new to you. The objectives of the chapter were to:

- Define leadership and introduce various concepts and models to the developing manager.
- Identify the nature and sources of power and influence available to the manager and introduce positive approaches to their application.
- Highlight ways in which teams can become effective.
- Discuss motivation and delegation in developing team members.
- Show how participation in the decision-making process can develop commitment.

How well have we, the authors, met these objectives?

More importantly, how have you approached and used the material yourself, and how much have you developed since the beginning of your course of study, or working through the chapter? You are strongly recommended to extend your research and study to include as much as possible of the material identified in further reading and references below, so that you can build on your expertise, incorporating more complex approaches and ideas as you develop further in your managerial role.

These objectives, if re-revisited over a period of time and put into practice in your job, will help you to achieve the personal competency of building teams, broken down into the elements identified in the table at the end of the chapter. In order for you to reflect on your own behaviour and that of others with whom you work, you might find it useful to use the table as a self-assessment check (reproduce as many as you wish) to re-evaluate your skills and knowledge.

PREPARING FOR ACTION PLANNING

Remember to review the checklist of questions, as identified at Appendix 1.

Analyse your own behaviour in terms of strengths (positive outcomes) and weaknesses (negative effects) in dealing with actual work-based occurrences with regards to the various situations discussed in this chapter, and summarized above.

Decide how you might deal with them differently in the future and what are your immediate training requirements and future development needs.

Discuss them with appropriate others and negotiate how you might address them.

FURTHER READING AND REFERENCES

Belbin, R.M. (2002) *Management Teams: Why They Succeed or Fail.* Oxford: Butterworth Heinemann. ISBN: 0-7506-2676-3 (pp. 147–153 as a minimum)

Guirdham, M. (2002) *Interactive Behaviour at Work* (3rd edition). Harlow: Pearson Education. ISBN: 0-273-65590-6 (specifically in support of leaders adapting a participative decision-making approach within teams)

Handy, C.B. (1985) *Understanding Organisations* (3rd edition). London: Penguin Books. ISBN: 0-140-09110-6 (specifically for the power of leaders as discussed in this chapter)

Mullins, L.J. (2002) *Management and Organisational Behaviour* (6th edition). London: Pitman Publishing. ISBN: 0-273-65147-1 (specifically for detailed analyses of motivational theories—as outlined in this chapter—may be found)

Tannenbaum R., Schmidt W.H. (1958) How to Choose a Leadership Pattern. *Harvard Business Review* 36 (2): 95–101.

Whetton, D., Cameron, K. and Woods, M. (2000) *Developing Management Skills for Europe* (2nd edition). Harlow: Pearson Education. ISBN: 0-201-34276-6 (specifically for the effective team-building aspects of the book)

Recommended journal articles for readers' further development

Balkema, A. and Molleman, E. (1999) Barriers to the development of self-organizing teams. *Journal of Managerial Psychology* 14 (2): 134–149

Cacioppe, R. (1999) Creating spirit at work: re-visioning organization development and leadership: Part II. *Leadership and Organization Development Journal* 21/02/2000: 110–119. Massachusetts: MCB University Press. ISSN: 0143-7739. Website: http://www.emerald-library.com

Goldberg, R.A. (2000) Awake at the wheel: a study on executive team development. *Leadership and Organization Development Journal* 21/05/2000: 225–234. Massachusetts: MCB University Press. ISSN: 0143-7739. Website: http://www.emerald-library.com

Poundsford, M. (2000) The era of them and us is now in the past. *The Guardian* 23/09/2000

Prichard, J.S. and Stanton, N.A. (1999) Testing Belbin's team role theory of effective groups. *Journal of Management Development* 18 (8): 652–665. Massachusetts: MCB University Press. ISSN: 0262-1711. Website: http://www.emerald-library.com

Scarnati, J.T. (1999) Beyond technical competence: the art of leadership. *Career Development Journal* 04/06/1999: 325–335. Massachusetts: MCB University Press. ISSN: 1362-0436. Website: http://www.emerald-library.com

Further recommended text

Conway, S. and Forrester, R. (1999) *Innovation and Teamworking: Combining Perspectives through a Focus on Team Boundaries.* Birmingham: Aston University. ISBN: 1-85449-392-2

Competency element	Competency level: 1 (low)– 5 (high)	Requires development	No direct experience	What can help? (identify oppor- tunities)	Who can help?	When can it be achieved?	How can it be achieved?
Build working relationships with others that are positive and effective							
Make time available to support others in assuming responsibility in and for their work							
Encourage and stimulate others to make the best use of their abilities							
Provide constructive feedback that is designed to improve people's future performance							
Show respect for the views and actions of others							

Show sensitivity to the needs and feelings of others	Use power and authority in a fair and equitable manner	Keep others informed about plans and progress	Identify what is required of and by others, whether this is clear and unambiguous	Invite others to contribute to the planning and organizing of work	Agree and set objectives that are both achievable and challenging

Check individuals' understanding and commitment to a specific course of action	Use a variety of techniques to promote good morale and individuals' productivity	Protect others and their work against negative impacts	Identify and resolve causes of conflict or resistance: between individuals, between teams, or those causes of conflict between individuals or teams and the organization	Communicate a vision that generates excitement, enthusiasm and commitment

CHAPTER 2

Communication and presentation: *how* to communicate with customers

Managers with skills in communication and presentation are able to share information, ideas and arguments with a variety of audiences.

LINKS TO THE CHARTERED MANAGEMENT INSTITUTE'S MODULE 'UNDERSTANDING YOURSELF'

This chapter aims to address the aims and learning outcomes as identified in the Introduction to this text under the heading *Links to the Chartered Management Institute's Module 'Understanding Yourself'* so that, in direct conjunction with other chapters (although less directly with Chapters 9 and 10), participants should be able to:

- Understand the impact of their behaviour on other people in a range of management situations (e.g. analysis of audience needs in the communication process).
- Demonstrate how they can gain more flexibility in their style and approach to others, to enhance the delivery of objectives.

INTRODUCING THE RELATIONSHIP BETWEEN THE PERSONAL COMPETENCY MODEL AND COMMUNICATION AND PRESENTATION

The Personal Competency Model (PCM) identifies the behaviours and skills that are necessary for you to develop before you are able to prove competence in any managerial function. This chapter attempts to deal with the various behaviours and skills necessary for you to apply across all managerial functions, transferring your learning to different occasions, at different times and under varying circumstances (contexts), consistently.

The outcomes below, as identified within this section of the model, should be borne in mind while you work through this chapter.

Outcomes required in communication and presentation

When developing *communication and presentation* skills, appropriate to various audiences and circumstances, there are a complex set of personal effectiveness behaviours required, the outcomes of which are that the manager:

- Listens actively, asks questions, clarifies points and rephrases others' statements to check mutual understanding.
- Adopts personal communication and presentation styles appropriate to listeners and situations, including selecting an appropriate time and place for the event.
- Uses a variety of media and communication aids to reinforce points and maintain interest.
- Presents difficult ideas, concepts and problems in a way that promotes understanding.
- Confirms listeners' understanding through questioning and interpretation of non-verbal signals.

- Encourages listeners to ask questions or rephrase statements to clarify their understanding.
- Modifies communication and presentation in response to expectations, responses and feedback from listeners as necessary.

These outcomes may all seem obvious, that we all instinctively know this. Unfortunately, we can see everywhere, all the time, how misunderstandings can occur between individuals and resentments build because people are not communicating effectively with each other. If this can happen between two people in private— causing apparently irrational and immature behaviour leading to negative results—it takes little imagination to understand how people become irrational towards each other in organizations, within nations and between nations, war being the worst of all possible outcomes.

INTRODUCTION AND OBJECTIVES

The objectives for this chapter are to:

- Identify aids to effective communication.
- Define the central role of communication.
- Identify barriers to effective communication.
- Introduce various concepts to effective interpersonal communication.
- Provide tips for effective reading and note-taking.
- Discuss ways to run effective meetings.

The nature of interpersonal communication

Definition: the exchange of information, verbally and through bodily expression, between two or more people in order to influence the occurrence of action, ideas or thoughts, at work, in leisure or community pursuits, or in individuals' domestic lives.

We communicate with each other, whether we wish to or not, in order to:

- Inform.
- Instruct.
- Motivate.
- Persuade.

41

- Encourage.
- Negotiate.
- Understand the views and ideas of others.
- Listen because we like to and want to learn.
- Seek, receive and give counselling, information, advice, decisions—and so on.

Types of information we wish to communicate to, and receive from others, can be categorized as:

- Knowledge.
- Data.
- Attitudes.
- Intentions.
- Emotions.

Interpersonal communication can hover between being easy, good, happy and positive, and being difficult, not so good, unhappy and negative. Communication, and thereby relationships themselves, often break down as the result of not *talking* to each other.

Verbal and non-verbal components to communication

We need to recognize the many forms of verbal and non-verbal communication and to *actively* listen to others. What we say, what we do, and even our refusal to talk, all communicate messages to those with whom we interact. Yet, however well we think we might communicate, there are still problems.

These problems, which are often caused by gaps in our communicating ability, are nearly always unintentional and they point to the difference between the intended message and the message received. Even with verbal communication, the words we use do not contain the whole of the message. Various commentators agree that a message is made up of 7% words, 38% voice tonality and 55% body language!

The receipt of any piece of communication, then, is based on individuals' impressions of what is being communicated. These impressions are complex agglomerations, which are the result of more than the obvious components that are being communicated. Any discussion of what communication is must therefore comprise more than a systematic analysis; it should also involve an understanding of the individual differences and expectations of those with whom we interrelate and whose perceptions are often based more on emotion, prejudice and guesswork.

First impressions

We tend to judge people based on very little evidence. It is quite well known in the selling business, for instance, that first impressions are extremely important. Various commentators have suggested that we make our minds up when we are interviewing in the first ten seconds, two minutes, or five minutes. Is it possible to elicit (or project) enough information in that time to give someone a rounded picture of character, personality and abilities?

On what information are such judgements made? Are they likely to be correct? Whatever the answers to these questions, researchers into the subject suggest, quite rightly, that we should maximize our opportunities by positively trying to create a good first impression. Conversely, we should attempt to defer judgement when meeting others for the first time.

WHAT FACILITATES INTERPERSONAL COMMUNICATION?

Active listening

The *active listener* will deliberately start by *taking in* information, rather than *giving out* information. In order to be effective communicators, we need to know other people's interests, needs and so on. We therefore need to demonstrate to others that we are interested in what they are saying.

It is therefore necessary for us to create an environment in which others can be honest and give information freely. To do this, it is important that we confirm to them that we have heard and understood their message, that we are supportive and not standing in judgement of them. We can do this by providing encouragement and constructive feedback, rather than constantly probing, interpreting and evaluating what they have said.

To listen actively to another person we should:

- Establish rapport.
- Make eye contact.

- Match body language—by mirroring actions, posture, gestures.
- Ask questions—to confirm, seek information and recognition.
- Not interrupt or change the subject—active listening means letting the other person *set the agenda*.
- Keep the focus on them, by using words such as *you* and *your* rather than *me* and *mine*.
- Use names.

Body language and other non-verbal communication

Body language is what usually springs to mind when we talk about clues to non-verbal, interpersonal communication. Body language will be discussed here in the normally accepted definition of the phrase, plus one or two other points for consideration, which might not spring to mind so readily.

Characteristics of non-verbal communication

These include facial expressions:

- Gaze and eye contact.
- Bodily posture.
- Gestures and use of hands in adding to, or contradicting, the spoken word.
- Proximity (some cultures expect to be in closer proximity when in discussion than others).
- Personal appearance (we are what we wear)—are we really telling people something about ourselves by the clothes we choose to wear?

Body language is important and it constitutes an integral part of the information that people consciously or unconsciously use to assess others. The interview is a situation in which this *activity* is particularly focused.

Important behaviours one might expect to see in others, and indeed portray oneself, at an interview, would include:

- *Appearance* This should be appropriate to the context of the interview (one would not normally expect to wear jeans to a selection interview, or to a formal review meeting or, by contrast, to turn up wearing a pin-striped suit for an informal counselling session at a job centre).

■ *Eye contact*
  To avoid eye contact implies dishonesty, even though this is not always true (e.g. it could be because of shyness, feelings of threat, etc.); therefore ensure eyes are levelled at the other person's eyes without staring or gazing for too long (this can seem like threatening behaviour)—above all *smile*.

■ *Body posture* The body posture is important, including the position of the feet. Slouching could convey lack of interest, splayed legs could suggest overconfidence.

■ *Stance* The body should be pointed towards the other person to encourage mutual interest and respect. To turn away implies disinterest, impatience or lack of time. Leaning towards the other person in a relaxed non-fidgeting way shows friendliness.

■ *Sit comfortably* The legs should either be side by side or loosely crossed to express comfort and a relaxed attitude. Unnecessary hand movements are best avoided (other than gestures that add to the positive meaning you are expressing; hand movements can be a distraction and even put across different messages to your words and facial expressions!)

■ *Show interest and enthusiasm* This will encourage the other person to relax, even to enjoy the session/interview by the warmth generated under these conditions.

■ *Listen and respond to what is said* Too often 'interviewers' are guilty of thinking far too much about the questions they want to ask that they actually forget to listen to the answers to the current questions! Not only will the *interviewees* stop making efforts when it is realized that they are not being listened to, but also the interviewers will look rather foolish if they then ask questions that have already been answered!

■ *Nod head to show understanding* Hold head upright, straight and level (to hold the head forward and high denotes aggression; to hold it forward and rigid denotes anxiety).

■ *Hold hands open and outstretched* Hold them away from the face and offer a firm handshake (pointed fingers and raised hands indicate aggression; clenched fists and folded arms show defensiveness).

■ *Clear and steady voice* This shows confidence; soft, pleasant tones indicate friendliness.

Verbal communication

Characteristics of verbal communication

Verbal communication, both face-to-face (including meetings) and on the telephone, involves conversations, listening skills and talking. all of which are supported by body language—even while talking on the telephone, one can *hear* when someone is smiling or frowning by his/ her tone of voice!

It is very important for managers to develop their conversational skills and to present ideas and opinions verbally. Demands upon verbal articulation will increase as areas of responsibility widen both informally in general conversations and formally in planned and prepared presentations.

People also communicate emotions and their innermost feelings through speech. It is possible to communicate all of these needs by using a variety of elements of speech, which can be controlled and used to good effect. Such elements would include:

- Voice *tone*.
- Speech *emphasis*.
- Speech *content*.
- Use of *figurative* language.
- *Humour* in speech.
- *Speed* of speech.
- *Pronunciation* used.
- *Pitch* of voice.
- *Inferred* speech.

Creating the environment

Some would say that a climate of independence within work-teams such that people do not feel threatened by the existence of other teams is im-portant in facilitating interpersonal communication. It is vital to make all information available within and between teams to facilitate good working relationships and by being aware of what others are doing.

If people are aware that they need to know what is happening in other areas of the organization for their understanding and development (they will then know where to send enquiries, and enquiries about their own work will be passed on to them in return), they will look out for and enjoy being able to pass on and receive information in this way.

Typically, if this kind of interaction is not encouraged, although people will still talk to each other, such talk is likely to be unproductive, creating cliques of individuals who have a tendency to gossip, start rumours and hold grumbling sessions about *the management*, other individuals and other teams.

Flexibility of staff to work in various capacities within and between departments might also be said to help effective communication; people become less *attached* to their assigned roles (which can make them insular) and more inclined to develop an organizational approach, thus creating greater and more effective channels within which to demonstrate their skills and abilities.

THE CENTRAL ROLE OF COMMUNICATION IN THESE ACTIVITIES

Why good workplace communications are important

Communication:

- Is a two-way process between people at all levels, within all functions and disciplines; it takes place upwards, downwards and sideways.
- Ensures efficiency and success.
- Is everyone's responsibility, from senior managers to the whole organization.
- Creates trust between people, especially when systems and procedures are being developed.
- Facilitates job satisfaction.
- Is vital in specific arrangements or agreements between managers and employees (e.g. consultation, negotiation, etc.).
- Reduces misunderstandings.
- Involves people—staff want to know:
  - What is happening and why.
  - The way their jobs can contribute to organizational prosperity and effectiveness.
  - The future prospects of the organization.
- Is vital in the fulfilment legal obligations in organizations, with or without union recognition.
- Requires the contribution of everyone.

Who is responsible for communications?

Communication involves everyone, but the function of management is primarily responsible for effective all-round communication, which should ensure:

- That there is a positive lead from the top.
- That policy is put into practice.
- That practice is properly maintained.
- That policy and practice are regularly reviewed.
- That adequate facilities and opportunities exist.
- That adequate feedback is obtained.
- That the chain of communication is clearly understood by those involved and that the chain is kept as short as possible.

The larger the organization, the more likely specialist functions such as, for example, personnel, as well as line managers, will take an active interest in employee communications—possibly involving direct responsibility and accountability.

The process of workplace communications

The means of workplace communication (which includes the medium used) can be various. For most purposes these include:

- Spoken—including non-verbal aspects.
- Written—correspondence, work proposals, reports, e-mail messages.
- Representational—often to external organizations, but also to other departments/teams, involving formal and/or informal presentations of materials.
- Team briefings.
- Meetings.
- Communication with self—thinking.

Effective workplace communication is:

- Clear, concise and easily understood.
- Presented objectively.

- Presented in a manageable form to avoid rejection.
- Regular and systematic.
- As relevant, local and timely as possible.
- Open to questions being asked and answered.

Maintaining effective communication will require:

- Monitoring.
- Reviewing.
- Communicators knowing their roles.
- Appropriate information being available.
- Information reaching all who need or want it.
- Information not being unnecessarily restricted.
- Communication bringing desired benefits.
- Practice matching policy.

This will depend upon:

- Appropriate training.
- The extent of employee co-operation.
- The quality of management decision-making.
- The level of involvement by senior managers.
- Absenteeism and labour turnover.
- The employee relations climate.
- Use of appropriate media, including communication and information technology.

Communication is one of the key skills for the competent manager. A commonly agreed definition of management is *achieving results through people*. In order to do this we need to practise the whole range of management competences, including the competencies underpinning them, and fulfil a variety of roles. These are all predicated on our ability to communicate with our colleagues at work (and sometimes with ourselves).

If we examine the management sequence illustrated in Figure 2.1, it becomes clear that communicating is involved at every stage of the process. It is therefore a critical component of almost every management skill. In this sense it can also be defined as a dimension of personal effectiveness (see Figure 2.2).

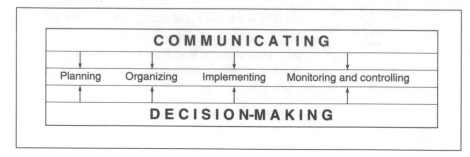

Figure 2.1
The management
context.

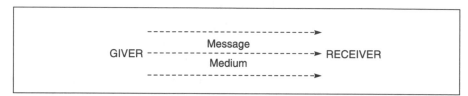

Figure 2.2
The components of
communication.

WHAT IMPEDES INTERPERSONAL COMMUNICATION?

According to the Open University (1990), in their 'Effective Manager' course material, there are a number of barriers to effective communication:

- *Uncertainty of message*—when we are simply not sure what to say, or how to say it.
- *Faulty presentation*—this might occur by choosing the wrong medium. For example, a memo when a *face-to-face discussion would be more appropriate.*
- *Limited capacity of target* or where the receivers of the message are not trained to interpret the information (e.g. financial statements), and receivers may feel threatened by being presented material with which they are not equipped to deal. Information thus provided is likely to be rejected or only selectively absorbed by the receivers.
- *Unstated assumptions*—where sender and receiver are unaware that they each have different assumptions about aspects of the message.
- *Incompatible viewpoints*—failure to communicate because the sender and receiver of a message view circumstances from a completely different perspective. For example, managers may view the introduction of a new computer system as pro-

viding opportunities for improving performance and saving people from the boredom of routine tasks, whereas others may see the introduction of information technology as a means of downsizing.

■ *Deception*—where the sender deliberately withholds certain aspects of information.

■ *Interference*—noisy telephone lines (e.g. the phone ringing while we are trying to write a complex letter), an emergency occurring in the office while we are trying to negotiate with a client, etc.

■ *Lack of channels*—where people who possess information with which others might usefully benefit, and vice versa, but who are unaware of the needs of each other because there are no formal channels allowing such exchanges of information.

■ *Cumulative distorted communication*—'Chinese whispers'. The longer the chain of people receiving and passing the information, the more distorted the message will be by the time it reaches the last in the chain.

If individuals and teams are encouraged to consider each other as 'customers' just like any other customers, they will have no reason or inclination to build resentments. They will begin to understand that everyone, including themselves, needs positive and friendly interaction in order to do their jobs to the best of their ability.

Conflicting views can present problems. Often we spend so much time thinking about what we ourselves want to express that we do not listen to what other people are trying to say. It is a hard, but very important, lesson if we can listen to others while remembering the main points of our own arguments; sometimes these become modified when listening to other viewpoints.

EXERCISE

Who has the responsibility for communicating within your organization? Analyse the effectiveness of the various modes of communication and determine how *you* might improve them.

IMPERSONAL COMMUNICATION

The written word (including writing reports and letters, reading and taking notes), meetings, public presentations, exhibitions and conferences, e-mail and other forms of electronic communication, information obtained/passed through the Internet or Intranet (internal, external—locally, nationally, internationally), facsimile, etc. are all examples of the impersonal communication with which managers must deal effectively and efficiently.

Use of business English

Written communication

Good writing involves not just one skill, but many. Writing skill is a continuum that ranges from basic information provided in notes and memos, to highly complex communication transmitted through reports and published papers. Each medium we use requires different skills and for most of us there is also a requirement for a technical or conceptual component.

The first principle in the use of business English is to *keep it short and simple* (the KISS approach), or as short and simple as possible. It is very tempting for managers and professionals to use jargon common to their organizations or professions. It would cause offence and be considered rude if used where the recipients are not familiar with it. The same would apply if a manager talks *down* to their correspondees, assuming them to be unable to comprehend the nature of the ideas they are trying to transmit.

A balance must be maintained between an acceptable, non-turgid/non-academic style of writing free of any jargon, and a language that is common within and between English-speaking organizations. Indeed, the style of this book is intended to be easily readable, unambiguous and understandable! Please let us know if we have achieved it.

It is important to decide the purpose, target audience and format. This will inform the requirements for the content. Clear thinking is also required in both written and oral presentation. If you understand the issues and the rules for presenting them, you will be able to argue logically and to identify any problems in the arguments of others.

The purpose could be to:

■ Change behaviour or beliefs.
■ Answer a question.
■ Present facts.
■ Present results of an audit, survey or other research.
■ Describe situations, events, or ideas.
■ Provide information.

- Record past events.
- Recommend.
- Influence decision-making.
- Bring about action.
- Persuade.

(Adapted from *Effective Business Writing*, by W.G. Hardy)

Structure

Once the purpose of writing is defined, we then need to organize the important ideas into some sort of structure. We are lucky today; indeed, as I am writing this section of the book and tap out the ideas onto my computer keyboard, with the word-processing package I am using I can move whole sections around, break up sentences and reorder them, delete unwanted parts and add to ideas as I come back to them afresh, without wasting paper or time or running the risk of forgetting ideas as they come to me.

I can suddenly move between chapters as ideas flow from one source into another area that is more suited to another chapter, and return again to add further thoughts. For me this is ideal; it is not always possible to use a computer, however.

When it is not possible to use communication and information technology to develop ideas for writing, it can be a good idea to mind-map ideas first (see the diagram at the bottom of Figure 2.3), rather like you might do when sitting an examination and you think through in advance how you might tackle the answer, linking your ideas with arrows. You will find, especially if you are a lateral thinker like me, that your completed map will be far from linear, with main ideas and associated ideas circling and spiralling all over the page. However, it is possible, once you have completed this process, to order the ideas logically, making sections and subsections which also help to develop the ideas further.

Another way of developing from the subheadings would be to list ideas in bullet point format for each section. Both these approaches are called *top-down*. With reports, a good technique would then be to *top and tail* each section; that is, for each section, write a first sentence encapsulating the purpose or key point, then write a summary containing the conclusion, or key point. It then remains only to fill in the text contained in the mind map or bulleted list.

Whichever process you use, commencing all written communication by thinking about headings and subheadings is a perfect means for developing your ideas and allowing them to flow easily.

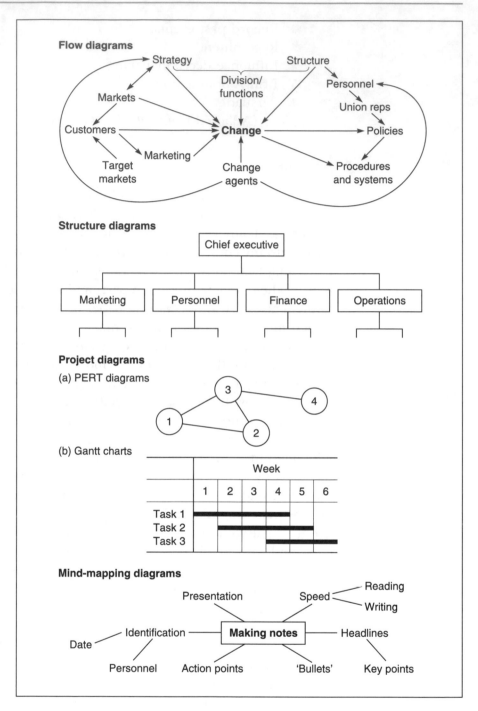

Figure 2.3
Examples of
diagrams used in
visual
presentations.

Sometimes you will add to them as you proceed, sometimes you will change or remove some of your original headings, but all will make writing easier to commence, develop and complete, whatever your purpose.

Good journalistic technique says that you should put the most important point first, and then any supporting information below it. Using this technique, the reader is then able to *cut off* the text at any point, as required, without missing the most important issues.

Logical reasoning

The logical form into which most arguments can be translated is known as a *syllogism* and consists of a:

- Major premise (or proposition)–the statement of a general law or principle or fact.
- Minor premise–connecting a particular case with the general law, principle or fact.
- Conclusion–a new fact validly inferred from the two premises.

Developing the theme

- *Serial arguments* These are commonly used in reports and technical papers where the *conclusion* of one argument becomes the *premise* of the next. For example, if we develop managers to *delegate* effectively to their work-teams, individuals will become more *competent* in their jobs and be more *satisfied* with their performance, which will, *in turn*, allow their managers more time to *think creatively*, which will also, *in turn*, provide the basis for the learning organization to evolve and *develop new areas of strategic thinking* ... and so on.
- *Lateral thinking* When we think laterally, we develop new and innovative solutions to problems by approaching them from entirely different directions. It is vital to write clearly and explain the rationale behind new ideas when writing. Where logical thinking is about linear, progressive, deductive approaches to problem-solving, lateral thinking is about the use of unorthodox or apparently illogical methods of approaching the problem and is likely to need a certain amount of defending (especially where information receivers' backgrounds are technical or scientific—i.e. they use logical thinking to support arguments!).
- *Writing style* The major objective here is to get over the key points in a way that is clear and effective. As already mentioned, this usually means the use of simple and clear lan-

guage. Many people forget this, but the most difficult ideas can often be put over in a simple way, using straightforward language.

■ *Correctness of language* Dictionaries record the accepted usage of words by the most educated people of the day, so that when we talk of correctness, in this context, we mean the speech or writing of formally educated people. However, it is necessary to use the rules as a guide rather than a rigid formula because English in all its forms is fluid and constantly changing. Without rules for language, however, there would be endless confusion of meaning.

■ *Obstacles to thinking clearly* If you identify any obstacles that might be inhibiting your own clear thinking, you can learn to overcome them. Such obstacles you might encounter include the following.

■ *Language* Language can be an obstacle. Names used for things are rarely ambiguous; however, more abstract terms can mean different things to different people—e.g. *right* and *wrong*, or *good* and *bad*. Different cultures bring different values to the workplace, and what may be considered *right* or *good* in one cultural setting may cause offence in another.

■ *Preconceived ideas* Attitudes and opinions can be major obstacles to clear thinking. These are based upon and have developed through our upbringing (our background)—education, at home, school and neighbourhood, as well as our individual experiences—and they have become our convictions. These preconceived ideas are often just prejudices, which prevent us from thinking clearly on certain subjects. They are strongly held beliefs that usually collapse if put to the test of logical reasoning. Prejudices should not be confused with criteria for judgement.

■ *Self-interest* Suspect your own opinions and those of others when it is obvious that the need to change them *appears* to threaten your own or others' security or happiness. This is not easy to do for yourself; however, objective scrutiny of your own motives is very helpful for self-development, as would be your facilitation of that of others.

■ *Generalizations* Be careful of making sweeping statements in arguments that might hide the important issues. They are sometimes also based on prejudices. It is helpful to make general statements more precise by inserting words such as *many, can, could, sometimes*, etc.

Attract and maintain the interest of the reader

Write to *express to*, rather than to *impress*, your reader. Inexperienced writers often try to impress others and, whilst they might talk with their own voice, they will try to be someone else when they write. The use of unfamiliar words and meandering sentences will result in vague, or even meaningless, writing, which will irritate rather than communicate.

One of the advantages of the top-down approach discussed above (apart from helping us to structure the information and the logical flow) is that it focuses attention on the main points of the argument. At the same time it also helps to attract and maintain the interest of the reader. There follow some useful guidelines:

- *Words* As well as avoiding jargon as already mentioned, avoid the use of complicated words and phrases where simple ones will do.
- *Sentences* The shorter you make your sentences, the better. It is not always possible, but if you aim for 10–20 words a sentence that makes your work very readable. *Punchy* statements are also more likely to be remembered.
- *Paragraphs* Three to five sentences per paragraph also break the words up into manageable chunks and are best if they contain details of one idea or issue at a time. Words that are spread out between paragraphs and sections, with plenty of blank paper showing, will encourage people to continue reading. Cramped paragraphs and lengthy sections are likely to bore readers and divert their attention to wondering how much longer they need to concentrate, rather than on how interesting or useful the information is.
- *Active verbs* These give a stronger and clearer sense of meaning. Why say, 'It is undergoing problems of a functional nature', when you really mean, 'It doesn't work'? The performance criteria in Management Standards have been developed making use of 'active verbs' so that the developing manager has no doubt as to what is expected of him/her.
- *Name it* Why go all round the houses to say something that would be better understood if you just said it? Ask yourself the question: if someone said to you 'But what does that mean?' how would you *tell him/her* what it means? If you rehearse a simple verbal explanation, it may help you to

write it. In other words, many people would be much better writers if they *wrote like they spoke*!

■ *Create mental pictures* So many words are abstract and represent concepts rather than things. It is then much harder to say just what you mean. In shifting from thinking to communicating, place yourself in the position of the reader. If that person is an outsider or a newcomer, try to remember how little you knew before you learned the special knowledge you now have.

■ *Assumptions* Many people start with the 'but ifs', before making the main point. This only obscures what they have to say. If you stick to the *point, evidence, conclusion* style, you will avoid this.

■ *Idea overload* It is common for people to try to say two things in one sentence. This usually results in *neither* having the required impact. If you want to make two points, write two sentences. A slight variation on this theme is the *sentence within a sentence* (or in parentheses—brackets, commas, dashes—where the sentence is complete without what is contained within them).

■ *Common mistakes* Search through some of your writing and check for the following:
  ▪ *This, it, they, you, we*, etc. Is it obvious what or who is being referred to?
  ▪ Typographical errors may lead to confusion: check completed work.

■ *Right first time* Many people agonize over their written work precisely because it is not right first time. You need to realize that nobody gets it right first time. It is much better to write it and then revise it, especially if the material is complex and possibly evolving as research, analysis and thinking continues.

■ *Perfection in grammar, style and spelling* People do get overly concerned about grammar, but, if it sounds right, it is likely to be right. As a final check, read it aloud. Real howlers should stand out when you say it aloud. There is not a great deal you can do about spelling—except that you should be honest if you are not always accurate. In which case use a spell-checker on your word-processor, or get someone else to check it for you. Even when you would normally spell something correctly, it is easy not see your own mistakes, but for someone else it is likely to *stick out like a sore thumb*.

■ *Punctuation* Do not punctuate to observe some rule; do it because the sentence you are writing demands punctuation if it is to be understood. Punctuation enables the reader to read quickly and without ambiguity. Common sense and logic are the best guides to punctuation.

■ *Fitness for purpose* Match your style to the application. A company annual report has to be formal, but most other documents do not. You can also use creative layout or other visual ideas. Above all, there is the need to know who your reader is. When writing to other managers, or sending them copies of letters you have sent to others, it is vital to be aware of the relevance of the information to them (and the language they use); it should be pertinent either to their jobs, their professions or to their wider interests. The large amounts of information received by managers means that anything that is not directly relevant will either be *binned* or, at best, *filed* unread. This is not only a waste of time and resources, but also impacts upon the wider environment and is an unnecessary waste of paper.

The presentation and interpretation of data

Most written communication is presented in report form for management purposes. Simple methods should be used to display the data in a way that captures the essential aspects.

In presenting any data it is important to use a neutral approach in your use of language, avoiding emotive words or statements, such as may be used by the popular press for instance. Avoid language as a smokescreen to hide features of your study—for example, obscure quotations, long and complicated sentences and excessive footnotes can be distracting and even completely off-putting for the reader.

Honesty is vitally important. Look for the strengths and weaknesses in the work of others you use (and discuss it) and also reveal in your report the strengths and weaknesses of your own work.

Types of report format

There are various types of report format. Some organizations require a lengthy and intricate approach to report writing; you must determine the *house style* as required. It is our intention here, however, to discuss concise and effective approaches to presenting findings in report format.

Reports are structured documents and are commonly organized in sections identifying:

- Title and author.
- Intended readership.
- A table of contents with actual headings and subheadings to allow readers to determine the nature of the report.
- Terms of reference: the authorization and purpose of the report.
- Summary of the main points of other sections, conclusions and any recommendations in order to tempt readers to delve into the detail within the report
- Background and history: generally speaking, it is necessary to devote a small section to the background of the report and the relevant history. This will usually identify the problem(s) or issue(s) requiring attention. It will also be useful if specific objectives for the investigation, or required outcomes, are identified here.
- Method of investigation:
  - Specific research will require the author to discuss alternatives and identify the preferred methods with full justification.
  - A general management report will require the investigator to identify which approach has been used.
  - Both types of report will need to include any constraints envisaged and how these may be overcome.
- General and specific findings of the investigation itself: this section will detail the circumstances and issues arising out of the investigation. This will be a factual account, reporting the findings in as subjective a manner as possible. If interviews have been carried out, these should be reported based upon the actual answers given to questions. When seeking information from others, particularly when researching attitudes and opinions, certain guarantees should be made. These might include:
  - All information obtained will be treated as strictly confidential (i.e. names of respondents will not be used when discussing their responses if they do not wish them to be so).
  - If interviews are carried out, the persons concerned will have the opportunity to see and verify the recorded statements.

- ▪ Those participating will be entitled to a copy of the final report if they wish.
- ▪ If the research is to be used by an academic institution for examination purposes, the question of subsequent publication will require the permission of participants.
- ■ Criteria for analysis, highlighting strengths, weaknesses, opportunities and threats.
- ■ The analysis itself.
- ■ Discussion.
- ■ Conclusions drawn from the investigation: these will be based upon the actual analysis of the data collected with no new material included.
- ■ Recommendations (where appropriate) based upon your enquiry or investigation. This is the *action centre* of the report and should meet the defined purpose of the report
- ■ Appendices: these are pieces of supplementary data that are not essential to the main findings, or updates of information, which will eliminate the need for re-writing. They may also include glossaries of technical terms and a list of abbreviations.
- ■ Acknowledgements: thanks to people who helped in the research or to prepare the report.
- ■ Bibliography: background reading used in the preparation of the report.
- ■ References: sources of references, actual quotations, used in the research, including unpublished material not generally available (e.g. company papers).

Reviewing the report

Having written the report, leave it for a day or two before revising and editing it. This allows time to think about what has been written and how. New thoughts may occur to you—their inclusion could improve the report. Type or print out the first draft, when it will be easier to:

- ■ Read the material objectively.
- ■ Assess the contents.
- ■ Decide if it looks good.
- ■ Review the language, logic and sequence of presentation.
- ■ Determine whether the main body supports the recommendations.

- ■ Decide whether it is convincing.
- ■ Know if you are proud of it.

Graphic communication

Graphic communication is the use of visual techniques to aid communication. There are many ways in which the techniques of graphic communication can enhance your ability to communicate clearly and effectively.

Among the many different types of graphic communication techniques are:

- ■ Lettering and typography.
- ■ Illustration and design.
- ■ Graphic enhancement—signs and icons.
- ■ Maps and diagrams (see Figure 2.3).

Both lettering/typography and illustration/design are really specialist functions best left to professional designers. However, they are usefully discussed in the context of word-processing and desk-top publishing.

We now live in a rich visual culture, and, in a technological and fast-changing world, we are used to dealing with huge amounts of information. We learnt a long time ago that much information can be assimilated quickly, and that graphic design and logos can help to carry numerous and simple messages with essential impact. Many organizations appreciate the importance of visual presentation, and will pay hefty consultants' fees to have their corporate material designed.

Of course, such devices can be used at a more modest level by all of us. We can incorporate icons or logograms into our documents and presentations to enhance the visual impact and the message.

The diagrams in Figure 2.3 are examples of the kinds of visual representations one can use simply in, for example, word-processing packages.

Information technology

The use of desktop personal computers (PCs) has opened up many more options for the graphic illustration of information. The main applications are:

- *Word-processing* As well as providing the ability to write in text, word-processors offer the ability to manipulate numerical information (e.g. financial information or stock/production levels) on a grid. The most sophisticated word-processing packages offer the ability to illustrate the information in diagrams such as pie charts or bar charts.
- *Desk-top publishing (DTP)* DTP adds to word-processing the ability to design pages, complete with illustrations. There have been many claims that the advent of DTP will turn us all into designers. Of course this is not true. It may well not be an efficient use of your time to spend hours slaving over a hot computer to produce a perfect document. However, for the computer-literate, documents and overhead projection (OHP) presentations can be produced with much higher quality if you can acquire the basic skills.

Statistical presentation

These forms of presentation are used almost exclusively for illustrating numerical data. They include pie charts, various types of bar charts and line graphs (Figure 2.4).

EXERCISE

Taking a report that you have, or a colleague has, written recently—on the basis of the above discussion—rewrite it to be more attractive to the reader.

Visual/aural presentations

Making information visually attractive is particularly important when making presentations to colleagues or potential customers. As well as

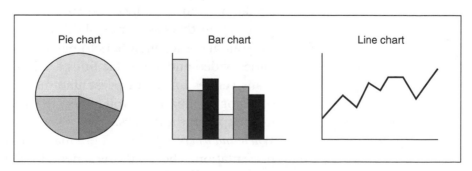

Figure 2.4
Statistical presentation of numerical data.

attention to the visual, this is an opportunity to use available technology to its full potential. When planning such a presentation, there are several elements to bear in mind.

Basic planning

- *Purpose* We need to identify what the presentation is intended to do. It is necessary to ask two things here: what is the purpose for you? and what is the purpose for your audience? There may be differences. This provides the focus, the structure and the style for the presentation.
- *Expectations* Both your own and the audience's expectations need to be considered.
- *Objectives* These too might differ between you and your audience.
- *Target audience* We are likely talk to colleagues in a different way than we do to potential customers. The nature of the audience will influence the level of formality. Also, the size of the audience will influence the style.
- *You–the speaker* You must ask yourself three further questions:
  - Am I the right person to make this particular presentation to the audience?
  - What makes me a suitable person to do this?
  - Why will I be considered credible?
- *Resources* Resources will be decided to some extent by the nature of the target audience, by what is available and by the nature of the venue. For a small informal group it may be appropriate to hand out copies of discussion documents. But it is possible, in most cases, to use an OHP or a flipchart. It can be very useful to hand out hard copies of any OHP slides for reference and note-taking. Figure 2.5 is an example of a Microsoft PowerPoint presentation handout. This package allows you to reduce the size of your slides to suit your purpose—in this case three slides per page—with the facility for your audience members to make notes next to each slide. Slides, video and audio facilities are increasingly available at many venues for major presentations. Many chief executives of major organizations will expect to use a teleprompter for a major speech these days.
- *When and where to present* These may be crucial aspects for any presentation. There may be a need to coincide the presenta-

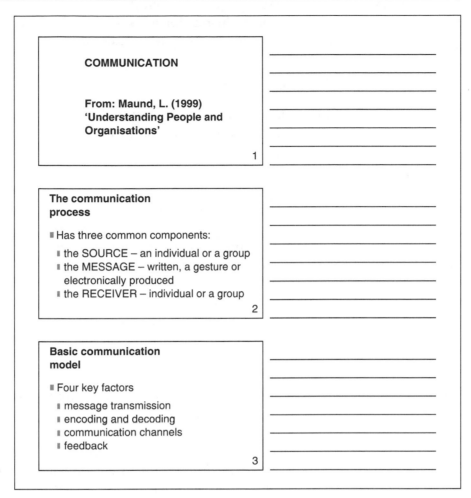

Figure 2.5
Example of a
Microsoft
PowerPoint
presentation
handout.

tion with the launch of a product or service, the introduction of new legislation or professional/organizational codes, stages in business planning and so on.

■ *Timing* As a general rule, the shorter the better, as few people can concentrate for longer than about 20 minutes on a single speaker. However, it is sometimes necessary to speak for longer. In this case, try to enliven your presentation by breaking it up, by adding an extra visual element, or by seeking the involvement of the audience. This interactive element always helps to interest the audience and can be done by simply asking questions at regular intervals.

■ *Physical surroundings* Consider the most appropriate place to present, the size of the audience and the seating arrangements in relation to whether everyone will be able to see, hear and take notes if they wish.

Planning the details

Once these basic planning factors have been analysed, you can then move on to the detailed construction of the presentation itself. In doing this you should pay attention to the following:

- *Structure* This should be broken down and organized into a coherent and logical structure: say what you are going to say; say it; summarize what you have said. Obviously the detailed structure is dependent upon the application itself, but it should include:
  - Purpose.
  - Overview.
  - Background/introduction.
  - The body of information (including claims and evidence, if appropriate).
  - Summary.
- *Visual aids layout* It is often tempting to put too much information onto an OHP (see Figure 2.5 for the ideal amount to include on any one OHP). It is better to limit text to a minimum. Your headings are a must, and *bullet point* lists are very effective. It is useful to remember that people seem to be able to remember points easier if they come in threes. When using an OHP it is very tempting for the presenter to read the words on the slide. This is a mistake, and a lost opportunity—the audience can read these for themselves. You should use your commentary to amplify, emphasize or to digress from what is written on the OHP slide.
- *Visual* Remember to use diagrams, charts, tables, icons, etc., where possible, as shown in the examples in Figures 2.4 and 2.5.
- *Commentary/style* You will need to make a choice of method of presentation before deciding how to remember the substance of it. You can read from a *highlighted* script, speak from prepared notes or speak without notes. The choice will depend on your skill and confidence, but remember to make notes only, or highlight the main points—which you can refer to—rather than read verbatim from a script. If you read, you will not concentrate your audience.

■ *Interacting with an audience* The rapport you create with your audience is a most important ingredient in ensuring that the message of any presentation gets across. This will depend upon you: looking and smiling at individuals (not the same ones all the time); maintaining good eye contact; asking questions where appropriate. It is also necessary to be relaxed, well prepared, well rehearsed, appropriately dressed, confident, enthusiastic, audible, and clear.

■ It can be effective if you make good use of humour. You must control the pace of your delivery, and you should never apologize for your presence or denigrate yourself. You should not distract the audience by your mannerisms (fiddling with a pencil, for example) or go on for too long about any one issue.

■ Creating a visual presentation is an ideal opportunity to use the facilities of the computer to help you create visual material of a high standard. Some people feel more at home using traditional aids such as the white board, OHP, films/video films, slide projector and handouts. Others are impressed by the techniques that can be employed using such media as Microsoft PowerPoint (PP) presentation. Personal experience has shown that students of management often become so absorbed by the numerous functions available to them by using PP, that they often allow the message to get lost in favour of style! So be warned. Again, Figure 2.5 shows how PP can be used effectively and modestly to get the message over.

■ Remember, too much visual material can cloud a point rather than illuminate it; the audience will concentrate more on the equipment itself and the techniques rather than on what you are saying. It is therefore vital to ensure that the use of any visual aid equipment illustrates and reinforces points; the messages 'projected' through them should be short, concise, simple and easy to see and hear.

EFFECTIVE READING

We all have to read—to keep informed, to keep up to date, and so on. But most of us could make our reading work much more efficiently for us.

- *Reduce your reading time* This can be done by judicious scanning. Before even beginning to read, you should look at the contents to identify sections of importance (and of no importance). Then you should look at the subtitles only, again to identify sections of particular interest. Thus, before you begin reading you should know what you are looking for, and where in the document you are most likely to find it.
  - When you do read, you should scan; do not expect to read every word. Most documents will contain only a few key ideas that you will wish to retain. The major task is to identify those.
- *Record what is important* When you have identified those few key ideas, you need to be able to remember them or to mark them for future reference. One way you can do this to use a highlighter pen to draw out the points as you go along. Another is to write a very brief summary and attach it to the front page of the document. Action points should be marked in a different colour, or a different style.

TAKING NOTES

Have you ever looked at the notes you have made of a meeting and wondered what on earth you have written? We often tend to take notes as a means of keeping ourselves occupied rather than with an eye for future use. We have all been guilty of reducing the effectiveness of our notes because we fail to record the most basic, and often the most important, information. Notes should always be dated, and should include the names of those present, if they relate to a meeting.

A good habit to get into is to begin notes with a statement of their purpose: why you are recording this information, and what the record is to be used for. Remember, we make notes in many circumstances and for many reasons. The following techniques should help to improve the effectiveness of your note-taking:

- *Be selective* Notes should not be too long, and should contain only summary information that can be of potential use later on.
- *Organize* The rules of any good writing apply. Information should be grouped, and organized into headings.
- *Presentation* Again, diagrams can be useful ways of illustrating information or dynamic processes. Bullet point lists,

again, help to summarize and show information in digestible form.

■ *Neatness* Reasonable writing, neatly presented, and without doodles helps the visual clarity of notes.

■ *Action points* These are among the most important items of information to record—whether they apply to you or others—yet they are often left out. Some visual device for recording action points can be helpful. Examples might include bracketing, use of coloured pens, or use of a special right-hand column.

MEETINGS

Purpose

Meetings should be useful ways to make things happen: to agree priorities, discuss and solve problems, identify new methods of working, agree and allocate responsibilities, follow up progress and so on.

However, these purposes can be, and often are, abused. Some people simply insist upon meetings because they have always had them. Others use them as a method of checking individual performance, assuming that group pressures will make people perform better. Others may use meetings as a method of group discipline.

We have all been to meetings that have been a waste of time for all concerned. Why does it seem so easy for so many meetings to turn out like this? Malcolm Peel (in his book, *How to make Meetings Work*), has identified six deadly sins:

■ Unnecessary attendance.
■ Lack of preparation.
■ Bad tactics.
■ Ineffective communication.
■ Personality problems.
■ Procedural problems.

A meeting should have a clear purpose, and this should be known and agreed by all concerned. This not only helps to integrate and focus the activities of the meeting, but it also serves as a way to measure its effectiveness.

Planning

A meeting should be properly planned and organized. Planning involves people, information and resources. The first and most obvious point is that a meeting cannot take place if any key contributors are not present. As well as being forewarned of meetings, participants should receive relevant information in good time before the meeting. If the purpose of the meeting is to discuss a report, no useful contributions can be made if the report is received cold for the first time at the meeting. Good organization will ensure that transport, rooms and other necessary facilities are available.

The conduct of the meeting will depend to some extent on the level of formality and the nature of the meeting. If planning a working meeting—to produce a draft document, or to solve a technical problem, for instance—it could take some considerable time and should be planned accordingly. Usually, however, the shorter the meeting, the better, as long as the objective is achieved.

Elements of an efficient and productive meeting:

- Purpose or objective known and shared by all.
- Agenda set and followed.
- Timetable set and agreed.
- Notes/minutes recorded.
- Input and involvement by all.
- Outcomes discussed and decided.
- Action points summarized at end.

There are three essential categories of membership at any meeting:

- The *chairperson*, who is responsible for calling the meeting in the first place, as well as identifying its purpose and the content of the agenda. This person must also, at the meeting itself, co-ordinate the issues, control participation and ensure optimum contributions from the relevant membership, as well as handle any conflicts. Above all, the chairperson must not dominate the meeting, must seek clarification of any technical or other complex concepts, and should make personal notes of the proceedings.
- The *secretary*, who is responsible for all arrangements before during and after the meeting. This will include the provision of all the necessary documentation, other specific information required for the meeting, equipment, materials and any

refreshments needed; he/she may also be required to take minutes unless another member is present for the purpose

■ The *other members*, who should ensure adequate preparation for their contributions at the meeting. These members will include the relevant experts required for the facts, someone who is able to identify compromise solutions, someone who is good at throwing up ideas (even if they are not all useful!), someone who can commit resources, and at least one person who is prepared to admit they do not understand, because most people are afraid to show their ignorance (see Chapter 1 for Belbin's nine ideal roles).

Construction of the agenda

There are specific stages with coherent progression, which must be addressed throughout the course of the meeting; the minutes will normally be recorded in order of discussion. The agenda should contain, as a minimum:

■ Apologies for absence.
■ Minutes of previous meeting.
■ Matters arising from previous minutes.
■ List of new items in order of urgency or importance.
■ Any other business.
■ Date and time of next meeting.

Recording of meetings

These should simply record the facts, any decisions taken and follow-up action required under each item. It is not necessary to record verbatim comments from each member other than when they directly refer to further action or further decisions required.

It is important to ensure that an accurate account of those attending the meeting be listed at the top of the minutes with relevant roles allocated alongside the names.

Item one should name those who should have attended the meeting but who have apologized, for urgent or important reasons, and who have been excused by the chair.

All members should have had sufficient time before the meeting to read the minutes of previous meetings and make any necessary notes in order to raise queries. Item two then requires that the minutes are agreed by all members and then signed by the chairperson and secretary.

Ideally, an *action column* should be ruled up on the right-hand side of the minutes to identify the initials of those who have agreed at the meeting to follow-up as necessary. Do not commit responsibilities to those absent from the meeting, unless they have previously agreed to be involved! This is a common mistake, which can result in the demotivation of those concerned, inaction and compromised objectives.

Item three will deal with the matters arising from those minutes, which may be taken in a different order, or be moved into another agenda item, depending upon any newly agreed priorities identified at the meeting, or newly acquired information.

This will then be followed by item four which addresses all new issues to be dealt with by the meeting, in order of priority. It is not unknown for discussion to take place to re-order the items in terms of newly identified importance or urgency (sometimes the managing director/chief executive is not available for the determined order of items for which she/he must be in attendance).

Item five covers any other business which may not be listed on the agenda and which has been identified by members as new, although perhaps not urgent, items for discussion.

The meeting members will then agree the time, date and place of any further meeting.

Techniques for effective communication at meetings

- *KISS* 'Keep it short and simple', as discussed earlier in this chapter. You must try to be clear and concise in what you say to ensure that it is fully understood by everyone at the meeting.
- *Know your own subject* Be familiar with all the written material made available before the meeting, and therefore be confident that you will be able to deliver your information and answer likely questions without fear of being unprepared.
- *Listen* Avoid interrupting others midstream. Let them make their points first, no matter how difficult it may be because you disagree, or are frightened you might forget what you want to say. Make your own notes, of course, so that you can come back to your points, but, by listening to others without interruption, it is possible to influence the discussion (or be positively influenced by the speaker) if the need for your

contribution remains. You will sometimes find that you do not need to make this contribution after all, that it is either covered by the speaker in the course of making her/his points, or that you simply change your mind.

- You will gain support and credibility as a good listener with the ability to acknowledge and apply what others think to your own thought development, without upsetting or embarrassing anyone. If you do not listen, not only the speaker but also others in the group are less likely to want to listen to you when it is your turn to speak.

■ *Use humour* This can be very helpful; it will relax everyone and help produce an environment conducive to open discussion and freedom of thought, especially where there are difficult problems to resolve or complex issues to debate. However, make sure it is relevant and that you do not become the scapegoat and ridiculed as the result of being known as a joker and never taken seriously.

■ *Speak* Speak when you have something constructive to add to, or ask about, the discussion and not just for the sake of being heard. One common mistake is for people to contribute only to their own function or specialism and remain quiet during the discussion of issues outside their immediate control or interest, when in fact they do have something to contribute. This not only makes them appear disinterested in the problems of others, but also that they are ignorant of them as well. Therefore, listen keenly to what is being said in all topics and allow your ideas to form accordingly. It can reveal to others where they have been less than efficient in transmitting information.

- Another mistake people can make is to be so anxious about not having said anything at all, that they will just say anything, no matter how irrelevant, unnecessarily confrontational, or simply pointless, in order for them to *appear* involved. It is best to say nothing, as long you remain focused on the subject at hand and *listen*.

■ *Compromise* Where necessary, and if you are able, don't just *stick to your guns* as a matter of principle. Uncompromising attitudes, unless the implications are too great for those you are representing—when you should explain them very clearly to the rest of the meeting—will achieve nothing. It could also damage your reputation as a good manager with the ability to view situations from a wide perspective.

- *When negotiating* identify those areas with which there is agreement and spell them out before making strong points over which you are seeking agreement, but which may be difficult for other members to accept.
- *Acknowledge the strengths and achievements of others* at the meeting This should include those who are not present. This also has positive effects on others' views of your abilities and perceptions. This must be genuine acknowledgement, of course, otherwise you will sound patronizing or condescending.

Smaller groups, better effects

One of the managers interviewed for this book found staff meetings very traumatic when she first arrived in post because of one individual's attitude within the group. No-one wanted to discuss things because the person concerned was always on the defensive, making it impossible for others to air their views and opinions. The manager then concentrated on holding small group meetings to much greater effect; others found it easier to contribute and develop their self-confidence.

When she finally ran a full staff meeting, the manager had been able to facilitate the removal of this individual's defensiveness, who then had little to say beyond relevant issues, making a more constructive and positive contribution to meetings. The manager's main tip for effective meetings: 'Always plan and prepare thoroughly, or you will look stupid. Take it from one who knows!'

As a final comment on the art of communicating impersonally, the manager would add: 'Remain focused on the end-product or desired outcome. Take time to read everything; policies, procedures, everything relevant. Past course materials make excellent reminders, especially if bad habits are creeping in. Keep up-to-date with things, it is no good having manuals of procedures and then allow the dust to settle on them. They have a purpose, so use them. Really understand the essence of their existence not just to act by the book, but to internalize their purpose and be party to their development.'

EXERCISE

Ask a colleague to observe your behaviour at the next meeting you run. Ask for feedback on your effectiveness:

- Was the agenda covered in time?
- Did you contribute appropriately and effectively?
- Did you make it possible for all attending to contribute?
- Did you handle any disagreements and how effective was this?

Telephone technique

The telephone is often the first line of response to customers, or the public at large, for many organizations. But what sort of impression do your customers get from your organization?

Try phoning your own organization from outside. What sort of response do you get? Is it prompt, helpful, informative and efficient?

It would be a pity to spend millions of pounds on a major media campaign to promote a product or service or a particular organization and have it spoilt because customers are treated badly by those answering the telephones.

Telephone checklist

Help your team to use the telephone effectively:

- Ensure the equipment is appropriate for the size and purpose of your organization.
- Give technical training. All staff should be able to use all available facilities provided by your equipment.
- Structure jobs appropriately. Good support and guidance for all staff answering the telephone are essential in helping them to give effective customer service.
- Establish good discipline. How to deal with various types of enquiry, making and receiving personal calls, peak time procedures and so on.
- Provide behavioural training. Make sure that the people answering telephone calls use the voice you would like your customers to hear. All organizations have their own preferred ways for staff to behave when dealing with telephone enquiries.

SUMMARY OF ACTIVITIES AND ISSUES

In working through this chapter, you will have encountered a number of issues and perhaps some ideas that are new to you. The objectives of the chapter were to:

- Identify aids to effective communication.
- Define the central role of communication.
- Identify barriers to effective communication.
- Introduce various concepts to effective interpersonal communication.
- Provide tips for effective reading and note-taking.
- Discuss ways to run effective meetings.

How well have the authors met these objectives?

More importantly, how have you approached and used the material yourself, and how much have you developed since the beginning of your course of study, or working through the chapter? You are strongly recommended to extend your research and study to include as much as possible of the material identified in further reading and references below, so that you can build on your expertise, incorporating more complex approaches and ideas as you develop further in your managerial role.

These objectives, if re-revisited over a period of time and put into practice in your job, will help you to achieve the personal competency of communication and presentation, broken down into the elements identified in the table at the end of the chapter. In order for you to reflect on your own behaviour and that of others with whom you work, you might find it useful to use the table as a self-assessment check (reproduce as many as you wish) to re-evaluate your skills and knowledge.

PREPARING FOR ACTION PLANNING

Remember to review the checklist of questions, as identified at Appendix 1.

Discuss your effectiveness as a 'person-to-person' communicator with your boss, your colleagues, subordinates, friends and relations.

Prompt their responses by asking about your behaviour under the various headings in this chapter and try to record them objectively (do not disagree with them, just think about what they have to say).

Were there any surprises? Were there areas of agreement between the various responses, if so, record your reactions and thoughts concerning them. What about the varying responses? Whom do you believe to be the most accurate in their observations of your behaviour and why? Be honest with yourself—this is all about self-development, not punishment for ineffective behaviour.

Do you have problems sifting through and reading all the material that lands upon your desk? Try out some of the simple rules discussed in this chapter and keep a log of the information you have gathered, recorded and stored.

Discuss with your boss the effectiveness of any reports you have submitted recently and make notes of any areas of development required. (Remember to assess your language, including use of jargon; any aids you have used to support your arguments—visual and otherwise; note-taking and other secondary information used in your reports.)

Discuss with those with whom you regularly 'meet' your effectiveness at meetings and group discussions. Detail your strengths and areas for development.

What are your particular strengths when dealing/liaising with people or agencies outside your own organization?

Would you say you had any particular difficulties?

What are your development needs in relation to the concepts and practicalities discussed in this chapter?

How do you intend to address them?

FURTHER READING AND REFERENCES

Cameron, S. and Pearce, S. (1995) *The Management Studies Handbook*. London: Pitman Publishing (Chapters 13–16). ISBN: 0-273-60346-9

Capon, C. (2000) *Understanding Organisational Context*. Harlow: Pearson Education. ISBN: 0-273-62162-4 (specifically for 'communications technology', pp. 59–63)

Cook, C.W. and Hunsaker, P.L. (2001) *Management and Organisational Behaviour* (3rd edition). New York: McGraw-Hill (Chapter 8). ISBN: 0-07-118032-X

Guirdham, M. (2002) *Interactive Behaviour at Work* (3rd edition). Harlow: Pearson Education. ISBN: 0-273-65590-6 (Chapter 7)

Hargie, O., Saunders, C. and Dickson, D. (1998) *Social Skills in Interpersonal Communication* (3rd edition). London: Routledge. ISBN: 0-415-08137-8

Hunsaker, P.L. (2001) *Training in Management Skills*. New Jersey: Prentice Hall (Chapter 3). ISBN: 0-13-955014-3

Jones, G.R., George, J.M. and Hill, C.W.L. (2000) *Contemporary Management* (2nd edition). USA: McGraw-Hill (Chapter 15). ISBN: 0-07-228147-2

Morris, M. (2001) *The First-time Manager* (revised 2nd edition). London: Kogan Page (Chapter 2). ISBN: 0-7494-3603-4

Mullins, L.J. (2002) *Management and Organisational Behaviour* (6th edition). London: Pitman Publishing (Chapter 17). ISBN: 0-273-65147-1

Open University (1990) *The Effective Manager*, Open University, Milton Keynes, UK

Recommended journal articles for readers' further development

Brinson, S.L. and Benoit, W.L. (1999) The tarnished star: restoring Texaco's damaged public image. *Management Communication Quarterly* 12 (4): 483–510. USA: Sage Publications, Inc.

Guiniven, J.E. (2001) The lessons of survivor literature in communicating decisions to downsize. *Journal of Business and Technical Communication* 15 (1): 53–71. USA: Sage Publications, Inc.

Halpern, L. (2000) You've got email: are you using it? *The Guardian* 30/11/2000. Net news: You are missing 100 million opportunities every day to raise your brand awareness

Hilpern, K. (1999) Why it's good to talk: companies are actually encouraging employees to chat in working time. *The Guardian Unlimited* 12/04/1999

Kelly, D. (2000) Using vision to improve organisational communication. *Leadership and Organization Development Journal* 21/02/2000: 92–101. Massachusetts: MCB University Press. ISSN: 0143-7739. Website: http://www.emerald-library.com

Leggett, B. (2002) Getting the sound to match the vision. *The Guardian* (12/08/2000

More, E.A. and Irwin, H.T. (2000) Management communication for the new millennium: an Australian perspective. *Management Communication Quarterly* 14 (1): 142–151. USA: Sage Publications, Inc.

Taylor, D. (2001) How to compile the perfect charity report. The Charity Commissioner's speech. Clear communication: changing the focus of the annual report. *Society* 12/02/2001

Ulmer, R.R. (2001) Effective crisis management through established stakeholder relationships: Malden Mills as a case study. *Management Communication Quarterly* 14 (4): 590–615. USA: Sage Publications, Inc.

Zorn, M. (2001) Forum: popular management writing. Forum introduction: gurus' views and business news. Popular management discourse and its relationship to management and organisational communication. *Management Communication Quarterly* 14 (3): 471–475. USA: Sage Publications, Inc.

Zorn, T.E. and Page, D.J. (2000) Nuts about change: multiple perspectives on change-oriented communication in a public sector organisation. *Management Communication Quarterly* 13 (4): 515–566. USA: Sage Publications, Inc.

Competency element	Competency level: 1 (low)– 5 (high)	Requires development	No direct experience	What can help? (identify opportunities)	Who can help?	When can it be achieved?	How can it be achieved?
Listen actively, ask questions, clarify points and rephrase others' statements to check mutual understanding							
Adopt personal communication and presentation styles appropriate to listeners and situations, including selecting an appropriate time and place for the event							
Use a variety of media and communication aids to reinforce points and maintain interest							

Present difficult ideas, concepts and problems in a way that promotes understanding	Confirm listeners' understanding through questioning and interpretation of non-verbal signals	Encourage listeners to ask questions or rephrase statements to clarify their understanding	Modify communication and presentation in response to expectations, responses and feedback from listeners as necessary

CHAPTER 3

Ethical perspective

Managers with an ethical perspective identify concerns and resolve complex dilemmas in an open, reasoned manner.

LINKS TO THE CHARTERED MANAGEMENT INSTITUTE'S MODULE

This chapter aims to address the aims and learning outcomes as identified in the Introduction to this text under the heading *Links to the Chartered Management Institute's Module 'Understanding Yourself'*. However, this chapter, whilst supporting the module, stands in addition to the material covered within it.

INTRODUCING THE RELATIONSHIP BETWEEN THE PERSONAL COMPETENCY MODEL AND AN ETHICAL PERSPECTIVE

The Personal Competency Model (PCM), as already discussed, identifies the behaviours and skills that are necessary for you to develop before you are able to prove competence in any managerial function. This chapter attempts to deal with the various behaviours and skills necessary for you to apply across all managerial functions, transferring your learning to different occasions, at different times and under varying circumstances (contexts), consistently.

The outcomes below, as identified within this section of the model, should be borne in mind while you work through this chapter.

Outcomes required to maintain an ethical perspective

This chapter invites the manager to develop behaviours which demonstrate that she/he:

- Complies with legislation, industry regulation, professional and organizational codes.
- Shows integrity and fairness in decision-making.
- Sets objectives and creates cultures that are ethical.
- Identifies the interests of stakeholders and their implications for the organization and individuals.
- Clearly identifies and raises ethical concerns relevant to the organization.
- Works towards resolution of ethical dilemmas based on reasoned approaches.
- Understands and resists personal pressures that encourage non-ethical behaviour.
- Understands and resists apparent pressures from organizational systems to achieve results by any means.

INTRODUCTION AND OBJECTIVES

The objectives of the chapter are to:

- Discuss the nature of ethical behaviour.
- Introduce concepts of ethical behaviour within the organization.
- Introduce concepts of ethical behaviour outside the immediate organization.
- Discuss environmental issues, ethics and management.

The aims of this chapter are to introduce the reader to the concepts of ethics that are relevant to the decisions that a manager has to confront. The chapter is not intended to turn the reader into an expert on moral theory. Neither will it transform an individual with fundamentally immoral or unethical beliefs into a fine upstanding member of society. However, we hope that it will pose some questions that will encourage you to think about the ethical dimensions of your behaviour as a manager.

THE NATURE OF ETHICAL BEHAVIOUR

In September 1993 the Institute of Management (now, of course, The Chartered Management Institute) conducted a major survey of its members on the subject of 'Ethics and the Professional Manager'. In the covering letter accompanying the survey questionnaire, Roger Young the then Director General of the Institute stated that:

> Recent events have led to a growing interest in the ethical issues faced by managers as they balance the competing demands of those with a *stake* in the organization. Yet despite this interest, there is little information about the experiences and opinions of managers themselves in relation to ethical and moral conflicts at work.

Roger Young then commented that: 'There is clearly a close relationship between professional management and ethics'.

The survey represents an important source of managerial perception of what constitutes ethical behaviour in the UK. Previously much of the work on business ethics had been carried out in the USA. There, business ethics had for a considerable time formed an essential part of both undergraduate and postgraduate business degrees. The question of *managerial ethics* is now making a significant impression on the content of equivalent courses in the UK, as can be seen by the recommended reading and references at the end of this text; academic authors are becoming aware of the importance of ethical, moral and environmental issues to the survival of the economy in general.

The survey found that about nine out of ten of those responding reported that they adopted an ethical perspective towards management and were prepared to speak out about ethical issues in the workplace. However, the findings indicated that a significant proportion of managers in the sample at that time said that there was an *ethical mismatch* between their own views and those that they reported their own organization held.

Significantly, the survey findings also revealed that managers appeared to see various behaviours identified in the questionnaire as more of an ethical issue for organizations in general than for their own organization in particular.

Ethics as tiers of issues

Matthews (1988) suggested that the demonstration of organizational ethics may be observed in terms of *tiers*. These tiers or layers represent a graduation of importance.

- *First-tier issues* are the most serious because they:
  - Affect large numbers of people.
  - Cause the greatest harm.
  - Are on the verge of illegality.

The sort of things that would be considered *first-tier issues* would be the manufacture of unsafe products, generating large-scale industrial pollution.

- *Second-tier issues* would be described as intermediate issues because they may affect a large number of people but are less serious in the amount of harm caused than first-tier issues. Examples of issues in this category would be the presence of monopolies, bribery, false advertising.
- *Third-tier issues* are distinguished by the fact that they are:
  - Less likely to be life-threatening.
  - Likely to have implications for social responsibility.

The sort of issues that might figure here are such things as a lack of community involvement and a failure to make charitable donations.

Absolute and relative ethics

As well as considering ethics as *tiers*, we can also consider the question of *absolute* as opposed to *relative* ethics. In order to understand this we need to understand two kinds of reasoning which you might use to guide your behaviour.

1 *Moral obligation reasoning* This is based on the moral thinking of the philosopher Immanuel Kant (1959). Kant claimed that morality consists in doing your duty according to *a priori* principles. By this he meant that you did not look at the particular circumstance but instead considered what basic principle should guide your actions. So if you consider that lying is *wrong*, then all lying is unethical and you cannot *pick and choose* according to the circumstances.

2 *Outcome reasoning* This is based on the writings of a philosopher called John Stuart Mill, who talked about something he called *utilitarianism*. In his view, you can ethically defend carrying out actions that promote the greatest good of the greatest number of people. Therefore, if telling a lie does this, then telling a lie can be ethical.

Application of moral obligation versus outcome reasoning

- *Lying* Moral obligation reasoning would not significantly distinguish between telling a lie to avert pain or to conceal an action. Outcome reasoning would accept lying to protect as acceptable, or even as ethically correct.
- *Corruption* Moral obligation reasoning would deem all corruption as unethical if corruption was in principle unethical. Outcome reasoning would accept that paying bribes to achieve a good outcome (e.g. getting food to people in areas of famine) was ethical.

Both moral obligation reasoning (MOR) and outcome reasoning (OR) are relevant. An integrative model could offer the following criteria:

- *Utilitarian outcomes* (MOR): the question would be 'does the behaviour produce the greatest good for the greatest number within the organization?'
- *Individual rights* (OR): here, the question would be 'does the behaviour respect the rights of all affected parties?'
- *Distributive justice* (OR): here, 'does the behaviour treat people equitably?'
- *Overwhelming factors* (?): a decision may be ethical even when it results in some good and some bad outcomes, when a person's behaviour uses questionable ends to achieve a positive end or when it is based upon inaccurate or incomplete information

Relativism in ethical behaviour

There is a school of thought which asserts that behaviour is judged by the standard of the local environment. This is the 'when in Rome do as Romans do' principle. In the commercial sector this has been defined by the views of Milton Friedman (1962, p. 33) as:

> In a free economy there is one and only one social responsibility of business—to use its resources and engage in activities to increase its profits so long as it stays within the rules of the game, which is to say, engages in open and free competition, without deception or fraud.

Thus Friedman asserts that, in business, to pursue any other goal than maximizing its profit, is tantamount to theft from the owners and thus could be viewed as immoral. Charitable intentions do not change this.

Carr (1970) also contended that business people had to engage in bluff and deception as part of everyday business activity both within and outside their organizations. He claimed that, as long as 'he complies with the law of the land and avoids telling malicious lies he is ethical ... A good part of the time (he) is trying to do unto others as he hopes others will not do unto him'. Ethical behaviour can be self-serving since it involves avoiding antagonizing competitors, suppliers, etc.

Carr argues that you can appear ethical yet also bluff and deceive in order to gain an advantage. Elaine Sternberg (1994) sought to set out the rules of the game, which she believed to include a ban on 'cheating', as well as a ban on 'losing deliberately'. Playing the game means playing to win. All activity within the game that is not devoted to winning is either not playing seriously or constitutes cheating.

Both Friedman and Carr argue that business (office) ethics are different from individual (domestic) ethics. Carr argues for the morality of the card game. Deliberate cheating is not acceptable, but bluff, deceit and misrepresentation have a role. Friedman argues for a clear duty to pursue profit to the exclusion of all distraction.

Narrow versus broad ethics

Tom Sorell and John Hendry (1995) suggest the existence of two categories of narrow and broad business ethics. They define *narrow ethics* as 'when it only relates to those employed or directly concerned with the organization (such as shareholders or current customers)'. *Broad ethics*, on the other hand, acknowledges the responsibility of the organization to society at large.

Environmental issues mean that increasingly organizations accept the broader definition of business ethics. The interesting question this poses is whether this represents a conflict with Friedman's claim that the only morally acceptable behaviour is profit maximizing (within the constraints of the law!). The argument might be that if the customers of the organization are concerned with its stand on environmental and social matters then it *is* profit-maximizing behaviour to recognize this. Accordingly, the organization adopts a broader view of business ethics.

The public image of organizations has become more important in a time of mass communication. A broader concept of business ethics can influence the narrower concept. Thus the way in which a company treats staff may be influenced by the pressure of the media and consequently of public opinion. The narrow code of business ethics (towards staff) can undergo a change as a result of this. For example, a practice of sacking employees before they acquire employment protection may be legal but, if exposed by the media, will give the company a bad image.

Similarly, narrow codes of ethics influencing how staff members behave within the organization may impact upon the broader business ethics towards the environment. A professional person, such as a doctor or a scientist, may feel constrained by a narrow code of ethics and reluctant to *whistle-blow* on a colleague whose behaviour is not acceptable within a broader code of ethics. Rather, the decision is to deprive the transgressor of *peer respect* for his/her actions.

Later in the chapter we will look at the concepts of narrow ethics as applied to stakeholders within, or close to, the organization, and broader ethics as applied more to the community or society at large.

EXERCISE

Identify a recent ethical dilemma (or potential ethical dilemma) you have experienced and analyse it for any moral obligation reasoning or outcome reasoning which you believe may have been employed. Would you recommend a different approach in the future—taking both a relativist and broad/narrow approach to ethical behaviour in your organization (or one with which you are familiar)?

Cultural and minority issues in ethics

The UK is a multicultural and multiracial society. One of the authors lives in a London borough, which boasts over 125 different languages within its boundaries. Many organizations incorporate *equal opportunity statements* into their recruitment material and include these statements on advertisements so as to attract the full *potential* population to their vacancies. The other author lives in the northwest of England, where ethnic grouping tends to be more widely dispersed, with isolated pockets of different ethnic minorities across the region. Although it has taken longer for organizations in the area to recognize the need for *diversity management*, because the issues are very different to those in London and the southeast, they have nonetheless addressed them more fully in recent years.

For many managers, especially those working in the public sector, there is no need for a book such as this to remind them of their ethical responsibility to behave in a fair and equitable manner at all times. Later on in the chapter we make reference to the legislation governing discrimination and equal opportunity. Here, we will draw attention to some of the issues associated with what is increasingly being called 'managing diversity' (see also Chapter 7 for more about *managing diversity*).

The evidence for the continued existence of discrimination in employment on the grounds of race, national origin, sex, religion, disability, accent, language, background and so forth is compelling. Studies carried out before and after the passage of relevant legislation have demonstrated that racial discrimination continues to take place. Newell (1995), summarizing these studies, suggests that the studies showed that 90% of white job applicants were successful as compared to 63% of Asian and Afro-Caribbean applicants *where the only significant difference was the race of the applicant* [authors' italics]. Newell notes that discrimination is often hard to prove and that this may account for its continuance despite the fact that it is illegal and has been for some time.

Where *female employment* is concerned, there has been a pattern of increasing workforce participation. This is to some extent linked to the growth of the service sector at the expense of traditional manufacturing, as well as to the expansion of part-time and temporary work. Studies have shown that women's work careers are less likely to be continuous and that there are likely to be periods 'out of the workforce' and of part-time employment. This has been associated with what Newell calls 'horizontal and vertical' segregation. The terms 'glass ceiling', 'glass walls' and, more recently, 'ice ceiling' (denoting a potential thawing) convey the notion that women are considered to be less *permanent* in employment and career development than men.

Horizontal segregation (glass ceiling), according to Newell, is associated with the lack of women in managerial jobs compared to their proportion in the overall workforce. As you look higher up the organizational ladder, the proportion of women declines even further.

Some would argue that this is a consequence of historic patterns of male recruitment and that, in time, women will move through the organization and into more senior roles. However, others would say that there is direct and/or indirect discrimination which serves either to discourage women from applying for promotion or which works against them being offered promotion.

Horizontal discrimination (glass walls) operates to restrict women to particular roles or functions within an organization or occupation. Thus women tend to be employed by airlines more in customer service roles (flight attendant and check-in staff) than in equipment-related roles (pilot, engineer and maintenance staff). This is in part a leftover from an image of women as best suited to a *caring* role. Possibly there is also a perception by some airlines that customers expect a male presence behind the controls.

Things have moved on considerably regarding women in employment since Newell's research, of course, not least of which, being the *end of a job-for-life* expectation, with more people of both genders moving between organizations in order to gain different skills, deeper knowledge and understanding, as well as organizations themselves needing to bring in/develop new skills associated with the constant environmental and customer requirement changes resulting in improvements to and changes in goods and services. Not only does this imply the need for change in more traditional views of recruitment and career development but also employers are becoming more amenable towards career breaks, which become less of an issue with these changing organizational factors. The *ice ceiling* demonstrates that attitudes towards what constitutes *commitment* from potential female managers no longer requires the long hours, no holidays and weekends at work which was traditionally required of men. There are still issues at the highest echelons of the organizations, but they are *melting* gradually.

General pressures to behave unethically

Before moving on to consider ethical behaviour within your organization, let us pause and consider what pressures exist for people to behave unethically. We could start by telling a story, a version of which most readers will probably have heard.

A person is asked by a colleague at a party whether they would take all their clothes off in public for £1 million. The person almost immediately replies that they would do it. The colleague then asks if they would do it for £1. The person refuses, saying 'What sort of person do you think I am?' The colleague comments 'Well you've already shown what sort of person you are, now all you're quibbling over is the price!'

You might want to consider this story when you read about someone who behaves unethically for an apparently minor reward. The temptations in organizations are relative. The car-park attendant may allow access to a car lot (to which you are not entitled) for the promise of a drink. Someone else from the same company could regard being offered a drink to behave unethically as an insult to his/her intelligence.

Temptation to act unethically is often linked to discretion. If a manager or official has any discretion over how to act and there is little immediate recourse by the client, customer or employee against the way the discretion is exercised, then there can be temptation to act unethically.

The expectations of organizations can encourage people to cut corners. Where the organization wills the *ends of an activity* and is indifferent to the *means taken to achieve that end*, then this is a powerful incentive to engage in unethical behaviour in order to achieve what is perceived as a desirable outcome. This is the area of the rogue dealers such as Nick Leeson, or the policeman who fabricates evidence in order to secure the conviction.

Similarly, where the organization is only focused on the process, rather than both process and outcome, the employee is tempted to avoid decisions and simply ensure that their paperwork is in order. Thus there are circumstances where unethical practices take place because a person is being denied a decision or resource that they have an *ethical* right to expect.

We would submit that, where there is an organizational or managerial indifference to *either* ends or means, the conditions exist to promote unethical behaviour. Where there is an indifference to *both* ends and means then you have an *ethical vacuum*!

ETHICAL BEHAVIOUR WITHIN THE ORGANIZATION

In Chapter 9 we look at the concept of stakeholders within an organization. Here we will be addressing ethics as defined more narrowly by stakeholders within the organization itself. You, as an employee, are such a stakeholder. Therefore, like it or not, your behaviour will have an impact within the organization.

We will raise here a number of questions about ethical behaviour. In some cases we can offer answers. Organizations are seeking to give people guidance through ethical codes of practice; perhaps your organization has such a code. Upon joining an organization, individuals might be formally trained by existing colleagues or managers, which will help provide a set of principles to guide behaviour. The informal socialization will certainly have an impact. This is when the naïve new member of staff encounters a discrepancy between what is *practised* and what is *preached*. Typically, it may occur through an aspect of *custom* such as an informal adjustment of working conditions. The employment contract says that you start work at 9.00 a.m. and finish at 5.00 p.m. with an hour for lunch. However, colleagues seem to all disappear at 4.00 p.m. on Friday! Is this unethical behaviour? Perhaps it has been accepted as a variation of the contract, perhaps not.

Ethical codes

Brigley (1994) commented that 47% of the organizations represented in the Institute of Management (as was) survey possessed an ethical code. He found that they were more likely in larger organizations and in public sector organizations. Trends in the USA suggest that such ethical codes are becoming more popular.

Respondents in the survey said that they knew their code well and generally felt that top management enforced the codes. They generally agreed that such codes demonstrated an organization's sense of social responsibility. Few thought that the code was too idealistic or difficult to apply in practice.

Perhaps significantly, the managers who responded to the survey were well educated (70% had a degree or higher qualification compared with 20% for all UK managers) and tended to be in the more senior managerial grades. This lends strength to a view that ethical codes are likely to be increasingly important in organizations in the UK.

Paul Harris, writing in the *Management Accounting Journal* in November 1995, suggests that even though 60% of USA businesses have ethical codes these have made little difference to what actually happens. He stresses that the simple existence of a code does not resolve the problem of implementing it.

When companies not only possess a code of ethics but also review and update it, then it can be inferred that it is taken quite seriously. United Biscuits produced an ethics booklet and provided it to staff and shareholders. This was done in 1987. In February ten years later the company had reviewed and revised the 1987 booklet. A code of ethics does not stand unaltered with the passage of time.

A code of ethics can be good for business. Companies such as the Body Shop and Tom & Jerry's Ice Cream are seen as 'good' by many consumers because of their *ethical stance*. The Co-operative Bank advertises itself as an ethical bank whose values dominate its investment policy.

However, there is some doubt about whether *codes of ethics* can be simply bought in. John Drummond, an expert in this area, comments that ethics are about actions not words. He helped NatWest develop its code of ethics and this included a 'hotline' for staff with a general guarantee of confidentiality for those who *whistle-blow*. The code encompasses such items as avoiding making disparaging remarks about competitors and not using employment status with the company to influence public officials or customers for personal gain or benefit. Drummond and Bain (1994) set out the advantages and disadvantages of ethical codes:

Reasons for employing ethical codes

- To clarify management's thoughts on what constitutes unethical behaviour.
- To help employees to think about ethical issues before they are faced with the realities of the situation.
- To provide employees with the opportunity of refusing compliance with unethical action.
- To define the limits of what constitutes acceptable or unacceptable behaviour.
- To provide a mechanism for communicating the managerial philosophy in the realm of ethical behaviour.
- To assist in the induction and training of employees.

Arguments against employing ethical codes

- Even a detailed list of guidelines cannot be expected to cover all the possible grey areas of potentially unethical practice.
- Like fair-employment practice statements, codes of ethics are often too generalized to be of specific value.

- ■ Rarely are codes of ethics prioritized; for example, loyalty to the company and to fellow employees does not resolve the potential conflict when a colleague is seen to be acting contrary to company interests.

- ■ As an individual phenomenon, ethical behaviour that has been guided by ethical codes of conduct will only be effective if the codes have been internalized and are truly believed by employees.

EXERCISE

Attempt to draw up a 'Code of ethics' for your organization, based on the industry within which it operates.

Staff

A well-known saying is that the biggest lie told in business is 'Your cheque is in the post'. Some claim that the second biggest lie is 'We value our staff'. The obligation between an organization and its employees is one rooted in law. Employment law is well beyond the scope of this book. It is sufficient to note here that much of the relationship between an employer and employee cannot be detailed in a legal document. This is especially the case when you move from routine simple tasks to the more technical and creative responsibility increasingly sought of staff.

There is an interesting question of whether an organization has an obligation to *find* work for employees. One of the authors did some consultancy work with a local authority, which made a commitment to *find work for staff*. Therefore, staff members, instead of being made redundant if their job disappeared, were offered redeployment into another part of the organization with some retraining. This was popular with staff at risk but some questioned whether it was fair to the customers of the local authority. The redeployed staff members were, in some cases, not as capable as people who could have been recruited through open competition.

An important point to make is that the moral obligations between employee and employer are two-way. With the growth of 'casualization' of the workforce, employers have taken the opportunity to relinquish certain obligations. Arguably an employer's obligation to a casually employed or agency member of staff is not as great as that towards a long-serving permanent employee. However, the relaxing of the obligation can be a *two-edged sword*. For example, casual or agency staff may feel a lesser moral or ethical responsibility to the organization. The European Commission (EU) when seeking to establish an equality of treatment between permanent and temporary employees in respect of such factors as holiday entitlement, an agency providing temporary staff, asserted that it already did this and did not require an EU directive.

Porter rules!

A real example is of an education establishment that decided to replace its permanent porters with contracted-in evening security guards. It enabled a saving in wage costs to be made. However, students objected when they found that they were being denied access to the library to return books because the security guards had been told to refuse entry to all who did not have a current identity card with them. The original porters knew most of the students and had allowed students to return books, even if they did not have current identity cards with them. The porters understood that returning library books was important both to the organization and to its customers and made judgements accordingly.

Colleagues

In most organizations of any size there will be some kind of division, which leads staff to identify colleagues as opposed to other employees of the organization. Sometimes it is based upon levels of responsibility; it may derive from time served or it may be based upon professional training or recognition. Sometimes it can become strongly entrenched, as in the legal profession with its division of solicitors and barristers.

Should there be a different ethical obligation between colleagues than between employees in general? A doctor witnesses a porter in a hospital handle a patient rudely and sees that the patient is noticeably upset. Is the doctor likely to respond differently if it is another doctor rather than a porter? In the first instance, the doctor may reprimand the porter directly or even report the porter to a manager. In the case of two doctors it is less likely that the matter would be reported formally and possibly it may not even be mentioned. One factor is whether there is some kind of common bond of training or professionalism that makes people colleagues. In such a case, the measure of acceptability/non-acceptability of behaviour may not be the same as the standard applied by the organization. Musicians in an orchestra or actors in a play may be harsher in their judgements on their colleagues than the organization itself would be.

On the other hand, in some organizations or occupations there are the equivalent of 'old Spanish customs' that govern behaviour. 'Old Spanish customs' were particularly common in the pre-Wapping print industry. Print workers would sign up imaginary employees and draw their wages.

There is a danger inherent in the natural feeling of loyalty towards colleagues where ethical issues are concerned. Most occupations have an unwritten taboo, which operates against reporting colleagues for unethical behaviour. Rather, the expectation is that the guilty individual is discouraged through professional disapproval or social pressure.

In the education sector this is a particularly contentious issue. Most academics in our field have a definite impression of their colleagues. They know who works hard, who is never available for students and who is doing the minimum amount of work to get by. Yet despite the weakness of the trades unions in the higher education sector, few academics would choose to stand up and point the finger at (relatively few) non-productive colleagues. There is a feeling that it is not the sort of thing a professional academic should do.

Senior managers

Writing in the *Financial Times* on 22 March 1996, Rob Goffee and John Hunt stressed the continuing need for managers, in the face of the removal of organizational middle layers, to value ethical behaviour and to focus upon such concepts as *vision* and *mission*. They quote a survey of top managers in which the characteristics of most effective top managers were considered to be:

- Force of personality (33%).
- Competence in the job (26%).
- Good with people (22%).
- Flexibility (10%).
- Ethical beliefs (6%).

The fact that ethical beliefs rated at all is encouraging. However, that the rating of it was so low is disappointing. Organizational members look to senior managers as role models to indicate desirable, acceptable and unacceptable behaviour. If you read about the horrors of the holocaust, one of the most chilling aspects was the cold *managerial efficiency* with which the victims were rounded up, transported and dispatched. The account of the operation of the death camps given in books such as *Schindler's List* portrays managers, stripped of ethical considerations, struggling with resource constraints. Without an ethical dimension to senior management, what is to prevent such further abominations?

A key responsibility held by senior managers is often to balance opposing considerations. Perhaps a reduction in the workforce has to be made. The shareholders might wish for the minimum legally required redundancy to be paid. The manager knows that the workforce would ideally wish for no redundancies, but, if there are going to be any at all, they would want the company to be far more generous than to give the legal minimum. To which stakeholder should the manager give the most credence? Certainly resources and company policy will influence the decision. However, there is an ethical dimension as well.

Redundancy at Ford's

The decision by Ford in early 1997 to make staff redundant from their Liverpool-Speke plant was heavily criticized. The company was accused of making the Liverpool workers redundant because they were cheaper to lay off than Ford workers elsewhere in Europe. The management could have simply responded that it was their responsibility to make the decision that minimized the costs and . . . so what! Such a response would have not been ethically defensible (assuming it were true).

ETHICAL BEHAVIOUR OUTSIDE THE IMMEDIATE ORGANIZATION

Where are the ethical boundaries of the organization in behavioural terms? There is no simple answer to this question. We asked a group of managers from public sector organizations to categorize a range of behaviours in terms of whether they were ethically acceptable or not. Factors such as talking about their clients in social settings varied in the extent to which they were seen as unacceptable depending upon the type of organization.

Some organizations are very extensive in their definitions of ethical boundaries. Staff members at the Government Communication Headquarters at Cheltenham were at one point denied the right to join a trade union. The reason given was that it might represent a conflict of loyalties given the secrecy of the work. Yet the staff members are also expected, as part of their responsibility, to intercept private communications usually without the knowledge or agreement of the communicating parties. This is justified on the grounds of *national interest.*

There are stakeholders that are close to the organization and the individual manager, such as customers and suppliers. There are ethical considerations that enter into communications with them regarding how you as an employee or manager relate to them. Similarly, if you are a professional, then you may well be governed by a code of behaviour particular to your occupation. Legislation also has a bearing upon the way many people make moral or ethical decisions.

Customers

The mottoes 'The customer is always right' and 'Give the customer what they want' have a certain cachet to them. Sorell and Hendry (1994) note that the consumer can be seen as victim as well as king. Much of the concern expressed over the ethics of the national lottery is based upon gullible consumers being conned into spending more than they can afford. The law is there to protect consumers. Organizations such as the Advertising Standards Authority stress the need for businesses to observe certain principles in trying to sell their products.

Of course, you are a consumer as well as an employee or manager. In some situations you are a very powerful consumer. If you are buying fast-moving consumer goods such as CDs, DVDs, audio- or video-cassettes, then you can shop around and compare prices. If you buy a disk or cassette that is defective then you find this out very quickly. There is an element of trust, but not as significant as the trust you place in the supplier of a less-tangible product such as your retirement pension.

There has been considerable concern expressed about the mis-selling of endowment mortgages and personal pensions. These are very different products to CDs. The consumer is less informed about the product and relies upon guidance from the person selling it. It may not be obvious that the product is inappropriate until many years later. They will then, of course, be grossly disadvantaged by that.

EXERCISE

Use the following questions to determine ethical approaches to your dealings with customers. It is helpful to put yourself into the frame of mind of your customer (to have empathy—seeing things from their point of view) and to ask yourself some searching questions:

- If I were buying or using this product or service what standards of advice would I expect?
- How vital is it that I understand the implications of the purchase decision or decision to use the product or service?
- How significant is the nature of the purchase or usage, which I, as a consumer, am making?

The exercise of what has been described as the golden rule of 'treating others as you would have them treat you' is always worth bearing in mind.

Suppliers

Much of what has been said about customers is also true of suppliers. Suppliers are often larger players than customers. Thus the agreement to supply may be accompanied by a more formal contract.

A senior government minister came in for considerable adverse criticism some years ago, when he suggested that companies could save money by delaying payments to suppliers. This illustrated what is possibly a significant difference where suppliers are concerned. If a company goes out of business then it is usually more likely that the suppliers will suffer immediate financial loss than the customers. The lack of customers may well be the cause of the company going out of business but it will be the suppliers to the company who are left at the end of the queue to be paid after the banks and the Inland Revenue!

Suppliers are sometimes heavily dependent upon particular pur-
chasers. Marks & Spencer was always well known for the close and
exclusive relationships that they had with their suppliers, until the
reality of changing markets and economics caught up with them a
few years ago. The difficulty then presented to Marks & Spencer
was how were they to deal with their suppliers? Sadly, a number of
them are no longer used because the business had to reposition itself
in order to remain solvent; these decisions were not taken lightly by
Marks & Spencer.

This does, of course, raise the question as to the extent to which a
company can or should *carry* a supplier who may be going through a
bad patch. In ethical terms the company may be regarded as failing to
meet an obligation to shareholders to safeguard resources if it allows
a supplier too generous or lax terms of business. Although the figures
are important, in many cases the goodwill that has built up over years
of doing business is a factor as well. These are not easy decisions for
managers to make.

Professional codes

In some organizations such as hospitals or research laboratories many
of the staff would regard themselves as professionals first and employees or managers second. Professions often lay claim to a particular set
of occupational values. Some professions such as medicine, nursing
and law are proud of the fact that they can enforce their professional
standards to the extent of expelling a member who falls short of the
required standard.

The standards exacted by some professional codes are well in
excess of what would be required by any normal code of organization
ethics. A doctor who has an affair with a patient risks being struck off.
Few employees who have an affair with a customer take the same risk
(though some organizations would certainly disapprove of it).

The area of medicine is probably most subject to professional codes
of conduct. These can run counter to the desire of managers to run
the health service in the most efficient fashion. Writing in the *Observer*
on 3. March 1996, Richard Norton-Taylor gave an account of problems in bringing a large health service computer network on line.
Doctors, lawyers and patients' organizations were concerned about
the level of confidentiality. The NHS management claimed that the
network would save over £2 billion each year by avoiding duplication
of services. The British Medical Association claimed the system was

insecure because it had been designed for the benefit of bureaucrats. The concerns were such that the various parties sought to introduce legislation to outlaw the use of illicitly obtained medical data.

If you, as a manager or as an employee, work in a setting where there is a significant professional presence, then you need to be aware of the likely reaction to proposed changes that challenge or impact on formal codes of professional behaviour. Indeed, sometimes the professional code is informal and just as strong.

Legislation and ethics

The requirements of the law and the dictates of conscience are not necessarily the same. Open any national paper on an average day and you will probably find an example of a person behaving in a way that you would question in ethical terms but which is perfectly legal. Have you ever witnessed an incident on the street where you were concerned that someone was being mistreated, but decided, for whatever reason, not to intervene? The law does not require us to be beyond criticism.

However, as we have indicated previously, there are situations in which behaviour is not only illegal but is also unethical. Discrimination in employment is such an example. The legislation that a manager needs to be aware of in this area would be the following:

- The *Equal Pay Act 1970* and the *Equal Pay (Amendment) Regulations 1983* set out to eliminate discrimination in pay and terms of employment between men and women where:
  - Men and women are doing work of a similar nature.
  - Jobs have been evaluated as similar.
  - Work is of equal value to the organization.
  This last category is significant because of proceedings against the UK Government under the Treaty of Rome. It raises the possibility of comparing jobs in terms of their value to the organization.
- The *Sex Discrimination Act 1975* lays down that it is unlawful to treat anyone, on grounds of sex, less favourably than a person of the opposite sex. This includes discrimination on the basis of marital status.
- The *Race Relations Act* was extended in 1976 and requires employers to treat people from different racial backgrounds

equally. This would include colour, race, nationality and ethnic or national origin.

For both of these pieces of legislation you need to be aware of the difference between direct discrimination—where a person is treated less favourably because of sex, race, etc.—and indirect discrimination—where the employer imposes a condition which one sex, race, etc. would find it harder to comply with; for example, imposing an unnecessarily high *minimum* height—which would discriminate against many women and people from certain nationalities—or requiring good written English for a manual job—which of course would discriminate against those whose first language is not English.

Ethics, fairness and integrity in decision-making

How can you apply fairness and integrity in the decisions that you make as an individual and as a manager? One proverb, which is useful as a guide, speaks of 'seeking to experience walking in another person's shoes in order to understand how they feel' (pure empathy). In the following two cases, we offer examples of people demonstrating empathy for how the other feels 'walking in their shoes'.

Ethics and the law

When one of the authors lived in the USA in the 1970s he came to know the father of a friend very well. The man was about to retire after many years as an FBI agent. The author noticed when visiting at Christmas the large number of cards the man had received. Surprisingly, many were from people the FBI agent had arrested and who had subsequently been to prison. How was it that convicted criminals sent the FBI agent who arrested them a Christmas card? The FBI agent explained that in his entire service he had never drawn his gun to make an arrest. When attending the house to arrest a person, he treated that person with respect. He was polite, he advised the person of his or her legal rights and would arrange that the person could call their lawyer from their house before leaving. He would suggest what sort of clothing and toiletries the person might need. Afterwards he would contact the person's family to reassure them that they were well and were being well treated. He commented to the author that just because someone had committed a crime did not deprive him/her of the right to decent and respectful treatment.

More recently, one of the authors was talking to a senior manager who had conducted a number of disciplinary hearings with staff whose conduct had fallen short of what the organization expected. The manager said that these hearings were very stressful for the staff members concerned. She had arranged that a long-serving, well-respected member of staff was available to spend some time with each person after their disciplinary hearing. She commented that people were often upset and sometimes angry after such hearings. She felt that it was important that there was someone supportive available, who was able to offer a sympathetic ear when the person came out of the hearing.

Taking responsibility for a decision is part of what you get paid for as a manager. We would hope that all the decisions that you make will be the most appropriate for the circumstances. In the real and imperfect world in which we all live, however, it is more probable that you will make mistakes. When you do make a mistake then ethically we would argue that you have the obligation to:

- Learn from the mistake, which means acknowledging it and endeavouring not to repeat it.
- Remedy, as far as is possible, any damage or loss that someone else has suffered as a result.
- Help and advise others in order that they also can learn from it.

These obligations we believe are common sense and most people would not dispute them. Nevertheless they do not sit well with organizational procedures where they instruct staff to 'never admit responsibility for anything to a customer or member of the public'.

EXERCISE

Analyse any recent events that you or your colleagues have dealt with for mistakes that were, or could have been, made; how these mistakes were actually dealt with; how you/they were able to learn from them or could learn from similar situations in the future.

ENVIRONMENTAL ISSUES, ETHICS AND MANAGEMENT

A few years ago, a rather unexpected hero was featuring on the pages of the national newspapers. His claim to popular fame was that he had obstructed the construction of a road for several days by tunnelling underground in the path of the construction machinery.

The green agenda is important for organizations and managers. Green products are sought by consumers and will become even more important. It is more probable now that you are a member or supporter of an environmental pressure group than you are an active member or supporter of a major political party.

Many years ago in the USA there was a saying that 'What is good for General Motors is good for America'. That saying would now be heavily qualified by environmental concerns. Many Americans are actively considering or pursuing claims against tobacco companies to seek redress for illness caused by their products. Will the next ten or twenty years see similar claims against car and petrol companies for illnesses associated with vehicle pollution?

The environmental agenda for a thoughtful manager cannot simply be a reactive one. You could wait until the popular pressure for internal or external stakeholders mounts up and becomes irresistible and then acquiesce in recycling, use of renewable energy or whatever the demand is. Alternatively, you can seize the initiative and set out either as an individual or as an organization to lead from the front.

The experience of organizations such as The Body Shop suggests that taking a proactive and ethical stand on environmental issues is good for business. But should this be the guiding principle? Suppose that a concern for the environment was not good for your business!

Where organizations fail to take an ethical stand then it is quite conceivable that the society in the form of the state may do so. In Denmark you will not find any canned drinks for sale. The government decided that this form of packaging was not environmentally friendly and banned it. Despite efforts to overturn this decision via the EEC, all the major drinks companies eventually had to accept the decision. Pepsi, Coca Cola and all the main beer companies have to package their products in bottles, which are recyclable.

Jennings and Wattam (1994) suggest a useful approach in assessing the environmental impact of a possible course of action. They divide the consequences of the course of action into primary (or immediate) impacts, secondary and then tertiary consequences, whereby each of the primary impacts has secondary consequences and each of the

Activity	Primary impact	Secondary consequences	Tertiary consequences
Relocate factory	Old factory lies empty	Old factory gets vandalized	Local authority takes action to deal with risk
			Factory site is sold for houses
		Loss of jobs in area of old factory	People find new work
			People move away
	New factory is less polluting	New factory needs less energy	Less environmental cost
			Lower energy costs
		Some jobs created in area of new factory	Some new house building

Figure 3.1
Consequences of factory relocation (based on Jennings and Wattam, 1994).

secondary consequences then has tertiary consequences. By following through these you can trace the impact of a possible decision. Figure 3.1 illustrates how this might operate for a decision to relocate a factory to a new site instead of refurbishing the current factory.

The question of the environmental impact of managerial and organization decisions may become an important consideration for government and regulators. There is frequently expressed concern over, for example, the growth of out-of-town shopping malls and their impact upon high street shops. The siting of shopping malls many miles away from town centres causes greater car usage and is seen by many as eroding the very soul of many town centres.

EXERCISE

Use the table in Figure 3.1 to analyse an activity familiar to you on the basis of primary impact and secondary and tertiary consequences.

SUMMARY OF ISSUES

In working through this chapter, you will have encountered a number of issues and perhaps some ideas that are new to you. The objectives of the chapter were to:

- Discuss the nature of ethical behaviour.
- Introduce concepts of ethical behaviour within the organization.
- Introduce concepts of ethical behaviour outside the immediate organization.
- Discuss environmental issues, ethics and management.

How well have the authors met these objectives?

More importantly, how have you approached and used the material yourself, and how much have you developed since the beginning of your course of study, or working through the chapter? You are strongly recommended to extend your research and study to include as much as possible of the material identified in further reading and references below, so that you can build on your expertise, incorporating more complex approaches and ideas as you develop further in your managerial role.

These objectives, if re-revisited over a period of time and put into practice in your job, will help you to achieve the personal competency of maintaining an ethical perspective, broken down into the elements identified in the table at the end of this chapter. In order for you to reflect on your own behaviour and that of others with whom you work, you might find it useful to use the table as a self-assessment check (reproduce as many as you wish) to re-evaluate your skills and knowledge.

PREPARING FOR ACTION PLANNING

Remember to review the checklist of questions, as identified at Appendix 1.

Analyse your own behaviour in terms of strengths (positive outcomes) and weaknesses (negative effects), in dealing with actual work-based occurrences with regards to the various situations discussed in this chapter, and summarized above.

Decide how you might deal with them differently in the future and what are your immediate training requirements and future development needs.

Discuss them with appropriate others and negotiate how you might address them.

FURTHER READING AND REFERENCES

Brigley, S. (1994) *Walking on the Tightrope: A Survey of Ethics in Management*. Kettering: IM Research Report. ISBN: 0-859-46247-1

Connock, S. and Johns, T. (1995) *Ethical Leadership*. London: CIPD. ISBN: 0-85292561-1

Cook, C.W. and Hunsaker, P.L. (2001) *Management and Organizational Behavior* (3rd edition). New York: McGraw-Hill (Chapter 12). ISBN: 0-07239662-8

Des Jardins, J.R. and McCall, J.J. (1990) *Contemporary Issues in Business Ethics*. Wadsworth. ISBN: 0-53412090-3

Dessler, G. (2000) *Management: Leading People and Organizations in the 21st Century* (2nd edition). New Jersey: Prentice Hall (Chapter 3). ISBN: 0-13-017780-6

Drummond, J. and Bain, B. (1994) *Managing Business Ethics*. Oxford: Butterworth Heinemann. ISBN: 0-7506-0663-0

Friedman, M. (1980) *Free to Choose*. Harmondsworth: Penguin. ISBN 0-7506-1705-5

Hannagan, T. (1995) *Management Concepts and Practices*. London: Pitman Publishing (Chapters 17 and 18). ISBN: 0-273-60773-1

Jennings, D. and Wattam, S. (1994) *Decision Making*. London: Pitman. ISBN: 0-273-60397-3

Kant, I. (1989) *Foundations of Metaphysics of Morals* (translated by L.W. Beck). Bobbs Merrill. ISBN: 0-02307825-1

Martin, J. (1998) *Organizational Behaviour*. London: International Thompson Business Press (Chapter 15). ISBN: 1-86152-180-4

Matthews, M.C. (1988) *Strategic Intervention in Organizations*. California: Sage Publications. ISBN: 0-803-93304-5

Maund, L. (1999) *Understanding People and Organizations: An Introduction to Organizational Behaviour*. Cheltenham: Stanley Thorne. ISBN: 0-7487-2404-4

Mill, J.S. (1910) *Utilitarianism, Liberty and Representative Government*. Dent

Newell, S. (1995) *The Healthy Organization*. London: Routledge. ISBN: 0-41510327-4

Sorell, T. and Hendry, T. (1994) *Business Ethics*. Oxford: Butterworth Heinemann. ISBN: 0-7506-1705-5

Watson, T. J. (2002) *Organising and Managing Work*. Harlow: Pearson Education (Chapter 12). ISBN: 0-273-63005-9

Competency element	Competency level: 1 (low)–5 (high)	Requires development	No direct experience	What can help? (identify oppor-tunities)	Who can help?	When can it be achieved?	How can it be achieved?
Complies with legislation, industry regulations, professional and organizational codes							
Shows integrity and fairness in decision-making							
Sets objectives and creates cultures that are ethical							
Identifies the interests of stakeholders and their implications for the organization and individuals							

Clearly identifies and raises ethical concerns relevant to the organization			
Works towards resolution of ethical dilemmas based on reasoned approaches			
Understand and resists personal pressures that encourage non-ethical behaviour			
Understand and resists apparent pressures from organizational systems to achieve results by any means			

CHAPTER 4

Focus on results

Managers who focus on results are proactive and take responsibility for getting things done.

LINKS TO THE CHARTERED MANAGEMENT INSTITUTE'S MODULE

This chapter aims to address the aims and learning outcomes as identified in the Introduction to this text under the heading *Links to the Chartered Management Institute's Module 'Understanding Yourself'* so that, in conjunction with Chapters 1, 2, 5 and 10, participants should be able to:

- Understand the impact of their behaviour on other people in a range of management situations (e.g. performance management, conflict situations, team-working, deadline delivery).

INTRODUCING THE RELATIONSHIP BETWEEN THE PERSONAL COMPETENCY MODEL AND FOCUSING ON RESULTS

The Personal Competency Model (PCM), as already discussed, identifies the behaviours and skills that are necessary for you to develop before you are able to prove competence in any managerial function. This chapter attempts to deal with the various behaviours and skills that are necessary for you to apply across all managerial functions, transferring your learning to different occasions, at different times and under varying circumstances (contexts), consistently.

The outcomes below, as identified within this section of the model, should be borne in mind while you work through this chapter.

Outcomes required in focusing on results

There are two major sets of behaviour addressed in this chapter. The first identifies that, when a manager is *planning and prioritizing objectives*, behaviour is developed which shows that she/he:

- Maintains a focus on objectives.
- Tackles problems or takes advantage of opportunities as they arise.
- Prioritizes objectives and schedules work to make best use of time and resources.
- Sets objectives in uncertain and complex situations.
- Focuses personal attention on specific details that are critical to the success of a key event.

The second set of behaviours contained in this chapter concentrates on the manager *showing commitment to excellence*. In showing such concern, it is believed by management gurus that the individual manager:

- Actively seeks to do things better.
- Uses change as an opportunity for improvement.
- Establishes and communicates high expectations of performance, including setting an example to others.
- Sets goals that are demanding of self and others.
- Monitors quality of work and progress against plans.
- Continually strives to identify and minimize barriers to excellence.

INTRODUCTION AND OBJECTIVES

The objectives of the chapter are to:

- Introduce the concepts of planning in organizations.
- Discuss the analysis involved in setting goals.
- Present the concept of managing by objective-setting.
- Introduce the concept of time management.

■ Present some examples of objective-setting and prioritization.

Planning activities are a key part of management work. Planning is linked closely to both setting and prioritizing objectives. After examining these, this chapter will look at the most precious commodity available to a manager in undertaking planning and goal setting. That commodity is *time*.

PLANNING IN ORGANIZATIONS

Planning is an activity that frequently gets pushed aside in the hurly burly of everyday pressures. Nevertheless, it is a key part of effective management. There is a link between the planning and management level in the planning process. The more senior the manager the more likely that the planning undertaken will relate to the organization's strategic as opposed to operational objectives. The relationship between the planning level and management level is shown in Figure 4.1.

The differences between planning day-to-day tasks and operational and strategic activities relate primarily to the extent to which the plans affect the way the organization operates. A salesperson plans the order of visiting customers as a day-to-day activity. The sales manager may plan that the customers in the Birmingham area, for example, should be the *target* of a particular sales drive. The sales director may

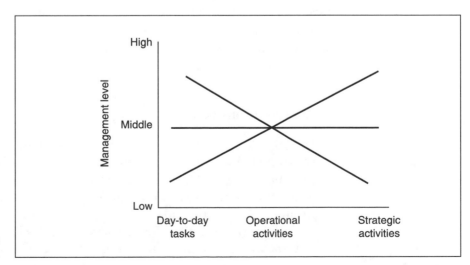

Figure 4.1
Amount of time
spent on planning.

plan to change the whole sales strategy for the company's products and/or services.

It is important to note that the distinctions are sometimes not always clear. A few years ago there was press publicity about conditions and practices in certain secure hospitals staffed by prison officers. It was reported that the prison officer staff brought a custodial as opposed to a caring approach to their duties. Clearly, the kind of approach adopted towards patients in these hospitals is at least an operational if not a strategic planning decision. Yet it would appear that it had been decided, possibly by default, by relatively junior staff.

Planning is important to managers in a number of ways. First, it enables the organization to achieve its objectives. Without the concept of direction that planning requires, then organizations are akin to a *drunk staggering from lamp-post to lamp-post*. The drunk has little plan beyond the short-term goal of reaching the next pool of light.

Second, planning, as Figure 4.1 shows, is a part of the managerial task irrespective of the level of the manager. Even relatively junior managers plan their activities. The main differences are the time frame and scope. The more senior the manager, the longer the time frame for planning and the greater the scope of the plans.

Third, planning is arguably the managerial activity that occurs before other activities. In order to organize resources, the manager, at whatever level of seniority, needs to plan. Sometimes the planning can have a macabre aspect to it. During the Falklands War part of the planning before the major battles of Goose Green and Port Stanley involved supplying the body bags for burying the dead.

Finally, planning is inextricably linked to effectiveness and efficiency (doing the right things, and doing them right). Cost-effectiveness has to be a key factor. The organizational world is full of examples of plans conceived at a cost far in excess of any possible savings that they could achieve. There is often a fine calculation over how much to invest in planning given the likely return.

Escape committee

During World War II a large number of allied military personnel were captured by the Germans and became prisoners of war. They were housed in well-guarded camps and a number of prisoners sought to escape. Initially, a large number of attempts failed and in part this was due to a lack of co-ordination and planning. In several of the larger camps this led to escape organizations being set up. If a prisoner wished to have the support of the organization he had to present a plan to a committee. The committee would then decide which plans to support.

The success of these escape organizations was considerable despite the fact that they had no formal authority to forbid escape attempts. The plans prisoners had to submit were similar to 'business plans', which bid for the limited resources available (food, tools, 'civilian' clothing, documentation, outside contacts and prisoners' skills).

There is a hierarchy of planning which operates in organizations of any size (Figure 4.2). At the top of the hierarchy is the mission or purpose of the organization. Sometimes it is described as the 'mission statement'. Possibly one of the simplest was that given to NASA (North American Space Administration) after the USSR was the first to put a man into space. President Kennedy told NASA that they were to beat the Russians in getting to the moon. The clear and straightforward nature of that objective certainly fostered its success. It is possible that the current lack of an objective of such clarity is creating a strategic problem for NASA.

Any well-run organization needs to be able to draw up a planned strategy for achieving the organizational mission. This will commit the resources of the organization and will involve making choices. For example, during the year 1992–1993, British Aerospace had to decide whether to sell or retain the Rover Group. Objectives were almost certainly in place to guide the company. These would have been at a strategic level. They were likely to be based upon a view of where the company saw its future: What mix of products? What customers? What market sectors or segments should be targeted? It would also have

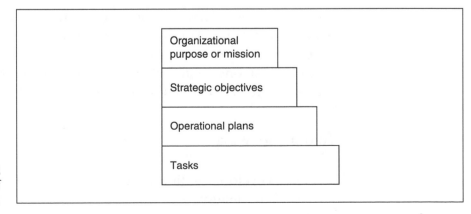

Figure 4.2 Hierarchy of planning.

been based upon the company's assessment of what was likely to be happening in the economy. Possibly most important of all, the company would have had a keen eye to the expectations of its shareholders.

Then there are *operational* plans that serve to direct the everyday running of the organization. For example, a few years ago, two large companies, IBM and BT, were engaged in reducing their workforce. For IBM this represented a major change in the ethos of the company since security of employment had been a key belief held by the company and its employees. IBM planned the workforce reductions in four phases in the UK, aimed at careful targeting of particular staff sectors. Extensive counselling was provided and the severance terms were not just presented in terms of cash. Employees were encouraged to set up in business with work contracts with IBM.

For BT the process was less drawn out and it was reported that about 19 500 left in a single day, representing one of the largest one-off workforce reductions in UK industrial history. The incentive offered was primarily financial and the redundancy offer was strongly marketed to staff. The demand for the offer was such that unions described BT's policy as one of compulsory retention, with many people applying being refused redundancy.

The operational plans drawn up by the two organizations led to a two quite different outcomes. The human resources plans of both organizations probably included the following planning elements:

- Recruitment plan.
- Training plan.
- Re-development plan.
- Productivity plan.
- Redundancy plan.
- Retention plan.

Operational plans create a hierarchy of tasks that need to occur in order to meet the plan's objectives. These tasks often imply a planning activity in order to ensure that they are carried out. Thus, if we consider just one of the above operational plans—the redundancy plan—we can list some of the activities that need to take place.

Redundancy plan

- Workforce audit (age, sex, seniority, skills, etc.).
- Consultation.

- Nature of redundancy offer.
- Costing and budget.
- Preparation of redundancy offer.
- Communication of redundancy offer.
- Decisions and any negotiation/appeal process.
- Communication of results.
- Implementation of payments/severance.

The above list is only a basic guide. Some items may be directed by company procedures or rules. Some may be the subject of legal requirements However, if we take just one item—the *communication of redundancy offer* —we can see that it too might break down into a further subgroup of tasks and activities.

Communication of redundancy offer

This could involve asking the follow questions:

- Media of message: verbal, individual letter, poster, leaflet, etc.?
- Wording?
- Timing?
- Messenger (who delivers the offer?)
- Printing?
- Costing and budget?

Each of these tasks or activities has a planning component. The old saying is applicable here, that 'For the want of a nail a shoe was lost, for the want of a shoe a horse was lost, for the want of a horse a soldier was lost, for the want of a soldier a battle was lost'. Consider the effect of a postal strike on a redundancy offer that has been communicated by letter to the employees' home address. If the letters have all been sent out, it is possible many employees will not receive them until the postal strike is over.

Most organizations will, as part of their planning process, identify possible problems in implementation. They will then take preventative action to reduce the possibility of the problem affecting implementation. In circumstances where the problem is a serious one, then there will be a back-up facility or contingency plan. Thus it is probable that the car you drive (or whatever public transport you use) will have a contingency device to ensure that a leak of the brake fluid will not deprive the vehicle of all braking power.

Preventative action is cheaper than contingency plans. It is cheaper to have office equipment regularly serviced than to have a back-up for each item of equipment. Besides, there is always the residual possibility that the 'back-up' may fail to work!

However, there is a trade-off between risk and the cost of a contingency plan. The loss of company records through a fire would generally be very serious. Research suggests that many companies fail to survive such a calamity. Therefore back-ups of computer data and perhaps having a back-up computer facility are usually worthwhile expenses. The likelihood of the fire occurring is small, but the implications of a fire are great. Therefore a company would be quite averse to taking the risk (see Chapter 9).

On the other hand, if a company is contracting with an advertiser for all households in an area to be leafleted about a new product or service, there is a high likelihood that some households may not receive the leaflets. They may not be delivered or may be picked up by other people, etc. The implications of this happening are probably not serious. A contingency plan to send out further leaflets would be costly and inappropriate. Preventative action would be a better way to deal with it, perhaps through arranging a check on a sample of households to ensure that leaflets were delivered (and letting the advertiser know you will be doing it). The advertiser, knowing that the company would be checking up, would be careful.

GOAL-SETTING AND ANALYSIS

Goal-setting and analysis can be seen as a process that has a number of logical stages, as shown in Figure 4.3. The process begins with establishing objectives. If we look back to the example of the company wishing to circulate product or service information to households in an area, then let's assume the objective was 'To increase public awareness of product/service Z in the area'. This might, in turn, have led to the following action plans:

- Advertising in the press.
- Advertising on radio.

Figure 4.3
The goal-setting process.

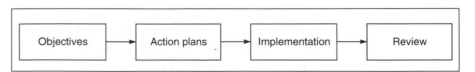

- Poster advertising on billboards
- Leaflet delivery to local households.

Implementation would involve the preparation of the advertising copy and placing it in the appropriate media. The leaflet distribution would probably require a contract with an experienced organization familiar with the area.

Review is the stage at which the nature of the original objective becomes crucial. We used the term *increase public awareness of product/service Z*. How are we to review how well our four action plans have done this? We could go out and ask people, but how do we know that their awareness afterwards is any greater than it was before?

> Goals should always be SMART:
> **S**pecific
> **M**easurable
> **A**ssignable
> **R**ealistic
> **T**ime-related
> We would add **C**hallenging to this mnemonic
> **A**ssignable can also be seen as **A**chievable

The original objective does not lend itself to being SMART. It is not specific (what is public awareness and in what area?). How do you measure an increase in public awareness? It does not specify responsibility for carrying it out. It may not be realistic depending upon what service/product Z is (no size of increase is mentioned). No time is specified.

So let us re-examine the objective. This will involve a certain amount of analysis.

Robert Mager (1991) offers a five-step process for analysing goals, consisting of the following:

1 Write down the goal.
2 Write down a list of what achievement of the goal would represent in terms of actions or speech.
3 Review what you have written down. Check for duplications and what Robert Mager described as 'fuzzies'.
4 Write a sentence that describes each item on the list.
5 Check to make sure everything is covered.

If we take Robert Mager's steps to analyse the situation we might come up with the following. Assuming that the company is profit-oriented then what really is at issue is *sales* of service/product Z. This does lend itself to specific measurement. Therefore, what we might write down as achieving this goal would be:

■ A substantial increase in sales of service/product Z over a period of time in an area that can be attributed to advertising.

If we examine this statement we see some words that are clear in their meaning:

■ Increase.
■ Sales.
■ Product/service Z.

There are some words that Robert Mager might describe as 'fuzzies', such as:

■ Substantial
■ Period of time
■ In an area
■ Can be attributed to advertising

'Fuzzies' are things that are abstractions; they do not lend themselves to general agreement over whether or not they have happened. Thus there would be little problem in gaining general agreement over whether there has been an increase in sales of service/product Z. However, whether this increase is substantial or not may be subject to disagreement.

The aim is to identify the 'fuzzies' and, as far as possible, turn them into performance-related statements. We might do this as in the following example.

Example

■ Substantial: an increase of over 20%.
■ Period of time: a period of 3 months.
■ In an area: Corby, Northamptonshire.
■ Can be attributed to advertising: following an advertising campaign in Corby.

Our objective thus becomes:

- An increase of over 20% in sales of service/product Z over a period of 3 months in Corby, Northamptonshire, following an advertising campaign in Corby.

If service/product Z was sold elsewhere, we could make the goal relate to an increase in sales in Corby compared to average sales elsewhere.

The reworded goal is Specific, Measurable, Achievable and Time-related and, no doubt, Challenging as well. The question of whether it is Realistic is only answerable in terms of the market and the product or service. If the market is very slow growing, then 20% over 3 months may be very unrealistic. The goal is Assignable in that the sales manager (or whoever) can be tasked with carrying it out.

The objective can then be turned into an action plan, or rather a series of action plans. Thus the plan to leaflet households might include elements aimed at:

- Identifying suitable leafleting contractors.
- Drawing up and agreeing contract specifications.
- Soliciting bids for the work.
- Awarding the contract.
- Monitoring contract performance.
- Evaluating the impact and reporting back.

Prioritizing objectives

Setting priorities is inevitable in any situation in which the resources are insufficient to meet all the demands placed upon them. Some managers have no system to work out priorities. They may rely on the guidance of other managers or staff. They may simply adopt the old engineers' maxim that 'The wheel that squeaks gets the oil' and simply focus effort on those objectives for which the clamour for action is the loudest.

However, there are several simple ways to set priorities. If used and communicated, these can enable a manager to target resources in a way that puts the manager in the driving seat. It is important to check that the priorities identified by the manager are agreed by the organization as appropriate. Therefore priority-setting should be a joint activity between managers and team members.

The ABC approach

This possibly represents the simplest method of setting priorities. Let us suppose that you have a list of tasks that may require your attention. You cannot do them all at once. You must find some way of establishing which ones are more urgent. Let us suppose that the list runs as follows:

- Prepare monthly sales returns.
- Arrange staff appraisals.
- Conduct fire drill.
- Visit northern region customers.
- Draft new sales brochure.
- Test new product.
- Negotiate maintenance contract.
- Review disciplinary code.
- Recruit clerk.
- Prepare budget.

You could then categorize the list in terms of:

- A: highest priority—cannot wait.
- B: next priority.
- C: do it if possible after A and B.

It is a simple system, which only requires a basic categorization of priorities. The resulting list might look as follows:

Prepare monthly sales returns	A
Arrange staff appraisals	B
Conduct fire drill	A
Visit northern region customers	C
Draft new sales brochure	C
Test new product	A
Negotiate maintenance contract	A
Review disciplinary code	A
Recruit clerk	B
Prepare budget	A

The list is then sorted according to priority:

Prepare monthly sales returns	A
Conduct fire drill	A

Test new product	A
Negotiate maintenance contract	A
Review disciplinary code	A
Prepare budget	A
Arrange staff appraisals	B
Recruit clerk	B
Visit northern region customers	C
Draft new sales brochure	C

The disadvantage is that sometimes it can prove difficult if many (if not most) of the tasks are seen as of the highest priority. Then the manager has to use some other criteria to prioritize the 'A' group.

Prioritizing by paired comparison

This is a more sophisticated method that takes more time and thought. Therefore it would not be appropriate for looking at your objectives for the next few weeks. It is useful in looking at longer-term objective setting. Let us consider an example of a training manager in an organization.

Example of prioritizing by paired comparison

The manager has established that there is a priority need for training in the following areas:

- Equal opportunities.
- Appraisal.
- Budgeting.
- Negotiating.
- Sales.
- Assertiveness.

The problem the manager confronts is how to prioritize these six areas in terms of both managers' time and training resources. The ABC method is seen as insufficiently sensitive since all the areas have high priority.

Paired comparison is a way of developing a priority ranking. The easiest way to do it is to set up a matrix so that each item can be compared with every other item. This is done in Figure 4.4.

The manager (or perhaps the management or staff group) will then consider the first training item—*equal opportunities*. They compare it with each alternative item in turn and decide whether:

- Equal opportunities is more important: give it 2 points (and the other item 0 points).
- Equal opportunities is less important: give it 0 points (and the other item 2 points).
- Equal opportunities is equally important: give it 1 point (and the other item 1 point).

Thus *equal opportunities* is seen as equally important as *appraisal* but more important than *budgeting* in this example.

After you have completed all the paired comparisons you add up the totals and obtain a point score for each item, as per the following example:

- Equal opportunities: 6
- Appraisal: 4
- Budgeting: 1
- Negotiating: 5
- Sales: 6
- Assertiveness: 8

The method is useful in establishing priorities between a number of objectives which all seem equally favoured. If using the alternatives of 2, 1 or 0 result in a deadlock, then the choices could be widened to include 3, 2, 1 or 0. Alternatively, a forced-choice rule could be used to prevent the allocation of 50% of the points to each item. A computerized variety of this method was developed by Jimmy Algie at Brunel University to enable social services departments to rank-order their priorities.

	Equal opportunities	Appraisal	Budgeting	Negotiating	Sales	Assertiveness
Equal opportunities	X	1	0	1	1	1
Appraisal	1	X	1	1	2	1
Budgeting	2	1	X	2	2	2
Negotiating	1	1	0	X	1	2
Sales	1	0	0	1	X	2
Assertiveness	1	1	0	0	0	X
Totals	5	4	1	5	6	8

Figure 4.4 Training priorities for an organization.

124

MANAGING BY OBJECTIVE-SETTING

Back in the 1980s, there was a popular concept called *management by objectives* (MBO), which was described as a:

- Strategy.
- Process of planning and control.
- Process of participation.
- System for getting results.
- Attitude of management.
- Time orientation.

Paul Mali (1986, p. 35), a leading American expert on MBO, has defined it as:

> a participative system . . . in which managers look ahead for improvements, think strategically, set performance related objectives at the beginning of a time period, develop action. . .plans, and ensure accountability for results at the end of the time period.

MBO contrasted with *traditional* management practices in that it involved the worker in objective-setting.

Although the MBO concept is no longer popular, mostly because it implied that only *managers* could fulfil the function, much of the process and practice of it has remained useful and popular when applying the newer concept of *performance management*. Most particularly has been the development of the concept of two-way objective-setting, whereby individuals agree the objectives with their line manager in the process of *appraisal or performance review*.

To involve individuals in their own objective-setting, the organizational purpose has to be made clearer. If responsibility is pushed down the hierarchy as far as possible then knowledge and understanding must also be encouraged.

The focus moves from effort to accomplishment. Individuals and teams agree targets that are measurable and which are reviewed. There is a future orientation in planning. The stress is not upon examination of the past but rather upon where things are going in the future. The progress made towards objectives is strongly tied into assessment at time intervals. Time is a vital component in managerial effectiveness and it is considered at greater length later in this chapter.

Participation in objective-setting

If you have contributed to, or better still been responsible for, an agreed target, then you are far more likely to be committed to achieving it. The 'R' (realistic factor) in SMART is addressed by *empowering* people to set their own targets and objectives, rather than imposing them. The evidence is that given encouragement and support people will usually set themselves challenging targets and work hard to accomplish them. Clearly, there can be no excuses about a target being *handed down* is not available when the individual had a major say in setting the goal. Communication, both verbal and written, is central to achieving participation. Chapters 2 and 6 provide you with some understanding here.

Getting results through objective-setting

Earlier in this chapter we discussed how to express goals in the form of measurable, desired outcomes. Organizations that are *for-profit* have a number of obvious result measures (sales, costs, profit margin, gross profit, etc.). These are explained in greater detail in other books in the series.

Organizations that do not have a tangible *product* or that are *not-for-profit* have *result* or *outcome* measures that are equally as effective. A charity might look at the percentage of administrative costs, the effect of fund-raising drives, the speed of response to requests for help and so on.

In fact we would argue that anyone working in an organizational context is able to set objectives that are measurable. There may be an issue around how well the measures actually reflect the organizational mission. How well does church attendance show that the church is promoting the gospel, for example?

THE CONCEPT OF TIME

There is a popular story in which a person advises another to invest their money in land. When asked why, the response is: 'Because they are not making any more of it'. Time is a commodity which, for you as an individual, is similar to land. You only have so much of it. Unless science comes up with a magic potion which enables you to work without sleep or beyond the current limits of our biological span you have to confront the reality that the only option you have is to improve on your management of your time.

Thus time is different from many other resources available to the manager. The ways in which it differs are crucial to understanding its importance.

- It cannot be stored up like a charge in a battery.
- For each person the amount of time available is limited.

Some professionals, such as lawyers, charge for the use of their time and thus have to record it in order to bill the client. Trades-people such as plumbers or electricians also usually charge an hourly rate. Do you know what you cost per hour? It may come as a surprise to you.

Time is money

Let us assume that your salary is £18,000 p.a. What you actually cost your employer is more than this. For professional, managerial and administrative staff the *on-cost* of pension, national insurance contributions, etc. is often about a third of salary. This added on makes your annual cost £24,000. Let's say you take 3 weeks paid annual leave and there is another week that is counted out because of statutory holidays. This makes your weekly cost £500 (£24,000/48 weeks).

Your working week is 36 hours but there is about 6 hours in total spent at lunch to be taken off. This leaves 30 hours. Then you have to allow for other *dead time* such as tea breaks or waiting for something before you can continue. Let us say, conservatively, about another hour per day. So this leaves 25 hours effective working time per week. You cost your employer £20 per hour.

That does *not*, of course, include all the support services such as accommodation rent, equipment (minimum today is likely to include mobile phone and PC), company car, electricity, support staff, etc., without which you probably could not function. Depending on your geographical location, position, job and other factors this could *double* or even *quadruple* your hourly cost.

> **EXERCISE**
>
> As an exercise to focus your mind you may wish to calculate your hourly cost to your employer.

The usage and wastage of time

Sir John Harvey Jones (1988, p. 288) offers these thoughts on the use of time:

> I suppose the most essential part of this struggle is the management of one's time, and here there are a number of key things that can be done. I have always believed that when I am at work I should work as hard and effectively as I can, all the time that I am there, but that equally, when I am not working, there should be a clear line between the two experiences. In order to cover the sheer amounts of work, of contact, reading and writing and so on, it really is necessary to use every moment of enforced working time to the best effect.

Sir John offers various personal suggestions for the use of time. These include being in a position to work when travelling by carrying portable recording equipment; this would include lap-top computers and electronic notebooks now, and suitable reading matter and visiting people in *their* offices rather than asking them to come and see you. His comments upon the cost-effectiveness of private aircraft and chauffeurs are unlikely to apply to more than a small proportion of managers!

In 1750 Edward Young said 'Procrastination is the thief of time'. Procrastination is putting things off to a later day or time. By *not* putting things off until later is not to advocate the simple resolving of issues by *knee-jerk* reactions and trying to do everything immediately. But ignoring things (so they might go away?) is a syndrome characterized by a willingness to defer an action or a decision, which has become a habitual form of behaviour. The question asked by someone *suffering* from this syndrome is 'Can I put it off?' as opposed to 'Why can't I do it now?'

Problems in use of time

The indicators of time-management problems have been described as the following:

- Having to work long hours.
- Insufficient time for planning.
- Frequent interruptions from people in person.
- Frequent telephone interruptions.
- Resolving team members' problems.

Managers describe the following ways to address these problems:

- Set goals and priorities.
- Make time to plan.
- Delegate.
- Focus time on the key activities.

Research has identified particular kinds of people who are prone to use their own or others' time ineffectively. These people are often:

- Recognition-seeking.
- Complainers.
- Resentful.
- Spontaneous.
- Fearful.
- Indifferent.
- Over-organized.
- Activity-driven.
- Time-obsessed.

We can consider these types in terms of brief pictures of the behaviours involved:

- *Recognition-seeking* Everyone knows how much work Lee does. Lee is at pains to let them know. Whatever the task, Lee rushes around struggling to make deadlines with the sweat pouring out. However, planning is a low priority.

The recognition of the pressure is vital to Lee. People comment on how Lee always takes too much on.

- *Complainers* Sam is never short of a reason for why the job cannot be done. 'The organization is badly set up, the people are incompetent and nothing can be done.' Certainly Sam is not going to sort out the problems. Telling everyone about them takes up all the time available!

- *Resentful* If you want co-operation and support do not go to Pat. Pat is nursing such a grudge about the organization. The basis of resentment may be short-lived or long-standing. The effect is that Pat has no desire to do anything to help the objectives of the organization.

- *Spontaneous* Beverly hates predictability. Planning and work diaries smack of regimentation. Beverly likes to *go with the flow* and take each day as it comes. There is little point in staff asking Beverly for deadlines or boundaries.

- *Fearful* Jo never makes a wrong decision. Jo rarely makes any decision at all. Jo feels that the organization is always blaming people for wrong decisions. All possible risks have to be thoroughly explored and discounted first. This takes a lot of time.

- *Indifferent* Lesley is a real *jobs-worth*. When asked to do anything, Lesley's most likely response is 'It's more than my job's worth'. Lesley is indifferent to whether projects are finished on time. Lesley is bored with the job and the only exciting day is payday.

- *Over-organized* Nikki is a 'list person'. There is a list for everything and they cover every eventuality. Nikki spends most of the time updating the lists. The one list Nikki does not have is a list of things actually achieved.

- *Activity-driven* Mel is a real dynamo. Mel organizes everyone and is a constant source of energy. However, whether the activities relate to the real world is another matter. Mel would have been great at arranging deck chairs on the sinking Titanic.

- *Time-obsessed* Karel has the biggest diary in the office. It is full of appointments and every minute is fully accounted for. At every meeting Karel becomes anxious as soon as any delay to (Karel's) timetable seems likely to occur. Karel has worked out a faster way to go to the bathroom. It may even save 30 seconds a day. Karel never has enough time for all the things in the big diary!

Do you recognize yourself or a colleague in any of these descriptions of (mythical!) people? If so, do not despair, for there are certain simple things you can do to manage your time more effectively.

Knowledge essential to good time management

There is an old proverb which says 'Know thyself'. This is particularly true of time management. Before you can set about improving your use of time you need to know *how* you currently use it and what attitudes affect how you structure this, your most precious resource.

This involves undertaking a certain amount of personal research. Usually this is through completing what is called a *time log*. A time log is a record of how you spend your work time.

There is no form of time log that is precisely suitable to everyone. However, the model offered in Figure 4.5 may give you some ideas to use. The principles that should guide the time log are as follows:

- It should be completed over a reasonable length of time. For most people a period of 2 or 3 weeks is suggested. Obviously you need to be aware of whether this time period is *typical* of your work pattern. A period covering *annual festivities* may not be representative of how you spent the rest of the year.
- It should enable you to record the kind of activity quickly and in sufficient detail to analyse how you use your time. Therefore you should develop some kind of list of your activities. Here is a simple form one manager used:

Time (15-minute intervals)												
Activity	9.00	9.15	9.30	9.45	10.00	10.15	10.30	10.45	11.00	11.15	11.30	11.45
Outgoing telephone call	B→											
Incoming telephone call		F←										
Meeting (planned)			C←	C←	C←						B→	B→
Meeting (unplanned)												
Routine paperwork												
Non-routine paperwork						C←	C←	C←				
Planning activity									B→	B→		

Figure 4.5
A typical time log.

- - Outgoing telephone call.
  - Incoming telephone call.
  - Meeting (planned).
  - Meeting (unplanned).
  - Routine paperwork.
  - Non-routine paperwork.
  - Travelling.
- In recording which activity was happening during each 15 minutes the manager also used an arrow to show whether the activity was:
  - Self-initiated: →
  - Responding to someone else: ←
- The manager also used a method of shorthand to show who (if anyone) was involved in the activity.
  - B: Boss.
  - C: Customer.
  - T: Team member.
  - A: Admin.
  - F: Finance.
- It should use intervals of short enough duration to pick up activities that *interrupt* your planned activities. With management students we use intervals of 10 or 15 minutes.

From this you can see that if you record your main activity every 15 minutes over some 100 hours of work (3 weeks) you will end up with 400 pieces of data. Making useful sense of the data is the next step.

As an example, Figure 4.5 shows a morning from the time log of the manager. That day the manager came in at 9.00 a.m.; made a phone call to her boss confirming agenda items for a meeting later that day; received a phone call from someone in finance; held a planned meeting that a customer had asked for; spent time writing up aspects of that meeting; planned for the meeting with her boss, to which she then went.

The manager who keeps up the faithful and accurate recording on this basis over a period of 3 weeks will be able to look at the 400 (approx) entries and analyse them according to:

- Proportion of time spent undertaking various activities.
- Proportion of time spent on self-initiated activities.
- Proportion of time spent on activities associated with different people in the work setting.

- Sequences or patterns of activity.
- Duration of individual activities (or the extent you change from one activity to another).

The method you use for drawing up a time log is your decision, although, of course, the categories of activities that you use must make sense to you. It is often useful to include items to record interruptions to ongoing activities. Otherwise it is easy to lose track of the number of times someone *drops-in* while you are trying to get through your in-tray.

Measuring your use of time is not in itself sufficient. You also need to think about your approach to time management. Do you set priorities and deadlines for yourself and do you review them regularly? Whilst this is dealt with elsewhere in the chapter, it is an integral part of successful time management. What about delegation, which is dealt with earlier in Chapter 1? and how easily are you able to say 'no' to unreasonable requests? You may wish to turn to the section on assertiveness in Chapter 7.

EXERCISE

Use Figure 4.5 to produce your own time log. How much time do you spend on unnecessary detail? Perhaps you are the sort of person who tries to be accurate to five decimal places when one is quite sufficient?

IMPROVING THE MANAGEMENT OF TIME

Routine paperwork

Few managers enjoy handling routine in tray items. Henry Mintzberg, a well-known writer on all things *managerial*, suggested from his research that often managers desire to be interrupted and fight shy of routine humdrum activity. However, routine 'paperwork' is a *necessary evil* and is more and more being dealt with via the PC rather than hard copies these days. In some cases it is essential to accomplishing managerial targets.

Paperwork can be categorized as follows:

- Writing.
- Reading.

- Calculating.
- Searching.
- Scheduling.
- File retrieving.
- Delegating.
- Proof-reading.
- Filing.

There is an acronym that can be used to describe the possible ways of responding to a piece of paper arriving on your desk, which can be summarized as 'the four Fs':

- **F**ollow it up.
- **F**orward it.
- **F**ile it.
- **F**orget it (i.e. use the round filing cabinet located *under* your desk).

The chosen action is best undertaken immediately. A speedy follow-up almost invariably saves time later on. The more times that you handle the same piece of paper, the less efficient the use of time.

How the follow-up happens is often important in the use of your (and others') time. Consider the implications of the following responses to an internal memo:

1 Dictate a reply to your PC (unlikely to be a secretary these days).
2 Draft a reply to be word-processed later.
3 Reply immediately—maybe as an e-mail attachment.
4 Write a response on the memo itself and send it back (keeping a photocopy if necessary).
5 Telephone the sender with any information required.

Obviously the circumstances may rule out some of these options. However, the options are listed in order of the *total* time they would probably take (including the time of the person receiving your reply). If you only use the first option then you should review whether this is the most effective use of your time.

Forwarding items for action is a skill in itself. Winston Churchill reportedly distinguished items for quick response by writing on them 'Action today'. You may wish to review Chapter 1 to see if your skills in delegation are making the most effective use of your time. The use of Post-It-style notes can be a useful device if it is not suitable to write on the paperwork itself. However, there is always the risk of the note becoming detached from the associated document.

Filing information is a task many managers are able to delegate. However, in these days of leaner organizations and computerized information systems a secretary per manager is already becoming a thing of the past. The test of any filing system has to be the extent to which it helps you to do your job.

The increasing use of computers offers both benefits and risks. The benefits come from the sophisticated techniques for searching the memory for that memo you recall writing sometime in the last two years, and the vast storage capacity available compared to *paper-based systems*. (This whole book can fit on just one computer disk the size of a drinks coaster.) The risks come from the possibility of system/disk failure or theft of the actual computer itself, although you should always back-up your work onto diskettes that you should store in another location. You also need to be sensitive to the provisions of the Data Protection Act!

Recent research suggests that many people recall where information is by cues that are not usually incorporated on computer filing systems—for example, the colour or thickness of a particular document, or where it may be located (top drawer of the filing cabinet)—although, in our view and experience, people adopt similar approaches, if somewhat different techniques in themselves, for the electronic variety of filing systems.

Forgetting about or getting rid of pieces of information is sometimes the hardest thing for a manager to do. It is often quite surprising how much information you file which, like the clutter in your attic or garden shed, serves no useful purpose. Rather, it actively impedes you by slowing up the retrieval of documents that *are* essential.

A piece of advice was offered by a very successful (and paper averse) manager to one of the authors who, as a manager, inherited a huge paper mountain. It ran roughly as follows: 'I suggest that you put it all in a large cupboard. Throw out anything you have not had occasion to refer to within 3 months.'

Use of meetings

Meeting and chairing skills are covered in Chapter 2. However, your analysis of how you use time may well reveal that you spend a lot of it in scheduled or unscheduled meetings. Meetings cost organizations a lot. So as a manager you should ask:

- Is this meeting really necessary? Perhaps a telephone call or a memo would suffice.
- Is there a clear purpose for the meeting? It does not follow that every meeting has to have a formal agenda. Many meetings (and organizations) are not like that. However, if *you* do not know why you are going to a meeting *and* you are chairing it then we would suggest there is a problem. It is also hard to prepare for a meeting whose purpose is unclear. A subsidiary question, which often helps, would be: How will I know if the meeting has been successful?
- What do I need to bring to the meeting? Sometimes it may be something tangible, such as a report or an item. At other times it may be an opinion or informed comment that you need to think through beforehand.
- How much time is the meeting likely to need? The calculation of how much to fit into an agenda and in what order is the art of a good chair. However, if you are not the chair you can often help by identifying what time your items will need and how important they are.
- What records will be kept? Meeting minutes do not (usually) need to record matters in great detail. However, they do need to record decisions and actions. If names are attached to actions then it assists the communication of decisions and later follow-up. Records made at the time, even if brief, are usually far more useful than more lengthy records made at a much later date.

Handling interruptions

As already noted, managers are subject to frequent interruption and sometimes these are *self- inflicted*. A proper time log will reveal the extent to which you are so affected. There is no lack of good advice for handling interruptions:

- Avoid people coming to your office. Instead go and see them and then you control the length of the discussion.
- If people do interrupt you be firm but polite with them. Go straight to the point rather than engaging in small talk.

- Stand up and sit in the edge of your desk when someone comes in. This shows you do not wish a long interruption.
- Offer to call back.
- Give a clear indication of how much time you have—and stick to it or the word gets around that 'one minute means up to half an hour'.
- Display a clock prominently where a visitor can see it.

Use of the telephone

It is a source of some surprise that telephone skills have not been normally taught to managers until recently. Telephonists, reception- ists and secretaries (all posts that are becoming less prevalent) have had training provided yet the manager is a late starter.

Increasingly business is done by distance using the telephone, more especially the mobile phone now. Managers spend a lot of time 'on the phone'. Sometimes there is some kind of perceived status attached to being the one *receiving* the call. Yet if you can make the call at a time of your choice then *you* control the time not the reci- pient.

Therefore analysis of telephone usage can pay dividends in time efficiency. The following guidelines are useful:

- Plan telephone calls. Treat them as mini-meetings. Time the length of calls using that clock or a watch.
- Set time aside for making calls in blocks rather than making them in a sporadic fashion.
- If you are subject to frequent telephone interruptions which disrupt your work then try to have calls *fielded*. If you have no secretary or receptionist to do this then it is often possible to come to reciprocal arrangements with a colleague.

Use slack time

Sir John Harvey Jones is a strong advocate of making the best use of travelling or waiting time. He apparently carried several recording devices and plenty of spare tapes and batteries when travelling; as already noted, lap-top computers, mobile phones and electronic note-books more likely to be the used now.

Although you may plan your time well, it is inevitable that often circumstances may force you to wait to see someone or you may have to undertake a long trip. Being prepared for such eventualities is a sign of effective time management. Non-essential but important reading can be kept in a folder in order to provide a ready source of material.

In our time calculation of the work cost above, we allowed a total of 11 hours each week for breaks and meals. Often this time can be used very effectively for something similar to what the Americans call 'working breakfasts'. If there is someone who you need to talk to informally then, rather than scheduling a meeting in one of your offices, why not join them for coffee or a walk at lunchtime? Hewlett Packard and other companies often encourage such informal association. One local authority set up coffee areas throughout the civic centre for staff to meet informally.

Time-dualling

This is related to the use of slack time. It involves trying to find a way in which you can use the same time for several purposes. For example, maybe you have to meet a group of new staff and also you have get some views on how staff feel about the cafeteria for the next management meeting. Why not combine the two?

Use of routine

This last point is in many ways the most important. Managers like to think that they manage by exception and delegate all the routine work. But the reality is that virtually all managers have a substantial amount of *routine* work, such as the paperwork referred to previously.

The development of work habits, which effectively and speedily handle the routine aspects of your job, makes a major contribution to both freeing up time and minimizing stress. Some suggestions are:

- Set aside blocks of time for routine work.
- Have a simple diary system, which your staff and colleagues understand.
- Try to get routine aspects of your work as habitual as brushing your teeth. Then you might even be able to do other things simultaneously!

EXERCISE

Try planning how you might improve your use of time by employing some of the suggestions contained here.

EXAMPLES OF OBJECTIVE-SETTING AND PRIORITIZATION DRAWN FROM MANAGERS IN VARIOUS ORGANIZATIONS

Setting objectives

We have *performance related pay* and the guidelines say that there should be a quarterly review. We discuss their objectives and have a personal development plan for every member of staff. Every member of staff has their own job description and also a skills matrix, which sets out all the skills that are necessary or desirable and staff are encouraged to plan their own career. They are always aware that there is a limited budget in terms of time and money for people to undertake their training.

David Tait, Manager, Woolwich Building Society

Project realignment

The organization had decided to reduce the number of organizational layers and a large number of employees would be affected. Work patterns needed to change to meet a new concept of service delivery. This would involve a different contract for a group of the employees. Staff members were concerned and the trade union was resistant to the proposed change. Relatively junior trade union representatives were bypassing normal consultation machinery and going direct to the director. The project was widely seen as 'stalled' and not progressing. There was a sense of disbelief. The trade union had organized a large meeting to discuss the perceived threat to the current service.

Geri and her colleague took on the task of communicating the project to staff in order to get it moving again (see Figure 4.6). They undertook a 'roadshow'. This had the aim of giving the same message to the staff. Every member of staff had a

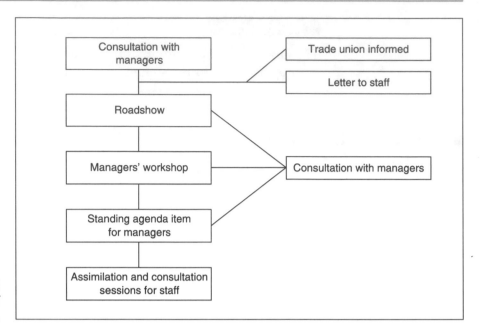

Figure 4.6
Example of
communication.

personal invitation to attend. The trade union was invited to be involved without any commitment to its objectives. The roadshow aimed to take the message of the project out to staff and visual aids (flip charts) were extensively used. There was a question and answer session afterwards. After that, staff members had an opportunity to discuss the project with the invited trade unions. The roadshow presenters deliberately withdrew to ensure free discussion took place. After each session the presenters checked with the managers present and got feedback to inform future presentations.

After the roadshow a workshop was held to enable managers to share their experiences. There was still a level of anger and managers had wanted the roadshow to 'lay down the law' to get things moving. People were asked to identify issues and action plans. It enabled managers to share fears about the changes. It also enabled information to be picked up and issues identified. Regular consultation continued afterwards.

Managers said they were unclear about budget issues so training seminars and consultation sessions were set up. The effectiveness of the roadshow was assisted by:

- The consistency of the message.
- The information was given to large groups of staff over a short time so minimizing the distorting effect of the 'grapevine'.

- The recognition that different groups of staff had different communication needs—hence the workshops for managers.
- The balance between supporting staff through change while conveying the reality of the change.

Since, the roadshow staff have shown more willingness to discuss the changes and the new jobs involved. Staff are taking up new duties voluntarily and accepting changes in conditions of work. Staff members are undertaking the training necessary for the adjustments. In some areas up to 80% of the staff affected have moved to new contracts.

The trade union has reverted to using the normal communication channels.

Geri Mitchell, Adviser, London Borough of Enfield

Goal-setting

We are driven by performance-related pay and we set quantifiable objectives for everyone down the line. It isn't MBO like Humble, which advocates bottom-up objective-setting. It's very much more top-driven; it's a performance management system that is linked to pay. It falls into two categories:

- There are quantified business objectives, which come out of strategic plans.
- There are qualitative objectives such as personnel ones.

The objectives are all 'deadlined' and quantifiable as far as possible and must meet the following criteria:

- Measurable.
- Achievable.
- Relevant.
- Controllable.

I spend most of my time setting objectives for line managers to achieve on a shorter, sometimes daily, basis. I tend to operate on the basis that people develop plans. The plans need to be clear with itemized action-points and deadlines that are clear and acceptable to me.

I want to see one sheet of paper with action-points—task-related. I believe if you develop a plan that is a decent one and you monitor progress against it then there are only a couple of reasons why it doesn't work. Either the plan was wrong in first place. Maybe someone didn't fight for a principle or was pressured into something sooner than they could. If so, they should bloody well have said so. Or implementation failed somewhere along the line. Perhaps circumstances changed. Were they circumstances we could have foreseen and done something about? Or is it simply that you are not putting into practice what you put on paper?

If you are talking task-oriented things then this is a good way to operate. I find it is very successful. You can be flexible within it. If you are very clear with your managers. You say I want a plan. I want it to have bullet points. I put it in my diary system and monitor it. Something arrives on my desk. I can then say I've either got the response which says 'Yes I've done it it's OK' and I can check the quality and I can delve underneath and go and sample the work and say 'Oh well, you say you've done it but I don't think much of this' or I can say 'That was super, I've got some very good feedback on that'. It works very well.

Nigel Wright, Woolwich Building Society

Prioritization and goal-setting

I run several things at once, like a computer running programs that has several loaded up at one time. For example, if something needs checking out with a management team or involves a committee report then those events have their own time cycle. Something else may be more personal and be more flexible. Every time I pick up my in-tray at the other end of the office I find a couple of days' work sitting there, waiting for me. I manage that by avoiding going down to that end of the office. In terms of my own mail I think I'm fairly good with most letters that come in. Quite a lot of them I ignore or throw away. If I'm in at work just after Christmas and there are not a lot of people around or over the summer when things go quiet I have obsessive phases when I decide to deal with everything. I'm surprised then to find out that quite a lot of memos (sent to me) they've forgotten about.

I do find that a lot of time as a manager is reactive. It's a bit of the job I could do without. About every two months our training unit will have an attack of cockroaches or a solicitor will try and evict us from it. On those sorts of things I'll drop everything.

We have an MBO system. It's called the business process. It's meant to be that everyone can point to it and say that's my job there. It got a bit messy in social services because our job is about development—this project and that project. The business process is structured in a kind of task analysis kind of way. There is an aim, which is called a committee aim that is then broken down into key result areas of which we have about 15. Each result area has several action plans and then each action plan has several key tasks. When you get to a key task it is written in such a way as you'd know whether it was down or not. Every year from about February to May people review themselves against key result areas and action plans. For people who can't do that you write a report about what the hell you've been doing. The idea is that everyone should be involved—even social services' clients.

The director would cream out headline news and feed it back to the councillors to show if the committee aim is being met or not. Things are also used internally. We were asked to identify areas for cutting back or for growth. These are used in the annual budgeting cycle and in appraisal of managers. I use the review as a way of generating another year's work for the trainers.

Richard Hooper, London Borough of Enfield

The new QA group

I was asked to set up a quality assurance (QA) group. I was given a vague outline and was unsure about how to go about it. We were very busy and QA seemed a bit of a luxury. I found it hard to understand what QA was about.

I read up a bit about it and then wrote a report which I sent around to staff. I asked for comments and suggestions. There were none. So I held a staff meeting and 'nobbled people' beforehand. At the area meeting I aimed to put it across in a simple way. I asked for help and ideas. I stressed that only attendance and a contribution to the QA group was required. I told them that the QA group would only run for a limited time with a set number of meetings.

I got names of people who might be interested. I had to sell them the idea. I was aiming for a mixture of staff to get involved in the QA group. Sometimes it involved using someone to find others who might be interested. I was looking for creative people. The administrative staff showed an interest so I involved them. Some carers became involved and I put in a lot myself. It changed for me once the group was up and running. It was the attitude.

For the first meeting of the QA group I prepared an agenda and I spent a lot of time setting it up. I discussed what was involved with several people and provided some simple reading for the people attending. We split into two groups. Why? Mainly because I felt that the size of the group was such that dividing it was indicated to enable people to contribute.

The QA group produced a report on standards. I then wrote a short article for a local magazine. It was about attitude. It was a learning experience setting up that group. It helped when later I had to set up a community forum.

Why didn't people respond when you wrote to them initially?

It was seen as a luxury when we had had so much unallocated work.

What did you say at the meeting to change this?

Talking about it . . .'. By simplifying it. The original document wasn't very good. I explained that we needed to look at the services we offered and the standards we were meeting. I made it sound interesting and different from what we normally do. Someone suggested a questionnaire. I was able to put it across more simply. I caught their imagination. *How?* I suppose I had a very good relationship with some people and because I was asking for help. The names came from people who knew me or from specialist workers. It was looking to something in the future. I also emphasized that people wouldn't have to do any work—take minutes or whatever—all I was asking for was their time.

Writing versus talking—what I did was to send just one sheet—saying I wanted volunteers and we'd be meeting over 3 months and that there wouldn't be any need to take minutes or whatever. The end product was to be the report that I wrote.

How did the operation of the group help this?

I spent a lot of time setting up the first meeting and how to operate it. I discussed it with people. I decided that we needed to review the service and we split into two groups to discuss this. I found someone to lead the groups and the groups were given the same task. We split the group for a couple of meetings. I split the group—the only criterion was that there were staff members in each group. But in one group there was very little southwest representation. The main reason was to encourage people to contribute—carers and clients would find it hard to contribute in the larger group. Afterwards people said that the group had affected their attitudes and had enabled them to listen to others.

What has happened to the report?

Standards are being set as a result of this and other reports. Within the office there has been a continuing impact. One of the problems is getting information out to people. Managers have a copy and all those taking part; there is a copy on the notice board. People were excited when they got their copy.

  I tried to make the report interesting by using sample questionnaires at the end.

Vickie Golding, Area Manager, London Borough of Enfield

SUMMARY OF ISSUES

In working through this chapter, you will have encountered a number of issues and perhaps some ideas that are new to you. The objectives of the chapter were to:

■ Introduce the concepts of planning in organizations.
■ Discuss the analysis involved in setting goals.
■ Present the concept of managing by objective-setting.
■ Introduce the concept of time management.
■ Present some examples of objective-setting and prioritization.

How well have the authors met these objectives?

More importantly, how you have approached and used the material yourself, and how much have you developed since the beginning of your course of study, or working through the chapter? You are strongly recommended to extend your research and study to include as much as possible of the material identified in further reading and references below, so that you can build on your expertise, incorporating more complex approaches and ideas as you develop further in your managerial role.

  These objectives, if re-revisited over a period of time and put into practice in your job, should help you to achieve the personal competency of *focusing on results*, broken down into the elements identified in the table at the end of this chapter. In order for you to reflect on your own behaviour and that of others with whom you work, you might find it useful to use the table as a self-assessment check (reproduce as many as you wish) to re-evaluate your skills and knowledge.

PREPARING FOR ACTION PLANNING

Remember to review the checklist of questions, as identified in the Introduction to this book, at Appendix 1.

Analyse your own behaviour in terms of strengths (positive outcomes) and weaknesses (negative effects) in dealing with actual work-based occurrences with regards to the various situations discussed in this chapter, and summarized above.

Decide how you might deal with them differently in the future and what are your immediate training requirements and future development needs.

Discuss them with appropriate others and negotiate how you might address them.

FURTHER READING AND REFERENCES

Adair, J. (1988) *How to Manage Your Time*. Talbot Adair

Anderson, E.S., Grude, K.V. and Haug, T. (2001) *Goal Directed Project Management: Effective Techniques and Strategies* (2nd edition). London: Kogan Page. ISBN: 0-7494-2615-2

Armstrong, M. (2001) *Performance Management: Key Strategies and Practical Guidelines* (2nd edition). London: Kogan Page. ISBN: 0-7494-2628-4

Bratton, J. and Gold, J. (1999) *Human Resource Management: Theory and Practice* (2nd edition). London: Macmillan (Chapter 8). ISBN: 0-333-73208

Dessler, G. (2001) *Management: Leading People and Organisations in the 21st Century* (2nd edition). New Jersey: Prentice Hall (Chapter 5). ISBN: 0-13-017780-6

Hunsaker, P.L. (2001) *Training in Management Skills*. New Jersey: Prentice Hall (Chapters 7 and 8). ISBN: 0-13-955014-3

Jones, Sir J.H. (1988) *Making it Happen*. London: Fontana

Mager, R. (1991) *Goal Analysis*. London: Kogan Page

Mali, P. (1986) *MBO Updated*. Chichester: John Wiley

Maund, L. (2001) *An Introduction to Human Resource Management*. New York: Palgrave (Chapter 10). ISBN: 0-333-91243-8

Perkins, S.J. (1997) *Globalization the People Dimension: Human Resource Strategies for Global Expansion*. London: Kogan Page (Chapter 7). ISBN: 0-7494-3124-5

Peters, T. (1989) *Thriving on Chaos: Handbook for a Management Revolution* (2nd edition). London: Macmillan. ISBN: 0-330-30591-3

Redman, T. and Wilkinson, A., editors (2001) *Contemporary Human Resource Management: Text and Cases*. Harlow: Pearson Education (Chapter 3). ISBN: 0-201-59613-X

Treacy, D. (1991) *Clear Your Desk*. London: Random Century. ISBN: 0-091-74850-X.

Competency element	Competency level: 1 (low)– 5 (high)	Requires development	No direct experience	What can help? (identify oppor- tunities)	Who can help?	When can it be achieved?	How can it be achieved?
Maintains a focus on objectives							
Tackles problems or takes advantage of opportunities as they arise							
Prioritizes objectives and schedules work to make best use of time and resources							
Sets objectives in uncertain and complex situations							
Focuses personal attention on specific details that are critical to the success of a key event							
Actively seeks to do thinks better							

Uses change as an opportunity for improvement				
Establishes and communicates high expectations of performance, including setting an example to others				
Sets goals that are demanding of self and others				
Monitors quality of work and progress against plans				
Continually strives to identify and minimize barriers to excellence				

CHAPTER 5

Influencing others

Managers who are able to influence the behaviour of others plan their approaches and communicate clearly using a variety of techniques.

LINKS TO THE CHARTERED MANAGEMENT INSTITUTE'S MODULE

This chapter aims to address the aims and learning outcomes as identified in the Introduction of this text under the heading *Links to the Chartered Management Institute's Module 'Understanding Yourself'* so that, in conjunction with Chapters 1, 2, 3 and 4, participants should be able to:

- Understand the impact of their behaviour on other people in a range of management situations (performance management, conflict situations, etc.).
- Demonstrate how they can gain more flexibility in their style and approach to others, to enhance the delivery of the above objective

INTRODUCING THE RELATIONSHIP BETWEEN THE PERSONAL COMPETENCY MODEL AND INFLUENCING OTHERS

The Personal Competency Model (PCM) identifies the behaviours and skills that are necessary for you to develop before you are able to prove competence in any managerial function. This chapter attempts to deal with the various behaviours and skills necessary for you to apply across all managerial functions, transferring your learning to different occasions, at different times and under varying circumstances (contexts), consistently.

The outcomes below, as identified within this section of the model, should be borne in mind while you work through this chapter.

Outcomes required when influencing others effectively

Influencing others effectively requires development of behaviours by the manager (keeping ethical considerations in mind at all times) whereby she/he:

- Develops and uses contacts to trade information and obtain support and the necessary resources.
- Creates and prepares strategies for influencing others.
- Presents her/himself positively to others.
- Uses a variety of techniques, as appropriate to the audience and circumstances, to influence others.
- Understands the culture of the organization and acts to work within it or influence its change or development.

INTRODUCTION AND OBJECTIVES

The objectives of this chapter are to:

- Identify the nature of influence.
- Discuss methods of influence.
- Debate individual responses to influences.
- Introduce methods for exerting influence.
- Identify common influencing problems and their solutions.
- Introduce ways to cope with aggression.
- Discuss organizational culture.
- Debate the use of negotiation.
- Develop and use contacts to trade information, obtain support and resources.

Influencing other people is not about getting our own way all the time. Influencing is about being assertive (see Chapter 7 for more about developing assertive behaviour), making sure others know what our views and opinions are and *also* ensuring that we make it possible for others to contribute positively to general discussion, problem-solving, generation of ideas and decision-making. Decisions made in isolation of others are less likely to be owned by them, or gain commitment from them.

We therefore need to influence *each other's* thinking and behaviour for constructive and mutually rewarding effects, in order to reach conclusions that produce effective results. In other words, we all have a duty to *influence* the actions taken at work, and share responsibility for the effects of those actions.

THE NATURE OF INFLUENCE

In order to influence others, we may consider that we have a certain *power* over them. The power we may have, of course, can be negative as well as positive. Power can be a very effective motivator, depending upon its source and purpose (see also 'The nature of power' in Chapter 1).

According to Charles Handy (1985), when defining *power*, it can be said that it relates to the capacity to affect the behaviour of others, or the actual ability to do something. In being a holder of power, managers are able to *influence* the behaviour and performance of others. *Influence* can be the application and the effect of power and authority.

Charles Handy distinguishes between power and influence. He says that the difference lies in the fact that influence is an *active process* and that power is a *resource* providing the ability to influence. Recourse to any source of power is likely to provoke different kinds of response in those over whom it is exercised.

METHODS OF INFLUENCE

According to Charles Handy, influence can be overt (seen) or covert (unseen). For example, where individuals are in a negotiating situation, it is not difficult for the parties concerned to determine the areas in which influencing attempts are being made. In contrast, however, one might take any other situation where two or more people are involved in discussion; an observer can often identify where the individuals concerned modify their views or behaviour as a result of the discussion, although this frequently happens without the awareness of those being influenced. It is important for us to accept that both our influencing of others and their influencing of us are essential to the achievement of objectives and development of individuals and teams.

We can achieve this by taking specific opportunities to determine what happens between individuals during discussion by asking an objective observer to take notes of such interaction. In psychological terms we could say that by doing this we are becoming more *conscious*, or aware, of the influencing effects we have on each other. It can be difficult initially, because personal pride (or position in the company) may make us believe we should have more influence over, rather than to be influenced by, others. We would argue that this is not necessary; that it would depend upon the circumstances and which individuals have the most expertise or knowledge in any particular context, as to who should have the most influence.

The most import skill for an influencer is to *listen* to others as well as to ensure he/she is being listened to. Most people who remain 'stubborn' tend to be those who are, for one reason or another, frightened of listening to, and being influenced by, the views of others.

The following table shows some ways in which people may influence, or be influenced by, others both positively and negatively, seen and unseen—you could add to them if you wish.

Leading by example (positive)	Overt—honest—always willing to do her/himself what he/she asks of others—builds trust and facilitates mutual support
Manipulation (negative)	Covert until understood—dishonest, self-interested—assumes others are incapable or less intelligent (unlikely to notice the negative effects)
Stealing others' ideas (negative)	Covert—sometimes conscious, sometimes unconscious—dishonest, but at least he/she is being influenced by others!
Political game-playing (negative)	Covert until it is understood—tends to blame others, does not take responsibility for own actions. Politically (small 'p') aware, but very unpleasant if on the receiving end—'crawls' to people in authority or otherwise *influential*
Political wisdom and integrity (positive)	Overt—honest—this is being politically (small 'p') aware and working with those circumstances and in turn influencing positive political and ethical development as needed
Integrating all ideas (positive)	Covert—honest—mutual influence, mutual benefit and ownership—builds trust and facilitates mutual support
Add as you see fit:	

Leading by example

Where influence is *overt*, those who mean to influence others will be honest about it, explaining their reasons and providing evidence and supporting information as appropriate. These people are also more likely to be influenced *by* others in the process, accepting that other viewpoints—whether they are ultimately taken on board or not—are likely to provide a more effective conclusion as a result of including these viewpoints in discussions.

This approach will build trust and allow mutual support between individuals. It is a course of action often adopted by good leaders who believe that they should *lead by example.*

Manipulation

People often use manipulation in order to *get their own way*. They want their own way but do not want it to be obvious to others and therefore adopt a manipulative approach to make people do and say what they want. This is *covert* influence.

Those who perceive their position to be weaker than those they wish to influence sometimes use manipulative approaches: downtrodden house-people (not all house-people, and men as well as women); victims of familial pressure and demands; some secretaries or other support staff who may feel they cannot stand up for themselves; those who believe they do not have the authority to attempt honest influencing strategies.

Manipulation can sometimes become a more serious case of emotional blackmail, where the manipulator subtly convinces others to act in ways that fulfil their own needs, and who are usually opposed to what is in the best interests of others. Not a firm foundation upon which to build positive personal *or* working relationships.

Those concerned with *getting their own way* all the time are still being the *child* in a *parent–child* relationship. It is immature behaviour, demonstrating that they have not yet learned that other people's involvement in developing their own originally identified wishes or beliefs can, in fact, bring about more positive outcomes for all concerned.

Stealing the ideas of others

There are also times when people like to believe all ideas are their own, without any other influence. Such people will often adopt other's ideas as their own, retrospectively perhaps after a period reflection, which they did not consciously acknowledge at the time of discussion and generally do not realize that they have *stolen* them. This approach can form after years of these people believing that they must have the ideas and make them happen, until finally they barely know they are doing it. How many times have you heard people say 'It was my idea in the beginning and it received little acknowledgement at the time, but an hour later it came back as the boss's idea with full commitment!'?

Political game-playing

Organizational culture (see 'The organization's culture' later in this chapter) can itself *influence* the positive or negative approach of its managers in influencing, and being influenced by, others. It can be very subtle, especially when it is negative, and individuals are often unaware of the effects the culture can have on their behaviour. Ultimately, where this organizational influence is negative (and it must be understood that there may have been no intentional harm created here), internal politics will ensure negative development in the way people treat each other, and the higher the position individuals attain within in the organization often the more negative and destructive the behaviour may become.

Political game-playing invites individuals *not* to take responsibility for their own attitudes and behaviour, unless of course they are likely to gain in some way from them. Organizations that encourage this kind of behaviour expect individuals to 'always be right' and will discourage any risk-taking. This, of course, not only restricts organizational change and development, it also creates 'dishonest' individuals to work in a 'dishonest' climate. This kind of experience will lead individuals to blame others for their own shortcomings and mistakes as well as to be sycophantic towards more senior members of the organization, or those who are believed to hold some other kind of power. Genuine individuals will either leave the organization or abdicate from essential interaction for fear of retribution.

Political wisdom and integrity

The term 'organizational politics' has itself come to mean something negative and unhealthy. This is not the case. Of course there will be *politics* (small 'p') in any organization where people interact and need to influence each other in meeting their objectives. There is, however, a vast difference between negative politics, where people play games (often more than they actually do the real work required), and the development of a healthy, politically aware team of people who understand the process and results of both positive and negative politics. These organizations and their managers will strive for open and honest relationships between all members as well as to seek to create 'ethical perspective' within the organizational climate (see also Chapter 3).

Integrating all ideas

This is probably the ultimate aim of open, honest and effective leadership, to achieve mutual influence between organizational members, mutual benefit so that everyone feels that they have a sound contribution to make to the process of achieving objectives as well as providing mutual support between members at all levels of the organization. There is awareness that a senior manager may not be the most knowledgeable or experienced in all circumstances and that a junior member of the team may bring rare knowledge or expertise to the situation. Having recruited the right people for the right jobs, this kind of organization will ensure that everyone contributes everything they are capable of contributing from the beginning and will therefore grow and develop accordingly. There is nowhere to 'hide' because there is nothing to hide from.

> ### EXERCISE
>
> What kinds of influencing techniques do you employ? Are they always appropriate? Identify and compare various situations. How might you behave differently in the future?

INDIVIDUAL RESPONSES TO INFLUENCE

There are at least three main responses by people to the influence of others. These responses may or may not be the recognition by them of others' seniority or expertise. These responses can often be related to the presence or absence of self-confidence, self-reliance and self-esteem, depending upon the circumstances (see Chapter 7 for self-confidence and personal drive).

- Influence by others is *accepted* by those receiving it because it is in their best interests to do so. It could be, for instance, that those concerned feel they are in no position to influence the process undertaken or the decision being made; that they either have no authority, or the relevant expertise, and therefore must obey those who are in a recognized position of responsibility or authority.
- It is possible for recipients to adopt ideas or proposals because they admire or *identify* with the initiator of the influence. For some reason they are over-impressed with the individual concerned and feel they cannot add to what is being presented. They are, in fact, not only doing an injustice to this individual, but to themselves also by not contributing and adding to the *quality* of the results.
- Those being influenced may have been so by *adopting* the ideas or proposals as their own. They internalize them so that they become their own possessions. This is, of course, the most positive response, as long as those concerned do not think that they were solely responsible for the original ideas. Caution should be exerted by the influencer to ensure that his/her approach does not become another form of manipulation or they will ultimately not be trusted.

It can be helpful to discuss their perceptions of various responses to influence, under different circumstances, openly with team members. Try to keep the atmosphere light and friendly and, where responses are inappropriate because of any misconceptions that may be present, the individuals themselves can change their behaviour as views alter.

EXERTING YOUR INFLUENCE

There will be times when you must ensure your influence is accepted, identified with and/or adopted. The difficulty for you will be to identify when this is necessary, that no further arguments can be introduced and that you must stand firm. A further difficulty is to not lose your temper or withdraw from the discussion, to be assertive rather than aggressive or passive (see Chapter 7—self-confidence and personal drive).

- *When you know your arguments are just* Do not scale down any requests you make in order to fit others' authority or willingness. It may not, on some occasions, be appropriate to compromise or modify your position, especially in dealing with organizational objectives or procedures such as discipline or grievance.

■ *To ensure the best outcome for everyone* Where you are convinced that not to exert your influence would result in a less-effective or a somewhat diluted outcome. Sometimes it is all too easy just to sit back and say nothing after a series of failed attempts at being heard.

■ *Make allies not enemies* If an *excuse* is genuine, it is often useful to enlist the person's assistance in approaching those who can really help, or in assisting the person to identify the means of overcoming difficulties, whether they are perceived or actual problems.

■ *In dealing with an ultimatum* Do not panic and do take your time, an ultimatum is seldom appropriate. Test understanding and summarize often (the problem may not turn out to be as extreme as at first thought); be firm but flexible, do not gain a reputation as a *soft touch* (you must work out an agreement); widen the debate, employ lateral thinking and influence the thinking of others away from the ultimatum by proving that there may be alternatives to consider.

EXERCISE

Identify a situation in which you have recently found it necessary to exert your influence. What were the circumstances and the outcomes? Did you behave appropriately? What might you do differently under similar circumstances in the future?

COMMON INFLUENCING PROBLEMS AND THEIR SOLUTIONS

The following problems, and simple rules identified for overcoming them, are just as successful when dealing with influencing difficulties inside the organization as they are to outside selling situations.

■ *Overselling* People often *oversell* their position in order to be heard at all. However, too many reasons put forward or too much emphasis placed upon advocating a particular idea or position will result in others losing interest or simply not believing what is being expressed.

- *Recognize the intelligence, reasonableness and logic of others by being realistic about the claims you are making.*

■ *Diluting benefits* Again too many benefits will dilute interest. Seeking many reasons why someone should *buy into* something, or accept claims being made, will make benefits appear multi-purpose with no clear focus and detract from the value of the more legitimate specific claims.

- *It is more advisable to make an impact with the most important benefits of your claims, by concentrating on the specific areas for which they are intended and are best at addressing.*

■ *Irritating remarks* Such words as *be fair, be reasonable, listen to my points, if only you* ... are more often used in the attempted emotional blackmail of those in opposition, or who require more persuasion, and are likely to make others present concentrate on the interpersonal behaviour rather than the purpose of the discussion. Effective relationships are unlikely to be developed in this way.

- *Be positive and keep to the real benefits of your arguments and issues surrounding them.*

■ *Dealing with excuses* Excuses can often cloud issues, and lack of preparation by the person meaning to influence can result in him/her being distracted by those trying to excuse their behaviour or ideas.

- *As with all organizational activity, adequate preparation is key to encouraging effective behaviour and results. At the same time, it is important not to make people feel threatened by our attitude while they are trying to defend themselves. We must remain calm, helpful and assertive in order to help others identify the problems that are causing their anxieties.*

Situation: a problem of influencing

The scenario has been provided by an advertising officer, who is also a MMUBS student (the names have been changed for reasons of confidentiality, upon request). It is *Daniella* who talks us through this case study.

■ *The company* A 10-year-old, medium-sized, IT consultancy firm.

- *The culture* Each departmental member is used to reporting vertically to the respective head, who would accept or reject ideas, ways of working and outcomes, etc., depending upon his/her expertise and/or interests. Departments rarely consult each other, except at the highest levels of the firm.
- *The future* Following a lengthy period of wide consultation within and outside the company, an agreed decision has been reached to change the structure from a, hitherto effective, functional bureaucracy to a customer-preferred matrix structure (customer satisfaction surveys had highlighted problems of inefficiency and gradual reductions in speed of response to queries and enquiries) with named teams of individuals from across the company working on specific projects, instead of only in project teams involving the IT experts.
- *The project* To establish more effective project team-working arrangements. The team members below have volunteered for the project, but this is the first time any of them has ever worked in this way.
- *The scenario* This was an actual exercise in the management of change, whereby both positive and negative influence occurred between team members. The needs of both the team members and the project objectives evolved over a period of time, proving some of the team development ideas of R. Meredith Belbin, as well as Charles Handy's views on influencing in general as well as the *perceived* power to influence in particular.
- *Team members* The team leader had been selected by the MD in advance of the team's formation, based on Sonia's previous experience as a departmental head. She had been given clear instructions to ensure this team develop a 'project team selection strategy' which would result in the most appropriate and effective members from across the organization being selected for any given project, depending upon the specification and intended outcomes of each project. The team had also to determine the systems and procedures necessary to ensure the most effective and efficient response to external requests by any team.

Sonia: team leader (accounts manager—systems background)
Ephram: computer programmer
Lucinda: computer programmer
Yanis: finance officer

Daniella: advertising officer
Frederick: systems analyst
James: human resources management officer
Graham: administrative support

Establishing roles and spheres of influence

At our first meeting, we were all vague as to the expectations required of us and, although we had all volunteered, in fact we felt very uncomfortable in the presence of each other. The IT experts wanted to impose the way they worked on their IT projects onto the rest of us; we were immediately made to feel inadequate and out of our depth.

Although Sonia set out very clearly from the start that we were all valued for the contribution we were individually able to make and that it was up to us as a group to define our own roles as we saw them within this project, in discussion with each other, there were so many differences of opinion as regards the effectiveness of each of our contributions that it seemed impossible to do. It was a very difficult and uncomfortable time for all of us.

Frederick soon emerged as a self-appointed informal team leader, with Ephram, Yanis and Graham deferring to his views.

On a number of occasions, Sonia found it necessary to exert her own influence and ask Frederick to allow other members a chance to have a voice. Lucinda, James and I (Daniella) had each attempted to make points, but we found it easier to keep quiet rather than to be overpowered all the time.

At the end of the first meeting Sonia felt she had achieved little other than to have allowed too much antagonism to occur and to some extent create enmity (she told us this later).

In discussing the problems with the MD at the her next mentoring session with her, Sonia told us that she soon realized that she had perhaps made too many assumptions about people's views and opinions of their respective job roles and how they could contribute to the work at hand.

OUTCOME: At the next project meeting 3 days later, Sonia had each of us explain to the rest of the team what our job function was, the kinds of issues and problems we deal with, what we considered our particular strengths to be, who our contacts were, both inside and outside the firm, and how we might draw on any information, support and resources we could supply and obtain from these contacts, in meeting the needs of the project objectives. This was a real confidence boost.

Agreeing terms of reference, project parameters and objectives

After we were all able to place our roles in the context of the current project, Sonia was then able to get us to focus on what the project required in order to meet the overall objectives. Frederick was still coming forward with very specific, technical approaches to how the project should be defined and conducted, of course, but some of us felt that he had very little idea of *how* to manage the process as regards the contribution of different people possessing very different skills and knowledge.

When Sonia pointed out how effective his ideas were in the context of purely IT or other highly technical projects, but that he needed to broaden his views as regards the composition of the current project team, it appeared at first that Frederick thought he was being undermined by her (let alone be lumbered with a team of non-specialists like most us were) and spent the rest of the meeting in abject silence, communicating only by employing very negative body language! We thought this was a retrograde step to start with and just couldn't believe Fred was being so difficult again.

Sonia's answer to this was to meet with Frederick on his own to determine how best to move forward. Clearly there were at least three team members who respected his informal leadership and Sonia, whilst not wanting to undermine the rest of us, did not want to negate his influence either. They worked closely together over the next several days to see how they could develop their relationship to extend to the project team and their joint leadership of the team's progress. Indeed, it was Frederick who sought the views of James, the human resources management project team member as to how they could best influence the most positive response from the whole team. This might seem underhand saying it now, but actually it was fine; they told us what they did and how it panned out privately and we were only too pleased for them to do it because the result was so positive.

OUTCOME: At the next project meeting, Frederick actively sought support from James as regards how they could agree specific objectives against the project specification and the best people to contribute to their achievement. This resulted not only in Lucinda, me and James himself contributing and defining our own roles in the project, but also the identification of the occasional secondment of others from around the organisation (and sometimes even an outside specialist) with additional skills which would be required at specific stages within the project.

Allocation of tasks, responsibilities and accountabilities

It was but a short step from this outcome to then be able to ascertain who should be responsible for what, how, who and when to report, etc., as well as how the project should be broken down into subteams according to *planned* need and *emerging* perceived need at various stages of the project.

Needless to say it was Frederick who designed the Gantt chart and plotted the indicative outcomes, monitoring and review slots, with dates for achievement, etc. all on the computer. The rest of us were so relieved he did this because we felt quite inadequate to the task. But Frederick didn't leave it at that, oh no, he was beginning to find his feet as regards his *wider* role within the team and successfully coached the rest of us in the design and application of project plans. We're all like Frederick a lot now.

I would never have thought of this, although as advertising officer I obviously have to plan campaigns. Somehow, I always just manage to plot things in my personal diary and then transfer them to the systems diary so I can run off reports; now I know how much more you can achieve through the systems diary! Learning's a funny thing really; you set out to learn the things you know you need to learn, and in the process stumble across things you would never have dreamed of had you not made that first step to start with!

OUTCOME: Sonia learns how to influence an influencer, Frederick learns to value the expertise of others and influences their involvement, the rest of us learn not to be so awkward and open our minds to being influenced further and learn something that might never have occurred to us, had it not been for Frederick.

Attitudes and perceptions

We also learned that we had negative attitudes and perceptions of others in our company. There was obviously an element of resentment and jealousy, which we only overcame once we became more self-confident and aware of how negative we were being. These were more the *incidental* results of everything that went on, because it was impossible to pinpoint by anyone. It was only by being open and honest with each other that we were able to overcome things that we would have found difficult to voice ourselves, other than as very negative views towards others and their jobs. Both Sonia as the formal leader and Frederick as the informal leader helped us to value our own contributions.

The problems we had to overcome were:

- Thinking others were cleverer than we could ever be.
- That the IT team were recognized by the firm, but that although we were needed we were expendable.
- Our defensiveness made it very difficult for Sonia at times and I know she was exasperated by our attitudes. Mostly though she managed to keep everything in proportion and went through everything stage by stage as needed—she was great (I would not have said that six months ago!)
- Frederick, and others like him, we began to realize felt self-important because *we* made them think that way, not the firm. Our under-confidence made us look like wimps when we first formed as a project team.

What we achieved:

- A greater understanding of who we all were.
- Trust and support between all of us—not just the project team.
- Broader understanding and more knowledge of the company and everything it does.
- How to have fun while learning and working.
- Some great working relationships which are continuing to develop, not just for the life of the project
- New friends as a result of better working relationships.
- More awareness of what we want to learn, as well as what we need to learn, in our current and future job roles.

Daniella–MMUBS, June 2002

EXERCISE

Identify a situation in which you have recently had problems influencing the behaviour of another/others. What were the circumstances? What were the outcomes? Did you behave appropriately? What might you do differently under similar circumstances in the future?

COPING WITH AGGRESSION

Do you respond in kind when confronting aggression, because you believe no-one will be listening otherwise? Or do you back off altogether? Either way, you will not influence the aggressor to change their behaviour and nothing will be achieved; the problem will only be unnecessarily prolonged.

You need to respond by stating your own needs, wants, feelings and opinions, directly and honestly. Listen to the other person calmly, test your understanding and be flexible but, above all, the aggressor must have their approach redirected and be allowed to state their position despite the initial aggression. It is most usual for aggression to subside when dealt with positively, allowing the person to 'let off steam' as necessary for them to calm down, and, as long as the person does not lose sight of what she/he wants, or wants to say, then the situation can be smoothed out. You will feel very positive yourself afterwards.

Acknowledge the aggressive person's determination or anger and state the affect the aggression is having on you and others, for example feeling nervous or becoming angry in return (the situation could be embarrassing for other people present) or whatever it may be.

Make suggestions and direct the conversation towards a goal. It is possible that you will have to go round the cycle a few times before achieving your aim.

EXERCISE

Identify a situation in which you have recently dealt with aggressive behaviour (your own or someone else's will do). What were the outcomes? What might you do differently under similar circumstances in the future?

THE ORGANIZATION'S CULTURE

Although definitions of organizational culture vary considerably, they all point to something that is difficult define, that it is elusive and intangible, but which has a strong influence on all those involved with it. Culture, which may or may not be appropriate to the organization's current purpose, is imposed upon people by people. New members of, or new associates to, an organization often find that they have to conform to the prevailing culture, or the relationship will not gel.

Culture is learned—or rejected—by new organizational members, sometimes by coping with some threat to their individual values by building defence mechanisms, or sometimes through the *positive reinforcement* model where an individual will internalize different values because they work and are accepted by others within the group. Where thoughts, beliefs or attitudes are inconsistent for the individual, he/she will experience what is known in psychology as *cognitive dissonance* ('cognitive'—the mental action or process of acquiring knowledge through thought, experience and the senses (*Concise Oxford Dictionary*, 2001), which is how we develop our values, beliefs and attitudes; 'dissonance'—clashing, lacking harmony).

This also applies to individual cultures within any one organization, where one group of individuals will exclude other groups and, if any new member to that group does not conform, that person is made to feel uncomfortable and is unaccepted by the others.

Charles Handy (1985) identified four main culture types associated with organizations; he expressed these diagrammatically for easy recall (Figure 5.1).

As discussed above, whilst it is important to understand the cultures of those organizations and individuals with whom we deal, it is often also important to influence changes as may be required according to the direction an organization may be taking for its overall development and improvement. This requires strength of character,

Power culture

The power culture is entrepreneurial by nature, with one person or a small team of people at the hub of the 'wheel' exerting all the power, control and influence

Role culture

The role culture depicts organizations that tend to be bureaucratic by nature, with well-defined jobs within tight structures, specific areas of function, responsibility and accountability (expressed by the 'columns' of the temple in the diagram)

Task culture

The task culture is a fast-growing and apparently more acceptable culture for *team* and *project* management, where the *manager* will vary from project to project, depending upon expertise and the contributions individuals are able make and/or develop (expressed) as a matrix in the diagram, where the dots are different people at different times, or covering the different projects)

Person culture

The person culture is great fun, but quite a problematic culture, where the individual is the centre of his/her organization's universe! It operates in isolation of everything and everyone else. The culture is only concerned with meeting personal objectives without wider reference (e.g. professional practices)

Figure 5.1
Organizational cultures (from Handy, 1985).

resilience, commitment, self-confidence and personal drive (see also Chapter 9).

EXERCISE

Study your own organization and/or team (internal or external to the organization) in terms of its prevailing culture. What are the difficulties? How might a change in culture meet organizational objectives more effectively (now or in the future as appropriate to you)?

THE USE OF NEGOTIATION

Some people seem to have an inborn ability to get results in conversations and negotiations. This is usually because they have real powers of persuasion, network naturally and easily and have ways of exerting their views within their spheres of influence.

Although negotiating is not the same as just getting our own way, we recognize that there are skills needed to increase the benefit to us in any particular situation.

> Negotiation is the art of seeking agreement to the maximum advantage of all concerned—win:win

This statement does bear some analysis. Notice that it says *seeking agreement*. This means that merely trying to bully someone into accepting our position is not negotiation. It is not very effective either. We should not confuse the notion of seeking agreement with the notion of changing someone's mind. It is not necessary to do the latter to achieve the former.

The definition also uses the phrase *maximum advantage*. This is because it may not be necessary to achieve all that is desirable in order to achieve the most important goals. Sometimes an element of compromise on minor issues can secure agreement on the major issues more readily than may be apparent at the beginning. This suggests that we start out with a clear idea of what we want (and the distinction between what we must have, as well as what we would like to have). It also suggests that we use our efforts to find out what the other person also must have, and on what they are willing to compromise.

Separate the people from the problem	When self-esteem is threatened, then people react. This in turn can cause a reaction that threatens the other person. The swapping of such emotions and attitudes inhibits proper negotiation. It is important to recognize that the issue that causes the problem is distinct from the people themselves.
Focus on interests, not positions	Positions are not the same as goals. We can take a position as a point of principle, and let the real issue go. So, for instance, although someone might insist on a colleague being moved to another department (the position taken), the issue might really be to prevent adverse criticism (the interest).
Generate a variety of possibilities before deciding what to do	Active listening is all-important. Do not accept positions taken by others at face value. Focus on possible areas of agreement – not of disagreement.
Base results on objective standards	These ought to be quantifiable criteria. They are easiest to understand in the context of financial negotiations. It is always legitimate to ask 'How did you arrive at that figure?' However, objective standards can always be found, whether quantifiable or not.

Figure 5.2
Successful negotiation (Fisher and Ury, 1984).

Fisher and Ury (1984) offer four basic principles for successful negotiating (Figure 5.2).

HOW TO CONVINCE PEOPLE

- Tell people when you agree with them.
- Admit when you are wrong.
- Do not argue.
- Put the case, quote the evidence.
- Use rationality, not emotion.
- Deal with objections.

EXERCISE

Identify a situation in which you have recently negotiated, or otherwise convinced people. What were the outcomes? Did you behave appropriately? What might you do differently under similar circumstances in the future?

DEVELOP AND USE CONTACTS TO EXCHANGE INFORMATION, OBTAIN SUPPORT AND RESOURCES

This skill involves effective networking both within and outside the organization. It is vital for any manager to develop and maintain relationships with colleagues across the organization at all levels, and with those who are operating within all the professional disciplines represented within the organization. To be most effective, it also requires us to develop and maintain relationships with customers, suppliers, professional and trade associations and institutes, local government, charities and anyone else with whom the organization can improve its standing in the community and gain trust in the mutual sharing of information, support and resources.

EXERCISE

In the following box, list those individuals and groups with which you do and/or should be developing relationships and the purpose of such involvement (add rows and columns as needed). You should involve your immediate colleagues in this exercise. How might you improve your approach to networking? This must be mutually rewarding!

Info you can supply	Info they can supply	Resources you can provide	Resources they can provide	Support you can provide	Support they can provide
Inside the organization					
Outside the organization					

SUMMARY OF ISSUES

In working through this chapter, you will have encountered a number of issues and perhaps some ideas that are new to you. The objectives of the chapter were to:

- Identify the nature of influence.
- Discuss methods of influence.
- Debate individual responses to influences.
- Introduce methods for exerting influence.
- Identify common influencing problems and their solutions.
- Introduce ways to cope with aggression.
- Discuss organizational culture.
- Debate the use of negotiation.
- Develop and use contacts to trade information, obtain support and resources.

How well have the authors met these objectives?

More importantly, how have you approached and used the material yourself, and how much have you developed since the beginning of your course of study, or working through the chapter? You are strongly recommended to extend your research and study to include as much of the material identified in further reading and references below as possible, so that you can build on your expertise, incorporating more complex approaches and ideas as you develop further in your managerial role.

These objectives, if re-revisited over a period of time and put into practice in your job, should help you to achieve the personal competency of influencing others, broken down into the elements identified in the table at the end of the chapter. In order for you to reflect on your own behaviour and that of others with whom you work, you might find it useful to use this table as a self-assessment check (reproduce it as many as you wish) to re-evaluate your knowledge and skills.

PREPARING FOR ACTION PLANNING

Remember to review the checklists of question, as identified in the Introduction to this book, at Appendix 1.

Analyse your own behaviour in terms of strengths (positive outcomes) and weaknesses (negative effects), in dealing with actual work-based occurrences with regards to the various situations discussed in this chapter, and summarized above.

Decide how you might deal with them differently in the future and what your immediate training requirements and future development needs might be.

Discuss them with appropriate others and negotiate how you might address them.

FURTHER READING AND REFERENCES

Capronia, P. (2001) *The Practical Coach: Management Skills for Everyday Life*. New Jersey: Prentice Hall (Chapter 3). ISBN: 0-13-849142-9

Eysenck, M. (1998) *Psychology: An Integrated Approach*. Harlow: Addison Wesley Longman (pp. 369–385). ISBN: 0-582-29884-9

Fisher, R. and Ury, W. (1984) *Getting to Yes*. London: Hutchinson Business Books.

Guirdham, M. (2002) *Interactive Behaviour at Work* (3rd edition). Harlow: Pearson Education (Chapters 8 and 13). ISBN: 0-273-65590-6

Handy, C.B. (1985) *Understanding Organisations* (3rd edition). London: Penguin Books. ISBN: 0-14-00911-6

Howell, J.P. and Coistley, D.L. (2001) *Understanding Behaviours for Effective Leadership*. New Jersey: Prentice Hall (Chapter 1). ISBN: 0-13-028403-3

Huczynski, A. and Buchanan, D. (2001) *Organizational Behaviour: An Introductory Text* (4th edition). Harlow: Pearson Education (pp. 816–820). ISBN: 0-273-65102-1

Martin, J. (1998) *Organizational Behaviour*. Boston: International Thomson Business Press (Chapter 17). ISBN: 1-86152-180-4

Rollinson, D. with Broadfield, A. (2002) *Organisational Behaviour and Analysis: An Integrated Approach* (2nd edition). Harlow: Pearson Education (pp. 392–397). ISBN: 0-273-65133-1

Recommended journal articles for readers' further development

Gupta, S. and Case, T.L. (1999) Managers' outward influence tactics and their consequences: an exploratory study. *Leadership and Organization Development Journal* 20/6/1999. Massachusetts: MCB University Press. ISSN: 0143-7739. Website: http://www.emerald-library.com

Competency element	Competency level: 1 (low)–5 (high)	Requires development	No direct experience	What can help? (identify opportunities)	Who can help?	When can it be achieved?	How can it be achieved?
Develop and use contacts to trade information and obtain support and the necessary resources							
Create and prepare strategies for influencing others							
Present yourself positively to others							
Use a variety of techniques, as appropriate to the audience and circumstances, to influence others							
Understand the culture of the organization and act to work within it or influence its change or development							

CHAPTER 6

Information management: *what* to provide when communicating with customers

Managers with information search skills gather many different kinds of information, using a variety of means, develop important working relationships and produce better decisions as a result.

LINKS TO THE CHARTED MANAGEMENT INSTITUTE'S MODULE

This chapter aims to address the aims and learning outcomes as identified in the Introduction to this text under the heading *Links to the Chartered Management Institute's Module 'Understanding Yourself'* so that, in conjunction with all other chapters, this material can be used to help participants be able to:

■ Construct a short-term, one-year (SMART) Personal Development Plan based on an awareness of their strengths as a manager and their development needs.

INTRODUCING THE RELATIONSHIP BETWEEN THE PERSONAL COMPETENCY MODEL AND INFORMATION MANAGEMENT

The Personal Competency Model (PCM), as already discussed, identifies the behaviours and skills that are necessary for you to develop before you are able to prove competence in any managerial function. This chapter attempts to deal with the various behaviours and skills necessary for you to apply across all managerial functions, transferring your learning to different occasions, at different times and under varying circumstances (contexts), consistently.

The outcomes below, as identified within this section of the model, should be borne in mind while you work through this chapter.

Outcomes required in information management

In developing this skill, the manager:

■ Establishes information networks to search for and gather relevant information.
■ Actively encourages the free exchange of information.
■ Makes best use of existing sources of information.
■ Seeks information from multiple sources.
■ Challenges the validity and reliability of sources of information.
■ Pushes for concrete information in ambiguous situations.

INTRODUCTION AND OBJECTIVES

The objectives of this chapter are to:

■ Identify forms of information required inside and outside the organization.
■ Define the information needs for customers.
■ Introduce the 'marketing mix'.
■ Establish what would be the 'right' messages.

- Identify customer needs and introduce simple market research techniques.
- Discuss the value and use of advertising and public relations.

In the process of managing information, we can approach the issues from a *marketing* perspective. When we are marketing to our customers and potential customers, we are providing information about our organization and its products or services. When we are providing information to other parts our organization, we are *marketing* who we are, what we can provide and the skills and knowledge we possess to our *internal customers*. In other words, we are defining and establishing the role we have in the overall success of the organization.

COMMUNICATING OUTSIDE THE ORGANIZATION

Communication is a strategic activity. Not only is it a part of the process of developing goals and objectives, but it is also an integral part of incorporating those goals and objectives in terms of profile and branding. It is therefore essential that the information we provide when communicating outside the organization is appropriate, valid, ethically and politically correct and carries the right messages.

External communications are the processes by which we send the messages about our organizations, and/or products or services, to potential or actual customers.

For some organizations, communicating to the outside world is seen as merely advertising, but it is, in fact, a much more complex and broad set of activities.

In the 21st century there will be many challenges facing organizations of all types and, if they do not recognize the significance of these challenges to their own work practices, they are unlikely to survive to the end of the first decade.

Some of the challenges already having impact on the economy are:

- Increased market competition.
- Rapid technological change.
- The *ageing* working population, as demographic changes produce a reduction of available young people.

To meet these challenges, organizations are being prompted to invest in people and ensure that valuable human assets are given the best possible chance to maximize potential, just like any other asset of appreciating value. According to *Investors in People* (1990), this investment can only be truly realized through meaningful and relevant training.

The justification of this statement will become clear as this chapter unfolds—each section itself addressing the complexities involved in understanding, addressing and meeting customer needs in the coming decades.

COMMUNICATING WITH THE CUSTOMER

In the organizational context, communication, including the provision of information, is essentially a subdiscipline of marketing. Marketing has to do with an exchange relationship in which all parties derive satisfaction. The exchange need not be for goods or money. Initially conceived in the commercial world, and still mainly associated with commerce, marketing principles are being adopted in the 'selling' of ideology (political parties), of personnel (employment applications), of a social consciousness (Keep Britain Tidy), of health (anti-smoking) and so on.

The concept is based on the exchange of value for mutual satisfaction, which depends for its success on the correct identification of the buyer's needs by the seller and supplying what the buyer actually needs so that satisfaction actually occurs. The supplier is also concerned to be satisfied. This may be in terms other than the commercial notion of profit; for example, in the public sector, 'the effective, efficient and economic delivery of a service'.

Three elements must be present in order for an organization to claim it is truly marketing-oriented—communicating the information:

- It must be customer-oriented—concerned primarily with the needs of customers and of co-ordinating activities that allow the organization to determine those needs.
- Its efforts must be integrated to create consistency, avoid duplication, capitalize on individual skills and personal creativity and, by so doing, create *synergy* (the value of effects which are more than the sum of the individual parts).
- Clear objectives must be established with the identification of the performance indicators (outcomes desired to determine relevant organizational activities needed to ensure the successful achievement of these outcomes) which will facilitate

the development of appropriate control measurements to monitor performance and progress.

THE MARKETING MIX

The expression *marketing mix* is a term that was first coined in 1952 for the concept of marketing as an integrative function by Neil Borden, a US advertising executive, and has been used as part of the marketing vocabulary ever since. There are many elements to the marketing mix, but Jerome McCarthy (1960) popularized a four-fold classification of these variables, called the 'four Ps':

- Product.
- Price.
- Place.
- Promotion.

Communications are vital to every element of the marketing mix and good communications techniques that provide the right information can be applied to each element of the mix in the following ways:

- *Price and positioning* This involves messages about price competitiveness, value-added benefits, quality and style. Positioning is not what you do with a product or service, but the effects your messages have on the minds of the customers.
- *Products* This involves consumer information and analysis of benefits, etc.
- *Promotion* This involves processes from advertising and sales promotion to packaging and point-of-sale displays.
- *Place* This involves the physical distribution of the product or service where they will reach the targeted customer effectively and conveniently.

As with any other communication activity, we need to examine:

- *What* the message is we are trying to communicate.
- *Who* the message is for—the target market.
- *How* to reach them—the medium (or media) to carry the message.

■ Why choose the product mix we do. As the environment, the technology and the products change over time, so must the rationale behind the choice of product mix.

IDENTIFYING THE *RIGHT* MESSAGES

Getting the message across

The variety of messages required to keep a company functioning efficiently in the market-place is vast. So too is the variety of target audiences and media to carry them. In each case, the purpose is to ensure recognition, quality and consistency of the message.

Media campaigns can be very efficient at promoting a single, often simple, idea about a company or its products/services. They often concentrate on a unique selling point, with a memorable phrase or strap-line:

'When it positively, definitely, has to be there on time.'
'Probably the best lager in the world.'

To what or whom do these lines refer?

The recognition, quality and consistency factors apply in all aspects of an organization's communications.

Corporate branding

It is often very important for a company to promote recognition of its own name, as well as its products or services. This is often done with the enhancement of visual recognition techniques such as colour, corporate logos, and so on.

London Underground is recognized, not just in London, or even nationally, but the world over, by its very distinctive corporate branding. This is based on the use of its distinct roundel, and the use of its own typeface (called New Johnstone—a variation of the Gill typeface). Another very strong feature of this recognition comes from the distinctive London Underground map. It is unusual in that it is not a *real* map, in the normal sense that the distances shown are to scale. It is a topological map, which shows the spatial relationships of the lines and stations.

Figure 6.1
Telephone
checklist (adapted
from Peel, 1987).

1   *Get good equipment* Modern technology now enables real sophistication in call storage, diversion and transfer.
2   *Give technical training* (today this applies to all staff since most of us now have to use call divert, store, voicemail and whatever else is available — *authors' addition*).
3   *Structure the job right* Good support and guidance for appropriate telephone techniques are essential in helping everyone to provide effective customer service.
4   *Establish good discipline* How to deal with various types of enquiry, personal calls, peak-time procedures Are individuals allowed to take messages for others?
5   *Behavioural training* Whoever takes customer calls, they are the voice of the organization. Are they voices you would like your customers to hear when they call? Are their greetings courteous? Do they identify the organization in the proper way?

These are all important.

Figure 6.1
Telephone
checklist (adapted
from Peel, 1987).

This map was designed for London Underground in 1933 by Henry Beck, complete with the distinctive colours for the lines that existed then. In substance, it has changed very little since that time; the roundel, the insignia style and the underground map are protected very carefully by London Underground, so as not to dilute the power of their distinctive symbols.

The telephone

The telephone is often the first line of response to customers, or the public at large, for many organizations. But what sort of impression do your customers get from your organization when they call?

Try phoning your own organization from outside. What sort of response did you get? Was it prompt, helpful, informative, efficient?

It would be a pity to spend millions of pounds on a major media campaign to promote a product or service or your company and have it spoiled because customers are treated badly by whoever answers the telephone. Yet this does happen all too often. Malcolm Peel (1987) identifies five steps to help; they are adapted here to meet more recent requirements (Figure 6.1).

INTERNAL COMMUNICATIONS

It should be understood that effective techniques and standards should be applied both within the organization and externally to it. In much of the current literature about the effectiveness of management, and in the growing body of literature that examines successful organizations, a consensus is emerging suggesting that successful organizations are those that communicate their mission to their own staff, motivate them to perform, and train and empower them to make decisions and to achieve success. In other words, treating employees as *internal customers*.

At all times, communicating the right information plays a vital role. Obviously, an important aspect of this is the interpersonal communication that takes place throughout an organization and at every level. This is dealt with in more detail in Chapter 2. Organizational communication to staff as a body is in itself like a marketing exercise to a specialized target group of *internal customers*.

The need to provide information internally occurs for many reasons:

- *Information*—to ensure everyone receives the information they need in order to fulfil their individual and departmental objectives, based on the overall organizational mission.
- *Corporate branding*—to ensure that all *internal customers* have full understanding of the organizational image and reflect the agreed standards in all their activities.
- *Training and development*—to provide benefits to the organization that will be reflected in:
  - Increased profitability.
  - Increased turnover.
  - Higher quality.
  - Improved image/reputation.
  - Better ways of meeting client needs, etc.
- *Team-building and integration*—by defining and promoting cultural values and norms.
- *Motivation*—the organization's *internal customers* will be more highly motivated if they understand what, and grow to identify with, the organizational image.
- *Social bonding*—internal messages about organizational image and identity will enhance interpersonal relationships and create a sense of belonging.

ESTABLISHING CUSTOMER NEEDS AND SIMPLE MARKET RESEARCH

Market research

Marketing can be defined as the process whereby we 'identify, anticipate and satisfy customer requirements profitably', and as such we need systematic means of undertaking each of these stages.

Market research is the process by which we research the nature of customer tastes and preferences, and by which we measure their satisfaction with products and services. It is one of the means of forecasting demand in the market-place, which might be included among the following:

- Buyer intentions.
- Sales force assessment.
- Trends analysis.
- Market research.
- Leading indicators.
- Comparative studies.
- Experimental research.

The scope of market research

Market research is generally agreed to give information about:

- Buyers habits.
- Demography.
- Consumer product/service knowledge.
- Opinions/attitudes.
- Intentions.
- Motives.
- Perceptions.

It operates in two key dimensions. The first is in acquiring information about current products/services, and their position in the market. The second is in identifying new market opportunities.

Some of the most important techniques

- *Panels* These are a selected sample of a target population who give interviews and express opinions on a regular basis. A problem with using panels is in assessing the reliability and validity of the information they give.
  - A more specific technique is the retail audit, which is used to establish brand share and volume sales.
- *Qualitative* This is the acquisition of opinions, reactions and behaviour. The gathering of qualitative information can take

many forms and can be carried out by interview, questionnaire, or by less formal means.

■ *Media research* This involves identifying the size and nature of
audiences for advertisements in various media. It can also be
used to audit the effectiveness of specific advertisements.
Researchers look for evidence of *spontaneous recall* or
prompted recall of a product or service.

■ *Test marketing* This involves various processes by which new
products are tried out on customers to gauge reaction. Test
marketing is used to reduce the chances of expensive failures.

■ *Preference mapping* This is a specific technique for analysing
customer perceptions of the benefits of a product or product
range.

Interviews and panels are used to identify significant attributes. These
attributes are tested with sample groups to identify priority order, and
eliminate unimportant ones. For instance, with training shoes, the key
attributes might be price and style.

Then a selected sample of customers is asked to rate their ideal
product/service in terms of the attributes identified. This rating is
quantified so that the responses can be mapped onto a matrix, like
the one in Figure 6.2.

When more than two attributes are identified, the matrix becomes
multi-dimensional. In the final phase, real products/services are rated
and compared to the ideal product.

The advantage of this method is that a very clear picture of a
product or service can be drawn in terms of customer response. So,

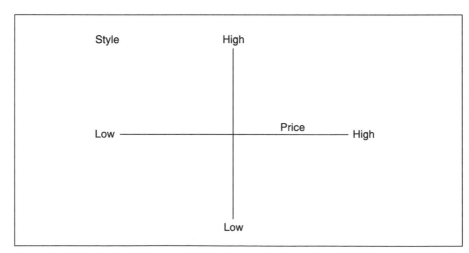

Figure 6.2
Example of
customer ratings
matrix.

if your product is identified as being too expensive, then countering strategies can be drawn up—either to reduce price, or to emphasize value-added aspects.

This technique works better for well-understood products or services, or ranges thereof, than it does for potential or innovative products or services.

Where customers or clients are also citizens with social needs

Some readers of this chapter may feel that marketing is of little relevance to them because they perceive that they serve a *market* of an entirely different sort. For instance, those working in parts of the public or voluntary sectors may believe that some of the concepts discussed here are quite irrelevant when addressing, for example, the needs of the elderly in residential care homes.

For the purposes of relating some of these theories to such situations, consider the following information obtained from interviews with the two managers quoted earlier in this book.

Enabling or disabling

Instead of enabling clients to develop their independence within one of the homes, a care assistant was actually leading others into *disabling* the clients by telling them what to do, how to do it, when, and what not to do, etc.

The manager herself believes it is simply a matter of educating both staff and clients who may believe that providing attention in a continued 'fussing over others and doing things for them' manner is the correct behaviour. According to this manager: 'It is difficult to convert to a customer care culture and to break down the "you do this and fit into our routine" approach, but it is an important challenge'.

Before the manager joined the care team, residents had no locks on their doors and the doors were also kept permanently wide open so that 'an eye could be kept on them'. When the manager discussed the idea of privacy and locks on residents' doors with the team, an uproar ensued. The general excuse made was that the 'corridor would be dark'. The locks were eventually fitted, but staff and residents alike found the idea very difficult to accept initially.

> Clothing was another issue. Care assistants had habitually produced whatever clothes they thought the residents should wear. Now the clients are being asked what they would like wear and proper discussions and questioning about such issues are replacing the well-intentioned, but inappropriate, control of client interests.
>
> The manager believes that staff must continue to identify residents' needs and wishes and work towards those, instead of always telling them what to do. If they continue to concentrate on residents' disabilities, the results will be negative. Therefore they must concentrate on individuals' strengths and abilities to ensure positive outcomes. The negative results, and indeed the disabilities themselves, she says, will then recede into the background.

This is clearly a deeply psychological approach to the provision of information and the communication thereof. This is not so different to providing or receiving information in the wider marketing context. If we all took the moral and ethical approach identified here by a residential care home manager, we would not risk accusations of misrepresentation of our organizations, services and products.

SIMPLE NEGOTIATION AND SELLING TECHNIQUES

Selling skills

If we consider selling to be 'convincing someone of the advantages of accepting your position', then we can interpret it in a relatively wide context. Some of us will be involved in selling products or services to customers face to face. Many more will have a marketing role. Nearly everyone will be involved in persuading internal customers to 'buy' an idea that we are 'selling', whether it be a new project, or a new system. The application of the theory and practice of selling involves *personal skills*—selling is the communication skill *par excellence*. By putting the theory and practice to good use, everyone can benefit—not just those who have the responsibility for moving products or services to individual customers. It can inform much of our persuasive activity.

Features, benefits and positioning

When we sell, we are looking to satisfy customers' needs. Clearly the most important element of selling is to find out what those needs are; this involves the seeking and supplying of information. This is interesting because it contradicts many people's notions of what selling is. They seem to characterize it as talking and persuading. In fact, listening is a much more important skill. Again, our active listening skills come to the fore. It is necessary to look more closely at our products and services, and what they mean to a customer.

- The *features* of a product or service are the technical or user characteristics that make a product or service interesting. On a video recorder, a seven-day timer is a feature. For a shop, seven-day opening is a feature.
- A *benefit* is the advantage gained by the customer by virtue of the features. So, if we are selling furniture, we might sell the benefit of comfort. For certain types of car we might sell status or speed.
- *Positioning* is about the way that we promote the image of a product/service, a range of products/services, or a brand name.

The most important aspect of this knowledge is that we sell *benefits*, not features. Most potential customers will not be interested in the finer working of the epicyclic overdrive capacitor. They will be seeking the answer to the question 'What can it do for me?' This can only be answered if we work to uncover what their needs really are.

Identifying needs

Most people have needs. They are not always explicitly and strongly expressed—particularly at the opening of a sales presentation. Initially, needs are often expressed as a *dissatisfaction* with some aspect of the current situation. The need grows eventually to a stronger and more positive commitment to a particular solution. Research shows that selling is much more efficient when it is directed to a strong explicit need than to a weak and implicit one.

A weak implicit need might be: 'Our order processing is not very efficient'.

A strong explicit need might be: 'I need a photocopier that will count copies used by our different departments.'

To return to some practical examples obtained from one of the residential care homes surveyed.

Providing the obvious

As a result of interviewing and finding out their client needs, the management team improved the information and facilities available to residents as follows:

- Brochures were made available from area doctors' surgeries.
- Special transport arrangements were made in the area.
- A suggestion book was provided.
- A simplified complaints procedure was developed.
- Computerized menus were produced, with large print for the short-sighted.
- Regular meetings for clients and relatives were introduced.
- Various clubs were introduced.
- Regular and special outings were arranged.
- Pictures for walls were provided.
- Public relations activities were introduced.
- Summer and Christmas bazaars introduced.
- Open days were arranged.
- Donations were encouraged from residents, families, local services, etc., and proper mechanisms for thanking them.

(Many things seem so obvious—after they have been discovered!)

If we know we are seeking to encourage customers to tell us their needs, we need to think about how to construct a sales presentation that enables us to do this.

The sales presentation

A one-to-one sales presentation should have structure and purpose, and should have the following phases:

- *Courtesy/introduction* This involves introducing ourselves and establishing rapport. We have already talked about the importance of good first impressions and nowhere are they *more* important than here. Look back at the rules for creating a good impression discussed in Chapter 2.

■ *Exploration* This phase is really the one where we identify the needs of the customer. It is vital that we give the customer the opportunity to tell us what their needs are—not the other way around. Research shows that successful selling occurs when buyers do more talking than sellers. Where we do talk, we should be actively seeking information at this stage—not giving it. What we need to do is to talk about the most interesting thing in the world to our customer—themselves! Again, our active listening skills are crucial here.

Once we have explored and identified explicit needs, we then move on to the next stage.

■ *Offering solutions* It is only now that we can offer solutions. The solution offered relates directly to the expressed need. The key idea is to match benefits to needs. This will be followed by discussion, objections, reinforcement.

Many books on sales technique talk about buying signals. These are basically where the customer is 'trying out' the ideas in their minds. They may range from vague interest to a genuine objection. Your job is to pick up these signals, find out their significance and respond accordingly. Once you see a level of commitment developing you should move on to the last phase.

■ *Closing the deal* There are really no rules about closing a deal, although there are many books that give advice, information, techniques and so on. The major objective is to seek a level of commitment. The level of that commitment will depend mainly on the customer and the circumstances.

'Would you like to pay cash or cheque' is a nice close, but it does not work like that every time. It may be that the maximum commitment a customer can or will give is to see the product/service in action, to use it for a week on trial, or any other commitment up to *on-the-spot* purchase. The skill is finding the maximum level of commitment that the customer is comfortable with (and has the authority to provide!).

More formal presentations have more formal requirements. The written presentation should:

■ Summarize your understanding of the customer's situation and needs.

- Describe key features and benefits of the proposed services and how they will meet customer needs.
- Summarize costs.
- Project your offer as different to and/or better than others'.
- Enable the client to evaluate your services, products and reputation.
- Communicate your message in a way that is appealing and intelligible to the decision-makers.

Oral presentations should:

- Get and keep the listeners' attention.
- Keep them interested in what you have to say.
- Spotlight four or five benefits or points of major interest to the customer.
- Answer questions and clarify any points necessary.

What you should find out about the customer

Assemble and evaluate information about:

- Technical, financial and historical information: this may be abstracted from client documentation to ensure accuracy.
- The personnel involved: their main interests; the level of their technical expertise, particularly in relation to your products and services; the interpersonal relationships between them (you will need to *pitch* your presentation according to the culture of the organization and the apparent power bases).
- The state of the relevant industry: whether it is a new industry; if it is expanding or declining; who are the major competitors, etc.
- Major problems currently faced by the organization: SWOT and STEP analyses are useful here, but at the very least you should discover whether the industry confronts the possibility of takeover; the implications of any major technological advances, important changes that are either pending or being avoided by the organization.
- The reasons why the customer wishes to consider your proposal: it may be purely economic—for example, a local authority may be more interested in in-company training provided by an academic institution than a leading consul-

tancy, based purely on the costs involved; whether they are seeking to short-circuit any improvements they should be considering; maybe your product or service is of higher quality standards than others, and so on.

Identify the prospective decision-makers and pitch your presentation according to expertise, degree of influence, the role they perform (their information needs will vary accordingly). Gain information quickly and effectively. Make full use of published material, knowledge held by colleagues and associates and use questioning techniques appropriate to eliciting free speaking (open-ended questions) and specific information (closed questions).

Find out what the customer needs and how you can meet the need

- Actively identify needs by responding fully to expressed (recognized) needs and seeking out unrecognized (but real) needs. Needs may be personal, task-oriented or organizational.
- Decide which services could be helpful in meeting needs and assisting in the solution of problems; identify the benefits and link a feature (attributes of the service) to the benefit (what's in it for the customer) it brings. Customers do not buy services; they are looking for a bundle of benefits.
- Analyse the strengths and weaknesses of your organization's services; demonstrate the strengths and seek to overcome the weaknesses.
- Demonstrate clearly what your organization can do more effectively than any other.
- Assess the personalities on your team as appropriate counterparts to the customer's team of decision-makers.

How to make the sale

- Be effective: the content of your delivery should match the customer's needs and your delivery should demonstrate that your are confident, perceptive, responsive and enthusiastic. You should use humour, listening skills and show ability to think on your feet; provide all information needed for the customer to make a decision; present information with different emphases according to the individuals in your audience.

- Present the right image—personal and professional.
- Communicate with skill (as discussed in Chapter 2).
- Deal with objections: anticipate them and formulate responses; seek to forestall them; if raised, respond to them by probing the nature of the problem raised—an apparent objection may be a device to seek further information.
- Find out about your competitors: who they are; where they are; what are their strengths and weaknesses and which major strengths you will have to compete against in this instance.

If you are unsuccessful!

Failure to obtain an organization's commitment is still a valuable learning experience. Capitalize on the investment put into it:

- Review the whole process.
- Identify precisely what you have learned.
- Identify other opportunities for your services or products.
- Build contacts.

THE VALUE AND USE OF ADVERTISING AND PUBLIC RELATIONS

Advertising

Advertising has been called 'the means of making known goods and services in order to sell them'.

It is easy to associate advertising with the high-profile, expensive TV campaigns, but advertising can be carried in many different media:

- Press.
- TV.
- Posters and transport.
- Cinema.
- Radio.
- Direct mail.

The choice depends on a number of factors, one of the most important of which is the budget available. There are, of course, other considerations. Examples would be the difference between trade and consumer advertising, and the amount of information needed to convey the message, or arouse interest. For instance, it would be difficult to describe the features of a high-tech item of equipment in a short TV advertisement, but it could be used to stimulate interest. Instructions can be provided for potential customers to seek further information.

Marketing tasks that can be performed well by advertising include:

- New product or service launches.
- Complementing face-to-face or telephone advertising activities.
- Entering new markets.
- Inviting enquiries.
- Direct selling.
- Creating images.
- Selling services.

Although many small and medium-sized enterprises will devise and execute advertising campaigns for themselves, larger companies will use specialist agencies to do this work for them. People who do this need to know how to get the best from such agencies, and their priorities and methods of working are instructive for the 'do it yourself' organizations.

Advertising agencies

Agencies have all the experience, expertise and resources necessary to manage the complex processes involved in any campaign. They are organized into specialist departments, which undertake different functional activities. These usually include:

- *Creative department* This department includes the thinkers and visualizers, whose job it is to create concepts and ideas from a brief.
- *Media department* They recommend appropriate media for a campaign, and can also 'buy' the space for the individual advertisements.
- *Production department* Their job is the writing, design, illustration, photography, film and print, to realize a concept.
- *Account management* Their job is to manage the whole process: to budget and schedule, and to act as liaison with the client.

Choosing an agency

Of course, there are many ways of choosing an agency. A common one for major accounts is called competitive pitching. In this, a number of agencies are invited to work up creative ideas in response to a written brief. This can work very well for the client, as they can judge the potential effectiveness of a campaign from the ideas proposed.

Not all agencies will expend the time and effort needed for this process. They will produce a credentials briefing, where they provide evidence of success based on completed projects. Only when they are contracted will they make full use of their creative team in developing the campaign further.

The brief

The needs of the client are specified in a document called a brief. Because it is the basis from which the creative team builds the campaign, it must contain all of the information they need, and it is vital to get it right. It is quite common for the agency to assist the client in drawing up the brief. Some are expert at turning the vague statements and ideas of the client into a powerful and workable brief. However, it is preferable for the client to control the whole process, and better results will be obtained if they can communicate their needs clearly to the agency.

The brief should cover five main areas:

- Objectives and tasks.
- Background to company and products/services.
- Target markets.
- Constraints/issues/interests.
- Media.

The more clues that are provided, the more accurate the response is likely to be.

Public relations

The function

Public relations (or PR) is the range of activities that seeks to place messages and ideas about organizations and products or services into the media. Unlike advertising, it does not prepare and control specific adverts, but seeks to gain profile through news and features.

However, it is not concerned solely with print media, and can encompass a huge variety of activities, including:

- Press releases.
- Research reports.
- Events, such as conferences (including press conferences).
- Personal appearances (e.g. on TV or radio talk shows).
- Crisis management.
- Information services.
- Specific briefings (e.g. for financial journalists).
- Sponsorship.

Quite often, some of the basic PR activities are covered by in-house press and publicity departments. Even where there is an internal service, one of its functions may be to brief and contract the outside specialist services of a PR consultancy. As well as having the whole range of expertise necessary to manage a campaign on a day-to-day basis, such agencies also have established contacts with people in the trade or consumer press, and can often place features, or gain exposure for press information that is beneficial to their clients.

As with advertising agencies, PR consultancies vary in their strengths, and in the services they offer. Some of this information can be obtained from trade directories, but a credentials pitch for a number of likely candidates is a better way to get a feel for the strengths of an agency. They differ in a number of ways:

- *Size*—from an individual consultant, up to the large consultancies.
- *Style*—from the traditional to the more youthful and up-market agencies.
- *Specialisms*—most agencies are generic, but all have particular specialisms such as finance, fashion, leisure.

Although it may seem like a *soft* spend, with little chance of auditing its own effectiveness, PR should be able to quantitatively justify its activities, like any other area of the business. If you wish to commission a PR consultancy you should expect them to project cost benefits from the work they do. One of the best measures of their effectiveness is the amount of column inches of advertising space that they have gained on your behalf. This can be costed quite easily.

The brief

As with advertising agencies, PR consultancies work best when they are properly briefed. The same criteria apply, and so, again, the brief should contain:

- Objectives and tasks.
- Background to company and products.
- Target markets (this could include customers, employees, shareholders, community and all other stakeholders).
- Constraints/issues/interests.
- Media.

In response to this brief, the consultancy should offer a complete service to manage outgoing information to reach target markets, whether they be trade or consumer, and it should specify the targeted media and the means of reaching them.

Campaigns usually involve a mixture of ongoing press activities, together with specific projects aimed at particular targets. In fact, it should be possible to list activities and target groups separately. Alternatively, they can be shown in a matrix, giving specific details (see Figure 6.3 for the example of a local building project described below).

In order to draw up a PR programme for a local building project, for example, it would be necessary to start by defining the target groups that need to be reached. These might include:

- Banks/financial institutions.
- Department of the Environment (DoE).
- Local planning authorities.

	Banks	DoE	Local groups	Politicians	National groups	Residents etc.
Information packs						
Visits to site						
Press releases						
Press conferences						
Photographs						
Competitions						
Exhibitions						

Figure 6.3 Matrix for the PR programme for a local building project.

- Local politicians.
- National pressure groups.
- Local residents.
- Press.
- Local pressure groups.
- Professionals.

Events and activities might include:

- Information pack.
- Visits to site.
- Press releases/articles.
- Press conferences.
- Photographs.
- Competition/education.
- Exhibitions.

OTHER MARKETING COMMUNICATIONS

There are a number of other means of promoting profile, products and services direct to potential customers. These can be broadly classified as marketing communications; highlighted here are a few of the most important ones.

Direct mail

Direct mail is the sending of information to specified and identified target individuals or businesses. As end-user consumers, we often call it junk mail. Despite their being some negative connotations to the concept, its wide use testifies to its effectiveness, when it is well done and properly targeted. It usually contains product or service information, together with some sort of inducement to buy. Two of the most popular forms are leaflets and letters.

As a receiver of junk mail yourself, you will know that the one thing you do not want with unsolicited mail is the need to work hard to understand its meaning, or to respond to it. Therefore, simplicity, directness and brevity are the key to its success. The most usual mistake is to try to send too many messages, and too much information. Ideally, there should be a single, simple message, whether contained in a letter or a leaflet.

In a letter, you should begin with a sentence that catches the interest and imagination. This should then be followed by the claim, and the justification for that claim. You must then make it clear how people should respond—and make it as easy as possible for them to do just that (complete the form, send it off ...). It is not expensive to arrange a FREEPOST reply facility that attracts potential customers, not only because it is easy, but also because they do not have to pay.

To summarize, an effective formula is:

- Did you know?—identify the problem.
- Look at this—here is the solution.
- Now do this-how to respond.

Information technology for direct mailing

Technology can help enormously in making direct mail effective. There are three main aspects to this:

- *Consumer databases* It is possible to buy names and addresses that correspond to specified criteria, such as income, status, demography, etc. The more constraints you specify, the more you pay for each name.
- *Word-processing/DTP* These systems can enable you to design and produce quite effective and inexpensive letters or leaflets within your organization.
- *Mail-merge* Lists of names and addresses can be supplied or entered into a database, and this can be linked to the word-processing package via a mail-merge package. This customizes each letter for the named individual and can also produce address labels.

As can be seen in Figure 6.4, this use of information technology connects to the much wider *architecture* that is now available in most large organizations. Note how the applications interlink and support each other to see how information can be accessed, applied and developed across the whole organization.

Brochures

Brochures and other specialist publications can be a very effective means of influencing potential customers. Not only can they carry written information, but photographs or illustrations can show pro-

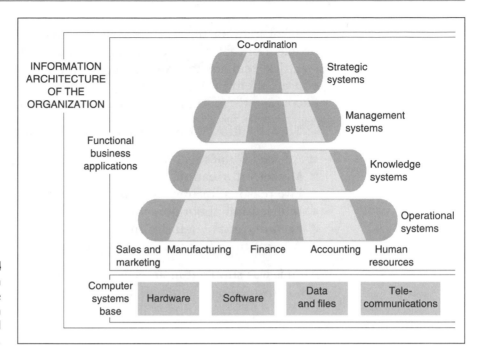

Figure 6.4
Information architecture of the organization (Laudon and Laudon, 1998).

ducts in a very positive light and design can be branded to promote very positive images. In order to achieve these effects, however, professionalism is required. Often, this expertise is available within an organization, but even large companies often subcontract agencies or freelancers to produce specific projects.

Whether the publication is to be produced internally or externally, it is the brief that is especially important. The brief should reference similar elements to advertising or PR briefs. In addition, they should also be explicit about content, style, the nature and extent of illustration and the format (size, number of colours, etc.).

Video recordings

Video recordings are now widely used. Use of the VCR can range from sales presentations or product briefings through footage for press and publicity purposes, to in-company newsletters.

In terms of execution, many of the comments about brochures also apply—i.e. use specialists and brief them properly.

Video recordings are a well-used and popular form of marketing communications. But all companies are individual in their needs and specific needs can often be satisfied by a different or more imaginative approach.

A major manufacturer of domestic electronic goods had a problem in that it was reliant on the sales staff of the major electrical retailers to promote its products. It needed to educate them in the benefits and features of its products and to encourage them to promote them to customers.

Their solution was to provide a sales training kit. It included:

- Advice on sales technique.
- Market information.
- Five reasons for buying their equipment.
- Information about how the equipment worked.
- Features and benefits of their products.
- A script for a face-to-face sales presentation.

All this was supplied in an electronic note-book format, which was known to be useful and attractive to sales staff.

SUMMARY OF ISSUES

In working through this chapter, you will have encountered a number of issues and perhaps some ideas that are new to you. The objectives of the chapter were to:

- Identify forms of information required inside and outside the organization.
- Define the information needs for customers.
- Introduce the 'marketing mix'.
- Establish what would be the 'right' messages.
- Identify customer needs and introduce simple market research techniques.
- Discuss the value and use of advertising and public relations.

How well have the authors met these objectives?

More importantly, how have you approached and used the material yourself, and how much have you developed since the beginning of your course of study, or working through the chapter? You are strongly recommended to extend your research and study to include as much as possible of the material identified in further reading and references below, so that you can build on your expertise, incorporating more complex approaches and ideas as you develop further in your managerial role.

These objectives, if re-revisited over a period of time and put into practice in your job, will help you to achieve the personal competency of information management, broken down into the elements identified in the table at the end of the chapter. In order for you to reflect on your own behaviour and that of others with whom you work, you might find it useful to use the table as a self-assessment check (reproduce as many as you wish) to re-evaluate your skills and knowledge.

PREPARING FOR ACTION PLANNING

Remember to review the checklist of questions, as identified in the Introduction to this book, at Appendix 1.

Analyse your own behaviour in terms of strengths (positive outcomes) and weaknesses (negative effects), in dealing with actual work-based occurrences with regards to the various situations discussed in this chapter and summarized above.

Decide how you might deal with them differently in the future and what are your immediate training requirements and future development needs.

Discuss them with appropriate others and negotiate how you might address them.

FURTHER READING AND REFERENCES

Brassington, F. and Pettitt, S. (2000) *Principles of Marketing* (2nd edition). Harlow: Pearson Education (Chapters 6, 17 and 18). ISBN: 0-273-64444- 0

Cadle, J. and Yeates, D. (2001) *Project Management for Information Systems* (3rd edition). Harlow: Pearson Education (Chapter 15). ISBN: 0-273-65145-5

Kotler, P., Armstrong, G., Sauders, J. and Wong, V. (1999) *Principles of Marketing* (2nd European edition). Harlow: Pearson Education (Chapter 8). ISBN: 0-13-262254-8

Laudon, K.C. and Laudon, J.P. (1998) *Management Information Systems: New Approaches to Organization and Technology* (5th edition). New Jersey: Prentice Hall (Parts 1 and 2). ISBN: 0-13-906462-1

McCarthy, E.J. (1960) *Basic Marketing. A Managerial Approach.* Homewood, IL: Irwin.

Competency element	Competency level: 1 (low)– 5 (high)	Requires development	No direct experience	What can help? (identify oppor-tunities)	Who can help?	When can it be achieved?	How can it be achieved?
Establishes information networks to search for and gather relevant information							
Actively encourages the free exchange of information							
Makes best use of existing sources of information							
Seeks information from multiple sources							
Challenges the validity and reliability of sources of information							
Pushes for concrete information in ambiguous situations							

CHAPTER 7

Self-confidence and personal drive

Managers with self-confidence and personal drive show resilience and determination to succeed in the face of pressure and difficulties.

LINKS TO THE CHARTERED MANAGEMENT INSTITUTE'S MODULE

This chapter aims to address the aims and learning outcomes as identified in the Introduction to this text under the heading *Links to the Chartered Management Institute's Module 'Understanding Yourself'* so that in conjunction with other chapters, participants should be able to:

■ Understand the impact of their behaviour on other people in a range of management situations (e.g. through being assertive, rather than passive or aggressive; keeping abreast of change, etc.).

■ Demonstrate how they can gain more flexibility in their style and approach to others, to enhance the delivery of the above objective.

■ Construct a short-term, one-year (SMART) Personal Development Plan based on an awareness of their strengths as a manager and their development needs.

INTRODUCING THE RELATIONSHIP BETWEEN THE PERSONAL COMPETENCY MODEL AND SELF-CONFIDENCE AND PERSONAL DRIVE

The Personal Competency Model (PCM), as already discussed, identifies the behaviours and skills necessary for you to develop before you are able to prove competence in any managerial function. This chapter attempts to deal with the various behaviours and skills necessary for you to apply across all managerial functions when developing self-confidence and personal drive, transferring your learning to different occasions, at different times and under varying circumstances (contexts), consistently.

The outcomes below, as identified within this section of the model, should be borne in mind while you work through this chapter.

Outcomes required for self-confidence and personal drive

In demonstrating this behaviour, the manager:

- Takes a leading role in initiating action and making decisions.
- Takes personal responsibility for making things happen.
- Takes control of situations and events.
- Acts in an assured and unhesitating manner when faced with a challenge.
- Says no to unreasonable requests.
- States her/his own position and views clearly in conflict situations.
- Maintains beliefs, commitment and effort in spite of setbacks or opposition.

INTRODUCTION AND OBJECTIVES

The objectives of this chapter are to:

- Introduce the notion of 'change' and present techniques for the identification and analysis of changes that have occurred, or could occur, inside and outside the organization.

■ Present ways to analyse individual behaviour and approaches to developing self-confidence and personal drive.
■ Introduce the concept of managing cultural diversity.
■ Discuss assertiveness and how to develop it.
■ Define conflict and present ways to handle it.

Organizations are presented with opportunities for constant change and improvement, requiring shifts in emphasis on skills requirements, external relationships, new methods of service and product development and provision. This constant need for change requires *growth* in ways rather different to the traditional economic term; growth in the new sense refers to growth of a more *personal* nature, contributing to the whole.

If organizations do not respond to, and then create, these opportunities for themselves, continued success will elude them. This factor alone places heavy responsibility on individual managers to keep two major needs in mind:

■ Managers must continually develop themselves to perform effectively against current and medium-term organizational objectives.
■ Managers must constantly predict future opportunities for organizational development and thereby ascertain their individual development needs accordingly.

The responsibilities and accountabilities of individual managers may once have been clear-cut, with obvious lines of authority, clear progression routes and career paths based on those ahead of them in the hierarchy. The responsibility now lies with individual managers to plan their own progression routes and career paths, identifying their own development needs as may be required of managers in general. It is also more likely that many managers will find that ultimately these paths may take them across various organizations, rather than progressing along the managerial ladder within any one organization. This is especially so where managers' emerging talents and potential direct them elsewhere because of either lack of opportunity in the current organization, or the identified need of developing particular skills, experience and knowledge in alternative industries.

Where organizational structures are becoming flatter, involving fewer managerial layers, the traditional view of a career in management is vastly altered. Not only would such a career involve moving between organizations to gain opportunities for learning and growth, but it is less likely that the title 'manager' will appear in job descriptions. Some would argue that it is the 'leadership' role that is becoming more potent, with spans of control becoming greater and the need for individuals at all levels of an organization to 'manage' themselves and lead initiatives and projects as is appropriate at any given time. In a sense all employees will become 'managers'.

The most important issue, however, whatever one's view of the future may be, is not whether one is officially recognized as a manager in one's current role, but more that being a manager—or leading a team of individuals—be regarded as a *profession* in itself. That where we aspire to, and have the potential to become, leaders and managers we learn what the role actually means; we gain the necessary knowledge, skills and abilities required of a management career, stay focused, in touch with society at all levels, continuously develop as new approaches and understanding emerge and demonstrate that we are *professional* in all we think and do.

These constant changes require all managers, potential managers, leaders—professionals in fact—to specifically focus on what their future requirements for self-confidence and personal drive actually mean. Many more of these professionals will need to identify the importance of this behaviour because they manage contracts for sponsors who are external to the organization. Such behaviour requires different applications to that which can be demonstrated within the organization and is often not only a matter of transferring their successes across different circumstances.

Much of our current behaviour has been derived through our experiences with known colleagues, a recognized organizational culture and existing managerial structures. Every new contract entered into with those external to the organization will require a more flexible view of individual behaviour and interrelationships. At the same time we must demonstrate the same outcomes as detailed at the beginning of this chapter.

In learning to become self-confident and to exhibit personal drive, you will need to analyse your behaviour in terms of your own activities and while dealing with others, which in turn affects their behaviour towards you and the effectiveness of the job they do. You will also need to use this chapter in association with Chapter 8 (Self-management), which discusses the management of stress and the management of personal learning and development.

Based on the assumption that you are using Chapters 7 and 8 together, you will understand that your personal skills will depend on your stage of personal development, the amount of managerial experience you have and what opportunities you have had for applying the knowledge you are acquiring.

Some of the following skills and techniques may, at first, seem somewhat strange used in association with *self-confidence and personal drive*, but it would be helpful to you if you remember that the more you know, the more you understand you need to find out, and the more you do find out, the more self-confident you will become, which will allow you also to develop your personal drive for improvement and development, to the advantage of all.

KEEPING ABREAST OF CHANGES

In building your self-confidence and personal drive, it is essential that you maintain and improve your managerial knowledge and understanding of external and internal changes and potential changes, which will influence your development needs. You should regularly scan appropriate news reports that can and will directly and indirectly affect the environment within which you manage.

People fear change, however negative or inappropriate a current situation may be; there is generally a tendency to trust 'the devil we know' rather than the one we do not. This fear may lead us to deny that change is in the air and we will often actively reject everything and everyone associated with its advocacy. Therefore, the first skill we must develop is the art of acknowledging the need for change; face up to what that means to us as regards our own learning and development, confront the challenges head-on and proactively contribute to positive implementation and progression instead of simply accepting the inevitable when it finally overtakes us and feel powerless as a result.

The case of a business school structure change

The scenario

A business school based in a new university is currently undergoing major changes to its structure and, inevitably, its culture. From the traditional faculty structure where each department was responsible for its own courses, administration and staffing, the business school is implementing a 'matrix' structure whereby part of the original organizational autonomy of each department will become *centralized*, leaving different specialist areas, or *projects* (as would be understood in the business world), with more freedom and flexibility than before (Figure 7.1).

This example simply demonstrates how some specialist subject areas will, to a greater or lesser extent depending upon the demand, be included within other specialist programmes, as well as having their own specialist programmes and routes to deliver.

For example, you might wish to gain a postgraduate qualification in marketing, which of course will be heavily marketing-oriented, but you would also receive elements of marketing in a general management course (e.g. the Chartered Management Institute's Diploma). By the same token, in the pursuit of your marketing qualification, you would also receive elements of general management so that you were equipped to be a fully rounded professional both within the context of marketing as well as having the skills and knowledge to manage people, resources, research and projects within any organizational context—*the transferable managerial knowledge and skills.*

Figure 7.1
One example of a matrix structure as applied to a business school. The number of co-ordinators (additional to tutors, mentors, administrators, etc.) is 1 per 500 programme / research participants or per 500 staff members and the associated resources, for the function in the far right-hand column.

	Executive head	Executive head	Executive head	Executive head	Executive head
	Undergraduate programmes	*Postgraduate/ post-experience programmes*	*Commercial/ company sponsored programmes*	*Research activities*	*Resourcing— including staff*
Subject specialist with leaders	Programme co-ordinators	Programme co-ordinators	Programme co-ordinators	Research co-ordinators	Resource co-ordinators
Management	********	********	*******	*****	****
HRM	*****	*****	****	***	****
ICT	********	********	*******	*****	****
Accounting and finance	*****	*****	*****	***	****
International	***	***	***	**	**
Government and corporate affairs	**	**	**	*	*
Marketing	********	********	*******	*****	****
Other					
Other					

These changes have been brought about by participant demand where most learners now require a modular and more flexible *programme* of delivery, learning and assessment, to blend more appropriately with other aspects of their lives: work, leisure, social commitments, etc., including today's undergraduate participants who generally have to work as well as study 'full-time'. They also require the flexibility to select modules appropriate to their needs, thus rendering a more traditional *course of study* inflexible and inappropriate.

In this model of flexibility derived from a matrix structure, it is considered more appropriate to provide *specialist subject areas* in place of *departments* whereby modules can be developed that are consistent across the business school, and fully up-dated as well as tailored to specific programme needs. By grouping the subject specialists (academics) in this way, they are more able to share best practice and take responsibility as separate teams of individuals for different modules, rather than each academic developing his/her own module as needed by specific *courses*. In the past, and one of the major reasons for this change, was that this approach to course development and delivery presented a business school with two increasingly serious problems: (1) repetition, or academics always 're-inventing the wheel' and (2) varying quality between similar modules, depending upon the commitment of academics to:

- Share their knowledge informally.
- Ensure continuous development and keeping up-to-date.
- Overcome any fear of change!

Such changes within academic institutions, reflect the changes and demands of the Quality Assurance Agency for Higher Education which was initiated by such research as that carried out by Dearing in the late 1990s. Higher education, along with any other institution and organization responsible for public services and accountable to the public, must ensure quality delivery and outcomes achieved against specified benchmarks at all times.

Returning to the example matrix structure in higher education above, the executive heads (five in this case) shown at the top of the table are each fully responsible for the *programmes* within the vertical columns across the business school; for example, marketing the programmes, recruiting participants for them, developing them so they continue to deliver what customers require, maintaining and continuously improving quality and academic standards, etc.—the total package. Programme co-ordinators, to whom much of this responsibility is delegated, are accountable directly to the executive heads because they are necessarily closer to the 'grass roots' of customer and staff requirements.

All this, of course, is carried out in conjunction with the executive head for staffing and resources so that requirements for recruitment and career progression can be determined, planned for and managed. It is also the responsibility of this executive head to ensure equity across teaching allocations by having an eye to the total requirement; where departments are responsible for their own *courses*, inequity can occur between them based on short-term needs, which can often become 'custom and practice'. This of course causes serious resentment when individuals discover, usually informally, that academics in certain departments have far fewer teaching contact hours than they do. This is one example of the advantages of *centralization* of certain responsibilities.

The subject specialist leaders, on the other hand, are responsible for ensuring that the staff delivering and assessing the modules are constantly updated and developed—exchanging best practice in teaching, learning and assessment of their subjects, individually and in teams, on a continuous development basis. They are also responsible, together with the various programme co-ordinators, for the appropriate allocation of specialists to the more specific needs of programme types.

The reality

As with any major organizational change, the implementation, on occasions, is less than ideal. The administrators are, in this example, generally pleased with the potential improvements that these changes will bring, and prove to be highly supportive and effective in making certain things happen. The same cannot be said, however, for all the academic and specialist management staff!

There is agreement that the changes being implemented will bring about the flexibility required by programme participants and their employers and, therefore, are considered to be 'good', both individually and collectively (the respective unions have been involved at all stages of these developments). However, there are serious misgivings demonstrated by some regarding the methods employed and timescales scheduled for some of these activities. During the consultation period strong influences brought about changes in anticipation of one particular deadline or a specific way of doing something, which is healthy and helps everyone to buy into the changes. However, not all of this influence was constructive and positive!

There are two major academic career types evident within this particular business school, demonstrating different aspects of fear of change by the individuals concerned. There are those long-serving individuals who, whilst having seen the move from polytechnic to university status, have nonetheless enjoyed many years of stability in a relatively certain and stable environment. A similar change was attempted a few years ago without success, which some of these academics enjoy relating to newer members. The view here seems to be 'ignore it and it will go away'. There are also those individuals who have worked across various organizations and cultures in order to ultimately bring their skills to the higher education environment. In other words, they may have observed this environment from afar and determined that this was their goal.

The positive views of all have been indicated above—the changes are needed and academia has finally had to confront it. Most business school members wish to make the transition seamless, transparent and well co-ordinated. But . . .

A number of people are feeling threatened, inadequate to the task and powerless to contribute effectively. Those of this number who are long-serving fear for their status and credibility which has been developed across thoroughly tried and tested approaches to the teaching, learning and assessment process; they are unable to determine how their invaluable experience can be applied to the new regime. Those of this number who are relatively new to the business school (or higher education in general) appear to have chosen this route to advance their career prospects based on more traditional views and values of the higher education system and tend to feel that they have somehow *'missed the boat'*.

The business school is currently offering as much advice and career guidance as possible to ease the transition and quell the fears of the individuals concerned. Only time will tell how effective it will be, but again if academics had only been encouraged 'to practise what they preach' and *keep abreast of changes* they could have gone to management with their own plans for change and improvement, rather than have them imposed from above!

Note from authors: there are no definitive outcomes to show for this case; it will be another two years before the changes are fully implemented. For this reason the name of the institution has been withheld, but there are a number of new universities that have either gone through this particular change, or are currently implementing something of this nature. However, you may wish to speculate in the meantime how the situation might evolve.

EXERCISE

Identify current or potential changes, or changing situations, influencing your organization and decide how you might personally contribute to these developments.

Techniques to allow change to be anticipated, issues identified and action to be planned

There are a number of techniques available to you that you can adopt, adapt or replace entirely with your own ideas. The important thing is that you have taken steps to anticipate changes so that you are ahead of, or at least in line with, current thinking and as far as possible, thus avoiding having changes some foisted upon you. We are introducing the concepts to you in this chapter. Chapter 9, however, provides you with more detailed approaches to help you develop these skills further while you are taking a *strategic perspective*.

Strengths, weaknesses, opportunities and threats (or SWOT)

Strengths and weaknesses are analyses of experiences *internal* to the organization and, as such, are based on the past. Strengths and weaknesses can be analysed by department, function, operation, or whatever your current organizational structure may be. You will need to discuss issues easily, honestly and openly with colleagues and other staff in order to produce an effective strengths/weaknesses analysis. This analysis can include products and/or services, staffing and recruitment, skills and knowledge, training and development, finance and investment—it is for you to decide and you should be as thorough as you possibly can.

Opportunities and threats tend to be 'external' to the organization and because they are *anticipated* they are projected onto the future. Although these may be 'external' to the organization, a number of 'internal' practices may themselves prove to be opportunities or threats to the survival of the organization in the 'external environment'.

In each of your analyses, remember that, for every 'strength' you identify, there is a commensurate 'weakness', and for every opportunity there is also a threat, *and vice versa*.

Environmental analyses

These include, for example, PESTEL (political, economic, social, technological, environmental—green, legal) analysis. Authors vary in their approaches to a number of 'environmental' analyses, but your common sense and circumstances will help you to determine the best approach(es) for you to take.

Essentially, each aspect of the environment, as it applies to you and your organization, should be analysed in terms of recent occurrences as well as those emerging.

All these methods of analysis can nowadays be facilitated by Internet searches, making any research much easier and simpler to carry out than ever before. Whenever you find an appropriate website, make a note of how you found it, as well as the actual address; it is all too easy to have searched and 'hit upon' something useful to your work, only to find at a later date that you cannot remember how you came upon it!

EXERCISE

Adopt whatever methods of analyses you prefer and provide yourself with some insights to what might happen to your organization as well as to the trade or profession within which you operate. Try producing some templates with headings to facilitate this.

INDIVIDUAL BEHAVIOUR

One of our more traditional attitudes has presented many of us, living and working in the UK, with difficulties in promoting our own strengths and good features. Our upbringing has determined that to demonstrate these characteristics would be seen by other people as conceited and inappropriate on our part. In general, this attitude has presented two extremes of behaviour in many of us, both resulting in the inability to identify and promote our strengths and, by definition, in being unable to positively address our weaknesses, which we have been encouraged by the prevailing national culture to hide and deny.

First, *false modesty*: this is where individuals say they are not good at something while, all the time, considering that they really are. Second, *under-confidence*: where individuals really believe that they are weak or lacking in some way, through years of either hiding their strengths because they have grown to believe they are inadequate, or genuinely denying that they possess them in the first place. This second attitude can, of course, become a self-fulfilling prophecy: believe that a thing is such and it will inevitably come about!

People who exhibit false modesty may also be under-confident, but in a different way. They know they have strengths, along with some weaknesses, which they are frightened of showing. Past experience may have taught them that they must not reveal any weaknesses at work because they may be penalized in some way. Rather than reveal them and seek support in overcoming them, they have been *shocked* into denying their existence.

In order to hide any weaknesses then, people exhibiting false modesty will openly deny any strengths at all, knowing that others can see how good they really are. Their intention in exhibiting this behaviour is to confuse others and hope that their weaknesses will be hidden beneath, what they believe, are their obvious strengths.

Other cultures, most notably the North American and some European cultures, do not share these problems in the same way. Indeed, it is considered a weakness *not* to highlight and promote their strengths, as to do so could limit their career opportunities and personal development. Only by acknowledging their strengths openly, it is believed, will it be possible for individuals to learn the opinions of others. In learning whether or not others agree, they will then be able to confront any differences of opinion, decide for themselves who is right and, most importantly, what can be done about it, or whether anything actually needs to be done. Self-confidence allows us to decide for ourselves and act accordingly.

In learning to deal with our strengths in this way, we are also able to confront and deal with our weaknesses. We can *balance our act*, so to speak. We know we cannot be good at everything; that some things come more naturally to us than others. Once we accept this, it is then less personally destructive to accept that we have to learn to overcome our weaknesses, or develop the behaviour we believe will ultimately be more positive and rewarding.

EXERCISE

What are your 'behavioural' strengths and weaknesses? How might you develop your strengths further and start to overcome some of your weaknesses? Ask your close friends and colleagues what they think and then ask yourself what, if anything, you might want to do to improve yourself. How might these characteristics affect your professional performance? Be as honest as you can—especially to yourself about yourself!

MANAGING CULTURAL DIVERSITY

Limited research has been carried out on the actual differences and how they are dealt with in the working environment, but managers are becoming more aware of the varying behaviours exhibited by people from different racial, educational, religious and cultural backgrounds. Equal opportunities legislation may help to ensure fairness of opportunity, but it does not and cannot change people's value systems, specifically their attitudes towards those who are 'different'.

It is clear that *cultural diversity* within an organization can offer opportunities far greater than *cultural unity*. However, it must also be understood that any thinking and action that may be considered *acceptable* behaviour, the *right* approach to take, or choice to make, by one particular group of people, could well be considered rude and unacceptable by another. These very differences exhibited by various people and groups of people represent the challenges faced by organizations in the management of them.

Traditionally, existing work-groups operating within a specific organizational culture have tended to apply pressure on newcomers to conform so that they think and behave as everyone else within the group, which of course can limit the opportunities and growth of both the individuals as well as the organization itself. Therefore, it is now incumbent upon managers to facilitate the integration of many different ways of thinking and behaving. By doing this and ensuring equality and fairness of those from varying racial, religious and cultural backgrounds, successful managers are also ensuring the integration of differences *within* individual groups, including the more traditional homogeneous groups, which will also help to overcome what Janis called *groupthink*. This concept identifies how any team will become insular over a period of time, resisting change and any influences from outside groups; they are so imbued with their own identity they only want to exist for their own sake. (Something you would also have considered when analysing the factors for, and resistance to, change.)

As managers, we all have a responsibility to get to know and understand those with whom we work. Even differences in people's *perceived* class status and regional background will affect their behaviour as well as others' behaviour towards them. If we spend more time getting to know about people in the beginning, the less time will be wasted later on as misunderstandings become greater and more serious through ignorance of the more subtle differences. It is these very differences that bring together the many and varied skills and abilities we need for effective work performance.

We should also study the differences between how men and women interrelate: woman to woman; man to man; woman to man; man to woman. There are significant differences between the way men and women interrelate and communicate with and between each other, and they are further affected by the differences between the racial, cultural, religious and educational backgrounds, as well as people's expectations, their prejudices, stereotypical beliefs, values and so on.

All this might appear to be a very complex and daunting task for the newly appointed manager, but it can be a fascinating challenge, which will help alleviate the longer-term frictions and conflicts that will occur if the need to understand the differences is ignored or postponed.

According to Torrington and Hall (1991), it is necessary to, first of all, identify who the 'disadvantaged' groups are when attempting to 'equalize employment opportunity'. They have identified:

- Women.
- People from other racial backgrounds.
- Disabled people.
- Older people.

This is obviously a somewhat limited list and could, no doubt, be added to. However, as a word of caution, it is essential to include other people's experiences as well as their awareness of these so-called disadvantages. We all bring our personalities to bear on situations, circumstances and issues and personality includes gender, physical appearance and age as well as all the other factors making up our whole person.

One of the authors is female and was born in 1944 (towards the end of the World War II) and is 5 feet 9 inches tall (taller than the majority of women of her age), but her experience has forever been far removed from what some might consider a 'disadvantaged' perspective. On the contrary, her experiences are all positive, having found being a 'tall, older woman' very much to her advantage both at work and in her private life.

It is interesting how times and 'fashion' also change people's perspectives, because at an earlier period in our history physical size and height was considered important (men should be tall, women should be shorter!); some people, especially other men, might have considered the other author to be a 'slight, short' man or, to be politically correct in today's language, *height-impaired*! (Please note that 'man' has not been put inside the inverted commas in this statement, whereas 'woman' in the previous paragraph was. Until more recently, being a man in business or the author of an academic text, was taken for granted, whilst being a woman was less usual and therefore had to be identified as such or else run the risk of being called mister!) It may have been harder then for his obvious intellectual and emotional stature to detract from his physical size because it was almost considered to be a 'disability' for a man to be short/small, but of course, today, one is unlikely to think about such a thing as someone's height.

Some feminists would (and have) accused the female author of being 'unaware' that she is looking at the world through 'rose-tinted spectacles'; her answer to that would be, 'Why make it into a self-fulfilling prophecy?' If we do not see obstacles to, or disadvantages in, who we are, then we are not going to come across to others as though we are expecting them to behave as such, thus putting ourselves at this 'disadvantage'! By giving people time to see and understand who we are, they will respect us for who we are and the influences and affects we bring to bear on any situation, just because of who we are.

Whilst there may be issues requiring discussion around being female and/or older, these issues are less problematic in the UK social culture today, in our view. There are a number of eastern cultures in which being a woman would definitely be an issue as regards the ability to work and progress in any career. We do not feel qualified to address these issues, but you may be able to. Many eastern cultures, conversely, have more respect for older people than can be experienced through our UK culture. However, since the UK workforce is now ageing along with the rest of the population, attitudes are likely to change and, although these issues will not be covered here, you may have your own ideas and experiences to discuss and pursue and please feel free to do so.

Torrington and Hall (1991) identify and challenge the perceived problems for 'Sikhs or Muslims being considered difficult to employ in the UK because of their religious holidays and practices'. There are also other assumptions that they challenge—for example, that 'Indians and Pakistanis are considered to overstate their qualifications and that qualifications gained abroad are believed to be not as good as those gained here'. By what standards are these judgements being made, one wonders? What about the different experiences gained, the richness that so much diversity can bring to any one organization? Public sector employers have come a long way in the last decade in improving employment opportunities, practices and conditions for racial and ethnic minorities, but what about the private sector?

What would be the positive side of the assumptions made above in inducing private sector employers to change them? How about the richness of cultural diversity previously mentioned? What about the ability to be able to add something very different to a discussion, for instance, about an organizational change currently under consideration? Do we not want to obtain the best possible outcome for the organization and the individuals working within it? Perhaps an exercise in lateral thinking would help us consider things from many different perspectives in the future.

Gender, age, religion, accent, cultural background, education, physical size (see below for disability), etc. are all irrelevant to whether a person is performing, or has the potential to perform, effectively and develop within any role. What is important are the finer qualities of the mind, the thinking and personal behaviour of individuals adding richness and quality to the process and outcomes of interaction and work.

EXERCISE

Consider the varying 'cultures' with which you have had experience (race, religion, ethnicity, gender, education, geography, language, accents, etc.). How do you see the people from these various groups? How do they perceive themselves within the working context (develop your empathy towards others: seeing things from their point of view)? Try to understand how/why different people behave as they do.

I can talk for myself!

I (Carol) recently met a woman—also called Carol—who was unable to walk, lift, write, or physically manipulate anything other than through her computerized wheelchair which was touch-sensitive to just the two fingers Carol was able to use. Her head was permanently angled to one side with her eyes tilted upwards. Try reproducing that appearance; on first meeting her, it looked as though Carol was permanently listening for something, or someone, outside the immediate exchange. What she was really doing was taking in every word, every nuance and every aspect of other people's body language as to be one of the sharpest, most astute, people I have ever met. Her concern was very much that most 'normal' people were embarrassed by her being dependent upon a fully equipped, electronic wheelchair and failed to see that she was more than able to contribute to the most involved and complex discussion. There is nothing wrong with Carol's hearing, or her ability to angle those large inescapable eyes of hers so that she also sees everything. Her speech is another matter. Although it is loud enough and clear enough, it has the intonation that might once have described as that of someone 'not all there'. How mistaken we would be if we thought of Carol in that way. She is young, vibrant, happy and thoroughly interested in everything she can lay her eyes and ears upon.

Unfortunately, Carol has never had the opportunity to work; she has spent the last 13 years in a care home with a number of others who are much less communicative than she. Most 'normal' people are extremely offended or embarrassed by Carol's appearance and cannot envision how she might contribute to any serious discussion. She is rarely spoken to directly by those who do not know her, because too many people think she cannot possibly answer for herself. How much 'opportunity' are we missing out on here, let alone the opportunities and potential Carol herself could realize.

Understanding and leading others

There are many aspects both within the organization and external to it that affect managers' ability to make things happen through their own self-confidence and personal drive. It is therefore important for them to know what these factors are and to understand how they influence their own behaviour as well as the behaviour of others.

Simply put, individual factors will have been created by upbringing, family background, class and ethnic culture as well as educational opportunities, all of which will have affected peoples' beliefs, expectations and values. On top of this, there will be personal work experiences, which people take with them from job to job, whether or not they are appropriate or valid. Individuals are often recruited who will reflect the appropriate culture, whilst others may be recruited with change in mind. Very often there is no certainty about this, only hope that people will integrate and adopt the cultural 'norm' and/or influence cultural change positively and promote effective and improved performance overall.

To quote Torrington and Hall (1991):

> Intentional discrimination is based on a set of clearly expressed beliefs about the differences between people. But much discrimination is unintentional and primarily arises from our unconscious learning experiences as individuals and as a society. We are conditioned by our experiences that, for example, women are nurses and men are surgeons, and these form a framework within which we operate and interpret and react to new experiences or the possibility of change. We make inferences from this framework, for example, that women make the best nurses and men the best surgeons. Frameworks determine our attitudes. Gradually, as more new experiences of a particular type arise, we change our framework to accommodate these. This is not a speedy process and may take many generations. For a long time many people will react defensively to new experiences and will reject or deny them.

Individual behaviour and customer relations

Everyone would agree that customers (internal and external) are important to any organization. However, not everyone demonstrates an understanding of the intricacies involved in meeting people's needs. In attempting to meet anyone's needs, we have to take into account individual human behaviour and how differences of opinion and attitude can have a bearing on how the organization is *perceived* as being concerned with meeting customers' needs.

Your organization may have an overall strategy to address needs in terms of the product or service provided, but somehow not quite meet those needs in the way the behaviour of individuals affects how activities are planned and carried out. As well as producing a statement of recognized need, the customer will have an expectation of the *way* in which that need should be met, which should also reflect an understanding of the benefits derived from having the need met.

When your organization plans to identify and meet customer requirements, it is in fact also planning to meet its own requirements—meeting objectives and retaining a *competitive edge* for long-term survival. Individual behaviour and the commitment of those carrying out the necessary activities are therefore crucial to these outcomes.

EXERCISE

Think of a situation where you to had to take a leading role in initiating and taking action (preferably at work—but any area of your social life will also be appropriate). Did you also have to control people's behaviour to ensure an effective outcome? If so, how did you achieve this? Consider all the above discussions when identifying and addressing any particular action you have taken.

ASSERTIVENESS AND HOW TO DEVELOP IT

What is assertiveness?

Assertiveness is about speaking one's mind openly and objectively, without undue emotion. It is the art of clear and direct communication. Being assertive enables you to: express personal feelings to others; be direct and ask for what you want; say 'no' clearly and firmly without causing offence when you do not want to follow a certain course of action. It allows you to take responsibility when necessary; say what you mean clearly and confidently and stand up for your rights (Hind, 1989).

The most important distinction that must be made is between assertiveness and aggression. It is much easier for some people to be aggressive, but it is ineffective. Those for whom aggression is the norm are unable to demonstrate their assertiveness for some reason; it may be that their experience has led them into this behaviour as the result of others not listening to them. It may simply be that they are insufficiently confident in their own abilities or the strength of their arguments and, believing others will not accept their 'reasons' under any circumstances, they have to force their opinions and beliefs onto others.

Aggressors tend to rally support from surrounding colleagues and subordinates; they achieve this either through others' fear of their power or as the result of perceived past successes.

Aggressors' behaviour towards those with opposing views who are not themselves sufficiently assertive will either breed aggression in return, or encourage avoidance by those whom they wish to influence or *bully*. Either way, nothing will be achieved and the problems will continue.

Assertiveness is about standing up for our beliefs and interests and at the same time taking into account the beliefs and interests of others. Whilst the display of aggression involves *forcefulness* in conveying our beliefs and interests and *not* listening to others, being assertive is to *confidently* and politely communicate thoughts and ideas, as well as to *listen* to others. Also, assertive people who know their own minds are not afraid of the influence of other peoples' views and opinions, where the outcomes may prove to be more positive or rewarding in the achievement of individual and organizational objectives.

Making and refusing a request

If we transmit to others the full facts relating to our reasons for making or refusing a request, in most cases people will genuinely understand and do their best to assist us when trying to achieve our objectives. By detailing exactly what our situation is, most people would respond positively, and assertively in return. Agreements are mostly reached when both parties are behaving reasonably and considerately.

As is implied in this statement, the tone of our voice and the inference behind the words we use are important factors in transmitting our views and opinions assertively. Politeness is essential, but extreme politeness is not assertiveness and would be seen as insincere and is unlikely to promote the desired response in others. (See also Chapter 2 for ideas relating to *body language, tone and pitch of voice* when communicating with others.)

Coping with refusal

There are bound to be occasions when you are denied your request. If this is genuine you need to accept the reasons positively and compromise accordingly, occasionally requiring a completely different answer, or approach, to the problem. Sometimes a refusal is made by someone without the *authority* to refuse that request. Again, there is no need to wield your own authority; a negotiated agreement can be reached and should be attempted before moving on to an alternative solution.

Standing up for your rights

Nervous or energetic people sometimes have difficulty in saying 'no', even when it is justified. Such people will often take on more and more work and then everyone is surprised when jobs are not completed on time or to the right standard. Managers must remember this when dealing with others if they appear never to say 'no' regardless of how busy they are. Managers must always be aware of the level of work being carried out by all those involved in activities or projects for which they are responsible, and peoples' workloads must be reviewed and discussed along with other factors in the process of work being carried out. The organizational objectives, as well as the control of individual stress levels, depend upon managers' personal skills in achieving them.

Managers can help others to say 'no' appropriately by keeping in touch with how they think they are doing; whether they are overworked or not; by finding out the level of work they may be receiving from other managers and so on. When people are asked frequently about their level of involvement, they find it easier to express how they really feel, because they will then become more relaxed and learn that the manager is being fair and reasonable.

The secret in you developing your own *self-confidence and personal drive* lies with your ability in recognizing the need for and providing the *wherewithal* for others to build their skills similarly. This approach will then help build positive working relationships and greater commitment to objectives. (See also Chapter 1 to 'Manage and obtain the commitment of others'.)

Passive behaviour

People exhibiting passive or compliant behaviour usually have come from a background where other people's expectations are that they should behave in this way. Women from many cultures, for example, have been brought up to be obedient to their fathers, brothers and, eventually, their husbands also. It is not too difficult to understand how that then becomes translated into *appropriate* and *acceptable* behaviour at work. The working environment itself often expects particular patterns of behaviour from people of varying backgrounds and particularly between the genders. Many organizations still hold traditional views about the roles of men and women in society.

Where men will largely be encouraged to be competitive, assertive, performance-oriented and demanding, similar behaviour in women is often criticized as being jealous, aggressive, over-demanding, bossy and selfish (or it's simply 'that time of the month')! Whilst many occupations are experiencing changed perspectives in the accepted behaviour of men and women, even the most enlightened organizations have their examples of work-roles occupied by women exhibiting the passive, compliant behaviours still frequently expected of them—or they believe these behaviours to be expected of them! (e.g. typists, administrators, cleaners, junior clerks, factory operators and assemblers, and so on). The jobs themselves often attract women, and sometimes older men, interested in part-time or flexible work requiring little commitment beyond the hours actually worked.

Most of the job-roles in question are of low status, poorly paid and often the first to be lost in times of recession. It is very difficult for people to exhibit assertive characteristics when their very livelihood is constantly under threat.

Giving and receiving criticism

In receiving criticism, it can be helpful to seek advice from your critic. In discussing the advice, objectively and positively, it is possible that the initial criticism will become less daunting for both parties and a better approach to future behaviour can be developed between you.

Similarly, in giving criticism, it could prove fruitful for you to start by questioning others about whether they believe the outcomes of their action were what they had anticipated. If they are unhappy with these outcomes, it follows naturally that you should then ask them why they believe this to be so. They may not have considered that their own behaviour could have brought about more desirable outcomes. Whatever discussions ensue, you should offer advice for future development. Those you are criticizing should be in no doubt that you are giving it but, at the same time, they will need assurance that you are prepared to help them to recognize their failings and how they might improve their behaviour.

Handling disagreements and conflict

Conflict exists everywhere, and often provides the basic context in which we need to negotiate. (See also Chapter 5—Influencing others—for further information on negotiating.)

We bring values, attitudes, beliefs, needs and perceptions to any situation and it is inevitable that we will be opposed by those people coming into these situations with alternative experiences and understanding and thereby different approaches. This then causes conflict. What is important is how we deal with conflict. We can ignore it, seek solutions, or seek to control it. An important element is whether it adversely affects relations within an organization.

However, we are used to and experienced in dealing with conflicts in our everyday lives: house-hunting, buying cars, how to be entertained, etc. It can create emotional reactions such as anger, hostility, frustration and even pain. We should recognize these and avoid them wherever possible.

There are also some important equal opportunities implications in the way we deal with conflict; from an interview held recently with a manager of a culturally diverse organization, it can be concluded that a lot of ignorance exists regarding the differences of opinion, attitudes and beliefs with conflicting results. The manager concerned believes there is the need for confrontation to promote awareness and education, but that, unless it is handled carefully with extra firmness and precision over the rules governing sensitive issues like equal opportunities, unhealthy conflict and stress will result.

Negotiation then, is often needed to resolve conflict. Resolving conflict does not mean just *winning*, which implies someone losing. It means satisfying the interests of all concerned. Satisfying interests on both sides of a conflict or negotiation situation is called a *win:win* outcome. It can only be achieved by understanding the needs or interests of all concerned.

Mediating

Mediating in a conflict is a task that often falls to managers and can be fraught with difficulty. Mediation is the facilitation of an agreement-seeking process by a third party (often the manager).

How to mediate successfully:

- *Acknowledge conflict* When conflict is ignored it will become difficult to control. Healthy conflict, when acknowledged and used with ideas being allowed to develop in this way, positive outcomes are likely. When potential negative, or unhealthy, conflict can be identified, it should be *nipped in the bud* and thus avoided.
- *Be neutral in relation to people* If you appear to take one particular side when trying to mediate, you will not be mediating at all, but applying extra pressures to influence the behaviour of the other party. Allow each to have their say and facilitate the parties' agreement for a way forward.
- *Keep to issues* Do not allow personalities to be discussed or questioned. The issues surrounding the conflict should be discussed openly and objectively thus keeping emotions to a minimum. It should be noted that sometimes it is impossible to keep emotion out of situations and those who feel that strongly about the issues should not be dismissed by anyone as irrational because of it.
- *Seek clarification* Be sure that everyone really understands what is being said by clarifying understanding and summarizing frequently.
- *Focus on agreement* Agreeing a way forward is what you should be trying to achieve. Ensure the parties are positively trying to agree on ways with which each can work.
- *Be facilitator not judge* A judge states the 'crime' and pronounces the 'sentence' or punishment. A facilitator allows discussion of issues, provides the wherewithal for agreement and allows the parties concerned to reach their own conclusions and decide upon methods for resolving the difficulties.

EXERCISE

Identify any situation with which you have been involved and analyse your and others' behaviour in terms of assertiveness, aggression, handling conflict, etc. How positive or negative were the outcomes of this situation and why do you think this?

SUMMARY OF ISSUES

In working through this chapter, you will have encountered a number of issues and perhaps some ideas that are new to you. The objectives of the chapter were to:

- Introduce the notion of 'change' and present techniques for the identification and analysis of changes that have occurred, or could occur, inside and outside the organization.
- Present ways to analyse individual behaviour and approaches to developing self-confidence and personal drive.
- Introduce the concept of managing cultural diversity.
- Discuss assertiveness and how to develop it.
- Define conflict and present ways to handle it.

How well have the authors met these objectives?

More importantly, how have you approached and used the material yourself, and how much have you developed since the beginning of your course of study, or working through the chapter? You are strongly recommended to extend your research and study to include as much of the material as possible that is identified in further reading and references below, so that you can build on your expertise, incorporating more complex approaches and ideas as you develop further in your managerial role.

These objectives, if re-revisited over a period of time and put into practice in your job, will help you to achieve the personal competency of self-confidence and personal drive, broken down into the elements identified in the table at the end of this chapter. In order for you to reflect on your own behaviour and that of others with whom you work, you might find it useful to use the table as a self-assessment check (reproduce as many as you wish) to re-evaluate your skills and knowledge.

PREPARING FOR ACTION PLANNING

Remember to review the checklist of questions, as identified in the Introduction to this book, at Appendix 1.

Analyse your own behaviour in terms of strengths (positive outcomes) and weaknesses (negative effects), in dealing with actual work-based occurrences with regards to the various situations discussed in this chapter, and summarized above.

Decide how you might deal with them differently in the future and what are your immediate training requirements and future development needs.

Discuss them with appropriate others and negotiate how you might address them.

FURTHER READING AND REFERENCES

Belbin, R.M. (2001) *Managing without Power: Gender Relationships in the Story of Human Evolution*. Oxford: Butterworth Heinemann. ISBN: 0-7506-5192-X

Cameron, S. and Pearce, S. (1995) *The Management Studies Handbook*. London: Pitman Publishing (Chapters 5, 11 and 12). ISBN: 0-273-60346-9

Davis, M.H. (1994) *Empathy: A Social Psychological Approach*. Oxford: Westview Press. ISBN: 0-8133-3001-7

Handy, C.B. (1985) Understanding Organisations (3rd edition). London: Penguin Books (Chapters 2 and 9). ISBN: 0-14-009110-6

Handy, C.B. (1989) *The Age of Unreason*. London: Business Books. ISBN: 0-09-174088-6

Hind, D. (1989) *Transferable Personal Skills*. Business Education.

Honey, P. and Mumford, A. (1990) *The Manual of Learning Opportunities*. Maidenhead: Peter Honey. ISBN: 0-9508444-4-6

Moss Kanter, R. (1990) *The Change Masters: Corporate Entrepreneurs at Work*. London: Unwin Hyman (Parts 3 and 4). ISBN: 0-04-658244-4

Peters, T. (1989) *Thriving on Chaos: Handbook for a Management Revolution*. London: Macmillan. ISBN: 0- 330-30591-3

Phillips, J.J., Bothell, T.W. and Lynne Snead, G. (2002) *The Project Management Scorecard: Measuring the Success of Project Management Solutions*. Oxford: Butterworth Heinemann. ISBN: 0-7506-7449-0

Rye, C. (2001) *Change Management: The 5-Step Action Kit* (revised edition, includes CD-ROM). London: Kogan Page. ISBN: 0-7494-3380-9

Straw, J. (1989) *Equal Opportunities: The Way Ahead*. London: CIPD. ISBN: 0-85292-422-4

Tolle, E. (1999) *The Power of Now*. London: Hodder & Stoughton. ISBN: 0-340-73350-0

Torrington, D. and Hall, L. (1991) *Personnel Management: A New Approach* (2nd edition). Hemel Hampstead: Prentice Hall (pp. 353–375). ISBN: 0-13-658667

Recommended journal articles for readers' further development

Cook, V. (2001) Best practice: continuing professional development. *Personnel Today* 10/07/2001: 11. Bradford: MCB University Press. ISSN: 0959-5848. Website: http://www.emerald-library.com.

Maurer, T.J. (2001) Career-relevant learning and development, worker age, and beliefs about self-efficacy for development. *Journal of Management* 27 (2): 123–141. Bradford: MCB University Press. ISSN: 0149-2063. Website: http://www.emerald-library.com

Rae, D. (2001) EasyJet: a case of entrepreneurial management? *Strategic Change* 10 (6): 325–337. Bradford: MCB University Press. ISSN: 1086-1718. Website: http://www.emerald-library.com

Van der Sluis, L. (2002) Learning behaviour and learning opportunities as career stimuli. *Journal of Workplace Learning: Employee Counselling Today* 14 (1): 19–30. Bradford: MCB University Press. ISSN: 1366-5626. Website: http://www.emerald-library.com

Wilson, I. (2000) The new rules: ethics, social responsibility and strategy. *Strategic Leadership* March: 12–16. Bradford: MCB University Press. ISSN: 1366-5626. Website: http://www.emerald-library.com

Competency element	Competency level: 1 (low)–5 (high)	Requires development	No direct experience	What can help? (identify oppor-tunities)	Who can help?	When can it be achieved?	How can it be achieved?
Takes a leading role in initiating action and making decisions							
Takes personal responsibility for making things happen							
Takes control of situations and events							
Acts in an assured and unhesitating manner when faced with a challenge							

Says no to unreasonable requests	States his/her own position and views clearly in conflict situations	Maintains beliefs, commitment and effort in spite of set-backs or opposition

CHAPTER 8

Self-management

Managers skilled in managing themselves show adaptability to the changing world, taking advantage of new ways of doing things.

LINKS TO THE CHARTERED MANAGEMENT INSTITUTE'S MODULE

This chapter aims to address the aims and learning outcomes as identified in the Introduction to this text under the heading *Links to the Chartered Management Institute's Module 'Understanding Yourself'* so that, in conjunction with Chapters 1 and 4, participants should be able to:

- Evaluate their use of time and resources at work and identify strategies for improvement.
- Understand the impact of their behaviour on other people in a range of management situations (identifying and handling own stress, managing time and planning personal learning and development).
- Construct a short-term, one-year (SMART) Personal Development Plan based on an awareness of their strengths as a manager and their development needs.

INTRODUCING THE RELATIONSHIP BETWEEN THE PERSONAL COMPETENCY MODEL AND SELF-MANAGEMENT

The Personal Competency Model (PCM), as already discussed, identifies the behaviours and skills that are necessary for you to develop before you are able to prove competence in any managerial function. This chapter attempts to deal with the various behaviours and skills necessary for you to apply across all managerial functions, transferring your learning to different occasions, at different times and under varying circumstances (contexts), consistently.

The outcomes below, as identified within this section of the model, should be borne in mind while you work through this chapter.

Outcomes required for self-management

There are two major sets of behaviour highlighted in this chapter. The first concentrates on the importance of the individual manager's *self-control*, whereby he/she focuses on her/his own stress management.

In order to maintain *self-control*, the manager:

- Gives a consistent and stable performance.
- Takes action to reduce the causes of stress.
- Accepts personal comments or criticism without becoming defensive or offensive.
- Remains calm in difficult or uncertain situations.
- Handles others' emotions without becoming personally involved in them.

The second behavioural set focuses on *managing personal learning and development*. In this situation, the manager:

- Takes responsibility for meeting her/his own learning and development needs.
- Seeks feedback on performance to identify his/her own strengths and weaknesses.
- Learns from her/his own mistakes and those of others.
- Changes behaviour where needed as a result of feedback.
- Reflects systematically on own performance and modifies behaviour accordingly.

- Develops self to meet the competence demand of changing situations.
- Transfers learning from one situation to another.

INTRODUCTION AND OBJECTIVES

The objectives are to:

- Introduce the concept of self-management and identify ways to develop self-help techniques.
- Discuss stress, how it occurs, how to deal with it and how to prevent it.
- Present concepts and theories and how people learn and what enables personal change.
- Discuss the idea of continuous personal development (CPD) and the notion of personal commitment.

This chapter focuses on the personal management of the individual, whereby effective outcomes will result in better relationships with others. As a person with your own unique strengths and development needs, your ultimate choice of techniques to achieve personal competency in *self-management* will depend very much on how you see yourself now, and where and how you wish to apply the skill in the future. The key to self-management lies within your ability to take responsibility for your own learning and development, identify and manage own use of time, stress levels, as well as the functional and behavioural aspects appropriate to your job role and/or perceived future job role.

HOW PEOPLE LEARN AND WHAT ENABLES PERSONAL CHANGE

In a sense everything that happens, nice or nasty, planned or unplanned, is a learning opportunity. Unfortunately, opportunities do not come neatly packaged and labelled as such. Opportunities tend to reside in the eye of the beholder, more a matter of perception and recognition than of incontrovertible fact. This means that learning opportunities, in common with any other sort of opportunity, are easily missed. A major task, therefore, for trainers and development specialists *and managers generally* is to get people to recognize and make use of opportunities for learning. The ultimate goal is the complete integration of all kinds of activities and learning. (Honey and Mumford, 1990—our italics)

This quotation from Honey and Mumford, in our view, begins with you, the manager or potential manager, for your own learning and self-development. The most important part of self-management is you taking *responsibility* for your own learning and development; identifying your needs, planning what do in order to gain the relevant opportunities for your learning, as well as how and when these should occur, and then making it all happen. Your Personal Development Plan (PDP—a generic term now being adopted across various organizations and sectors), which you have either started working on during a course of study, or from your performance reviews (appraisals) at work, should by now be seen as a good *habit* you need to pursue for your *continuous professional development* (CPD).

In the Introduction to this text, we introduced you to the idea of Kolb's learning cycle (Figure 1.3) and how we can systematically move around the cycle to ensure a more concrete, permanent learning experience. We also identified the various opportunities that you might determine in order to learn new skills and knowledge to contribute to your professional development. Honey and Mumford, in their various publications listed at the end of the chapter, can help you to identify and analyse these in more detail to ensure you become *conscious* of the opportunities around you as well as how *taking* them can influence and affect your personal learning and progression.

The Learning Cycle is meant to show how learning is an *iterative* process. This means that we do not just go round the cycle once in order to learn something thoroughly, although we will have learned something from just one trip around it. Undergraduate students, for example, when confronted with the idea of learning something more about what motivates people to work, are often heard to say 'We did motivation in the second year!'. By that they usually mean that they had one 1-hour lecture, followed by one 1-hour tutorial/workshop on the topic! What usually happens when we are learning something new is that we will revisit a topic or situation, gain reinforcement and/or new insights on second and subsequent trips around the cycle and thereby add to our overall store of knowledge and skills.

So much of what we learn is realized in retrospect. It is for this very reason that performance reviews and appraisals should be welcomed; not simply so that we can determine good and bad performance, but more specifically to determine what was learned during both positive and negative experiences so that this learning can be put into practice in the future. It is possible to do a really good job in some area of activity, only to find later, because we had not analysed *why* it was such a good job, that we cannot repeat the performance. Learning is about many things, but one of the most ignored is the value of recognizing and applying learning from our *strengths* to other activities, especially where we may be weaker. By doing this, we can then see more clearly where we need to take positive steps for more direct and sometimes structured learning.

Honey and Mumford use the model shown in Figure 8.1 to help show how learning takes place and subsequent change is effected.

Most people believe learning from experience to be an accidental, unconscious process, which tends to be haphazard and taken for granted. They consider such experiences to be a matter of *serendipity* (discovery by accident) if they happen to *consciously* realize they have learned something from the experience, though by and large this kind of learning tends not to be transferred to other situations—it is unrealized. Whilst such discoveries should remain valuable and exciting, we would maintain that much of this accidental learning can be planned for and realized in a constructive and worthwhile way.

Learning through competence identification and objective-setting can crystallize the meaning of experiential learning and facilitate clear action planning and performance criteria identification for further learning and development.

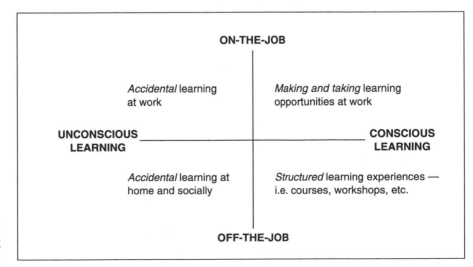

Figure 8.1 Learning opportunities.

The advantages of being a learning opportunist

Honey and Mumford say that learning opportunism (i.e. identifying and using learning opportunities) has many potential benefits, including:

- Adding an interesting, extra 'learning' dimension to all you do.
- Making learning from experience a more conscious and deliberate process.
- Making one more purposeful—determined to extract learning even from unremarkable, routine events.
- Helping one to learn from successes not just from mistakes.
- Making it more likely that one will transfer learning from one specific situation to a broad range of other situations.
- Meaning one can articulate what one has learned and communicate it to others.
- Provides a recipe both for one's continuous improvement and helping others to improve.
- Helps one to keep ahead of, and attuned to, change.

The learning opportunist, say Honey and Mumford, who reaps all these learning benefits finds that, in addition, their overall performance is enhanced.

Work-related experiences likely to provide learning opportunities

- *Situations within the organization:*
  - Meetings
  - Managing changes
  - Tasks: familiar
  - Social occasions
  - Tasks: unfamiliar
  - Foreign travel
  - Task forces
  - Acquisitions/mergers
  - Customer visits
  - Closing something down
  - Visits to plant/office

- *Situations outside the organization:*
  - Voluntary organizations
  - Professional meetings
  - Domestic life
  - Sports clubs
  - Industry committees
- *Processes:*
  - Coaching
  - Mentoring
  - Counselling
  - Public speaking
  - Listening
  - Reviewing/auditing
  - Modelling
  - Clarifying responsibilities
  - Problem-solving
  - Walking the floor
  - Observing
  - Visioning
  - Questioning
  - Strategic planning
  - Reading
  - Diagnosing problems
  - Negotiating
  - Decision-making
  - Selling
- *People:*
  - Bosses
  - Peers
  - Mentors
  - Consultants
  - Network contacts
  - Subordinates

(Honey and Mumford, 1990b)

Once people's minds are focused on the idea that every experience, generating reflection and self-appraisal, becomes an opportunity for development not previously perceived as possible, all experiences take on a new value and are seen as beneficial.

It is important to overcome any feelings of self-recrimination, embarrassment or shame over mistakes. The only time there is a need to judge ourselves is when we have wasted the opportunity to learn from such mistakes and simply continue to make them! Even then it should only be a judgement that is converted into a positive decision to ensure that we do not make this particular mistake again, and determine to learn from our mistakes in the future.

This process is common to all aspects of life; if we do not learn and develop as a result of experiences, the same *apparent* mistakes and unfortunate experiences will continue to confront us, and our progress will be arrested. When successes are accepted without understanding their meaning, then the actions taken to create those successes, being accidental, are less likely to be repeated.

Learning styles

From their learning styles exercises, Honey and Mumford identified four preferences in individuals' learning approaches: *activist*, *reflector*, *theorist* and *pragmatist*. They then took the Kolb Learning Cycle and adapted it to include the four styles of learner (see Figure 8.2). The process of understanding your actual learning style will help you to see how you may, or may not, complete the learning process effectively:

- The *activist* prefers to get on with the job and will try anything once.
- The *reflector* spends a lot of time thinking about what has been done and what is to be done.
- The *pragmatist* is happy as long as things make practical sense.

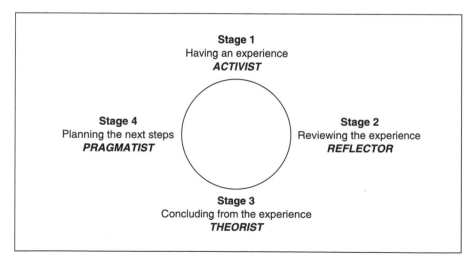

Figure 8.2
The Kolb learning cycle with Honey and Mumford's 'learning styles' added.

- The *theorist* likes to analyse situations and behaviour and make philosophical sense of situations, without necessarily needing to prove them empirically.

Different learning style preferences lead most people to distort the iterative process of the Learning Cycle by placing a greater emphasis on some stages than on others. Thus reflector/theorists tend to linger at stages 2 and 3, preferring to postpone getting into planning and action, whereas pragmatist/activists tend to leap-frog stages 2 and 3 in their haste to do something! There are, however, other tendencies, which become apparent when one examines how people learn from experience (Honey and Mumford, 1990b).

As the result of Mumford's survey of 144 directors, Honey and Mumford (1990a) have identified four different approaches to learning with hindsight and with foresight:

- The *intuitive approach* involves learning from experience, but not through a conscious process; it is claimed that learning is an inevitable consequence of having experiences.
- The *incidental approach* involves learning by chance from activities that jolt an individual into conducting a 'post mortem'—usually when something out of the ordinary has happened or when something has not gone according to plan.
- The *retrospective approach* involves learning from experience by looking back over what happened and reaching conclusions about it—especially provoked by mishaps or mistakes; these people are also inclined to draw lessons from routine events and success.
- The *prospective approach* includes all the retrospective elements, plus planning to learn before an experience, where future events are treated as opportunities to learn. The *prospector*:
    - Takes responsibility for meeting her/his own learning and development needs.
    - Seeks feedback on performance to identify his/her own strengths and weaknesses.
    - Learns from her/his own mistakes and those of others.
    - Changes behaviour where needed as a result of feedback.

- Reflects systematically on own performance and modifies behaviour accordingly.
- Develops self to meet the competence demand of changing situations.
- Transfers learning from one situation to another.

CREATE OPPORTUNITIES FOR YOUR OWN LEARNING AND DEVELOPMENT

Obtain support in creating learning opportunities

It is often necessary for you to involve other people in your quest for self-development—a key skill which is not always apparent or fully utilized. In fact, to quote Ben Johnson, and many have: 'Very few are wise by their own counsel, or learned by their own teaching. For he that was only taught by himself had a fool for his master'.

The essential fact here is that, whilst we should all take *responsibility* for our own learning, this does not presuppose that we always *know* what it is that we need to learn or develop. We often need mentors, facilitators, tutors or colleagues while learning and developing.

EXERCISE

Choose a particular situation and look for and accept help from others (this is not always easy). Identify who these people are (they may be inside or outside work) and how they may help you, for example:

- Recognize and use learning opportunities.
- Provide and encourage a learning environment.
- Give you opportunities to review what you are learning and doing.
- Provide constructive feedback.
- Provide coaching and counselling.
- Share and take risks when seeking and using opportunities.
- Undertake joint problem-solving.

Use various techniques to make full use of others' contributions—e.g. active listening (this involves body language which shows how well you are listening which, in turn, encourages further and deeper communication—see Chapter 2), observing, questioning; emulating.

■ Develop and use contacts to exchange information and obtain support and resources.

■ Create and prepare strategies for influencing others (this is not about winning all the time, but about listening and being heard).

■ Always present yourself positively to others.

■ Use a variety of means to influence others.

■ Identify and take opportunities when they arise to achieve longer-term aims or needs.

Seek feedback on performance

Feedback is a central part of performance management, as well as crucial for learning and development. It is one of your main tools for maintaining and improving your own performance as well as that of others. The following desired outcomes from effective feedback should help you improve both how you receive feedback as well as how you give feedback to others:

■ Measure your own current skills as a manager against appropriate standards and by getting feedback from appropriate others from inside and outside work, as appropriate to your situation.

■ Identify what it is about feedback from other people that is so important and how it can be used and integrated with your own ideas.

■ Identify the difference between constructive and destructive feedback.

■ Identify various types of feedback.

■ Identify appropriate opportunities when you might receive feedback.

■ Learn to: enjoy; actively listen to; ask for clarification; seek specific examples; look for ways forward; agree what each will do.

■ Avoid defensive reactions and offensive responses.

■ Compare feedback from others with how well you think you are doing, and improve your future performance as a result.

■ Change your behaviour where needed as a result of feedback.

Learning from your own experiences

Learning from both positive and negative experiences is important. When you have made mistakes, you should try not to make them again—find out what went wrong and why. When you have achieved positive results try not to take them for granted; analyse what you did and why it was that you were successful.

Evaluate your experiences

Share your experiences with others and decide what went well, and why, as well as what did not go well, and why, as a result of your behaviour.

Draw from these experiences for your own future use, by accepting that no-one behaves appropriately all the time, but that all experiences are valuable. It is helpful to try to imagine how you might transfer this learning to other situations. Any behaviour is only truly learned by applying it to various circumstances, involving different people and making some assumptions about how similarly or differently they might respond. It is helpful to evaluate your learning periodically and identify various situations where the results could be equally valuable. Take a positive approach to your mistakes, and those of others, to ensure further learning, rather than to simply take or pass blame.

CONTINUOUS PROFESSIONAL DEVELOPMENT AND PERSONAL COMMITMENT

It is essential that you maintain and improve your behaviour in understanding and responding to external and internal changes that affect both your routine and planned activities (see Chapter 7). You should regularly scan appropriate news reports which do/will directly and indirectly affect the environment within which you manage.

Keep abreast of developments that constantly occur within the working environment, which are both internal and external to the organization. You will need to display an understanding of how the different parts of the organization and its environment fit together and the effects of its culture; whether it is stable, dynamic and evolving, uncertain. Most importantly, you will need to identify the resultant behaviour of the people concerned.

Continuous professional development (CPD) is a process whereby managers update and develop their skills knowledge and behaviour through self-, and/or independent, assessment of their performance. CPD is about managers systematically maintaining and improving their 'professionalism' in line with organizational change, management development theories and techniques and national initiatives to improve UK competitiveness in world markets.

'Profession' in the context of management CPD may be associated with a specific profession (e.g. accounting, engineering, architecture or management in general). It is therefore for individuals to determine what they must do in order to improve their management skills whether: they are already managers and have management qualifications; are managers who have no qualifications; are not yet managing but wish to acquire the appropriate knowledge and behaviour.

In evaluating your effectiveness in your CPD you might wish to consider the following:

- Did the action I took meet my needs? What will I do next or better next time?
- To evaluate the CPD process, discuss it with relevant others during the process itself and on completion:
  - Did it work? Was it cost-effective? Was it enjoyable, etc.? From the identification of learning and development needs through to completion of each stage of the process?
  - CPD as a qualifications reassessment: will it update the qualifications you have already gained, or will it once you have gained them?
  - How might you use CPD as building blocks to gain a qualification, etc.
  - CPD should help you in the identification of further learning and development.
  - It is also helpful as an aid to equal opportunities monitoring (who you recruit, select, promote, provide advice and guidance to and so on).

CPD can be used in conjunction with any quality standards (e.g. ISO or Investors in People), as well as specific standard such as the national standards for management (see Appendix 2).

An important and helpful approach to take can be one of *focusing on the customer* and it is this example that we have used to help you focus the planning you need to do for your own CPD programme.

In determining the needs of *customers* who are both internal and external to the organization, it is possible to ensure that the learning and development you undertake is appropriate and mutually beneficial.

The benefits you can gain by working through such a process, and returning to various stages as your career develops, are:

- An opportunity to reflect upon your organization's approach to providing opportunities for learning and development.
- An approach to exploring the performance review techniques you currently use and assessing them for their effectiveness; or an opportunity to identify an approach suitable to your own circumstances.
- Helps you learn how to link organizational objectives to team and individual learning needs (whether you already attempt to do so or not).
- Helps you to think about the abilities and skills already available within your team, or from individuals, and assess any gaps between these and those required by the organization overall.
- Opportunities to identify and review who your customers are both inside and outside the organization.
- Occasions for you to reflect on your attitudes and approaches to customers, colleagues and staff, etc.
- The ability to explore and apply various techniques and develop those most appropriate to your current and/or changing situation.
- Make contributions to the effectiveness of your organization in meeting internal and external customer requirements.

The process will, after several reviews, take you to a point where *focusing on the customer* will become second nature to you, because you will begin to think about what you are doing and why, while you are doing it, as well as reflecting upon it after the event.

This reflection will be an indication of your on-the-job progress whereby you will also be able to identify any off-the-job requirements you may have, such as:

- Training courses.
- Reading requirements.
- Activity away-days with colleagues, etc.

You will thus develop your approach to learning by involving the whole of the *learning cycle* and taking opportunities throughout the four *learning styles* (as discussed earlier in this chapter).

You will also soon learn that there are no right or wrong answers to *meeting customer requirements*. The planning and action required will depend upon your own job role, the organization's and customers' culture, the goods and services you produce, the markets you operate within and so on.

Defining your customers

We have said that customers can be internal and external to your organization. *Customers* can be those who purchase your goods or services from outside the organization; they can also be departments or individuals who *purchase* or require your goods or services from within your own organization.

As well as customers in the obvious sense then, they may also include:

- Colleagues who may require your input on projects for which they are responsible.
- Colleagues who are seeking answers to specific questions in order to meet their own objectives.
- Another department or business unit that is *buying* your time for any technical or functional input.
- Any member of your senior management team requiring you to be responsible for a particular project or assignment.
- Any *sponsor* internal or external to the organization requiring your input.
- You are also an ambassador for the department or business unit to which you are attached, and communication and liaison beyond its immediate boundaries will require you to behave towards others as your *customers*.

In order to respond to these demands from others, you will be attempting to *meet your customers needs*. These demands will need:

- You to anticipate, in advance, all likely needs from all likely sources.
- You to plan and prioritize them in terms of time and other resources.

- Staff to be identified, trained and developed to ensure the required expertise is available and accessible.
- Individual objectives to be identified, agreed and set, so that collectively they are aimed to meet customer requirements.
- The development of an overall culture which is one of motivation towards both meeting customer requirements through objectives set, as well the flexibility to welcome any unexpected requirements through reviewed objectives.

Identifying your customers tangible and intangible needs

Tangible needs are the obvious goods and services that are more easily identified once you have accepted that the market for them is divided into segments that are different in their requirements.

Intangible needs are associated with your behaviour towards your customers. It is also about *how* you produce and deliver your goods and services. The cultures demonstrated by each of your customers will respond differently to the culture demonstrated by you and your organization. Often the intangible needs will have direct impact on the more tangible customer requirements.

For example, a customer who is a small company may have difficulties understanding why you, as part of a large, highly structured organization for instance, insist upon a 2 months' lead time for the delivery of your goods or service, when they are far more responsive to their own customers. In contrast, if you work for a small company or are self-employed but servicing a large bureaucracy, you may be valued more highly if your response time is faster than theirs.

Other examples of cultural differences likely to affect attitudes and behaviour are:

- *Clashing structures*: hierarchical *versus* team management.
- *Form of address*: first name terms *versus* formal address using title and surname.
- *Appearance of individuals*: formal *versus* casual dress.
- *Decision-making*: free, open discussion, sharing views and joint problem solving *versus* closed doors and private problem-solving.
- *Leadership styles*: maintaining control *versus* mutual trust, support and valued individual contributions.

Customers, then, might well select suppliers on the basis of their culture (which is more about behaviour than end-products) being compatible with, or complementary to, their own (depending upon their supplier success priorities). It will be helpful for you to identify benefits to customers based upon the culture of your business or organization, as well as the benefits to them of the more tangible outputs you are offering.

Customers' views of their suppliers' successes

In determining to meet customer needs, you must also take into account the kinds of supplier successes (your successes) in producing and delivering goods or services they might be looking for. Your customers may value the following factors among these successes:

- Price.
- Quality.
- Speed of delivery.
- Flexibility in delivery.
- Reliability.
- New ideas.
- Choice.
- Participation/consultation.

Agree specifications and plans with the customer

Having become open to responding to customer needs, you will be able to allow your creativity to come to the fore. It is not sufficient to just say to your customer 'Yes, I/we can do that for you'. You also need to identify what *added value* or *uniqueness* you can offer over and above the next supplier in a competitive environment. This is where your individual expertise and experience will benefit your overall offer.

Before you agree your customer specification and plan then, you will need to have a clear idea of what you are likely to be offering overall so you can put some *excitement* into the process, as you demonstrate that you are empathizing with the customer; seeing the desired results from the customer's point of view.

Review and evaluate the planning process

Although it is obvious that the planning process should always be reviewed along the way and evaluated at the end, it is worth stating it here, since the *focus on the customer approach* is not a one-off activity—it is iterative (repeated—and improved—in the light of experience).

You will also identify your own techniques as your confidence grows, which you will be able to add as necessary to the material, including approaches and behaviours most acceptable, or effective, within the markets and environments you operate.

Converting the 'business planning process' into your own learning and development planning or CPD

Most people find that, to plan and implement their own learning and development, they need some kind of focus; so, in order to complete the *cycle of learning*, you might find it useful to return to the change analyses you completed in Chapter 7 and convert the SWOT and PESTEL outcomes for organizational development into your own CPD requirements.

EXERCISE

What all the implications for your learning and development (CPD) when analysing the results of the environmental analyses you carried out in Chapter 7?

STRESS AND THE MANAGER

This section sets out to examine the nature of stress and how it might be managed. Stress, or excessive stress and pressure (distress), is a problem for many people as well as managers. There are various ways to identify the causes of stress and of taking action in order to reduce it. Some will be explored here; you are invited to analyse the effects of stress in your own working environment, especially as it affects you personally, and to determine how they might further be reduced.

Since everyone behaves differently, the diagnosis of stress symptoms can seem difficult. It is also a very sensitive issue for many people who might feel that to experience and show signs of stress is unprofessional and a serious weakness.

What is even worse is that you might not even know you are suffering from stress. It sometimes requires the intervention of a third party to point out that the behaviours you are exhibiting could be proof that your stress levels have increased.

You must first understand that the weakness lies in denying the potential and reality of stress and not in suffering from it. Once you accept the existence of stress, you can then take measures to reduce its effects.

What is stress

Stress is 'A mismatch between perceived demands and perceived ability to cope. It is the balance between how we view demands and how we think we can cope with those demands that determines whether we feel no stress, distressed or ... challenged in a way we feel we can handle.' (adapted from Looker and Gregson, 1989, p .29)

Almost everyone, from all walks of life, has a view about stress. Concern is expressed about the stress associated with such things as:

- Unemployment.
- Raising a family.
- Illness.
- Caring for a dependent relative.
- Moving house.
- Death of a relative.
- Relationship or marital problems.

EXERCISE

In order to start you thinking about stress, try to list at least three different sources of stress (other than those already listed above) in the everyday life of yourself or of a person familiar to you:

1	
2	
3	
4	
5	
6	

The things you have listed may have been associated with particular life events or changes—a holiday or someone leaving home.

They may have been environmentally related: 'It's not safe to go out at night on my own'.

Perhaps they were linked to particular people: 'My boss causes me stress'.

They may have touched upon how you (or the person you had in mind) *manage* life: 'I can never say NO to anything so I end up doing too much'.

People express a wide range of views about the causes of stress.

The sorts of comments you hear reveal a great deal about the views of everyday managers and staff. Cast your mind back using your own work and life experience. Recall the comments which either you or your friends, family or work colleagues, have made on the subject.

EXERCISE

On a sheet of paper complete the following sentences. There is no right or wrong answer. Photocopy the page to make it easier.

- I find I get most stressed when . . .
- The last time I felt under stress was because of . . .
- The most stressful thing about my particular job is . . .
- The most stressful aspect of working in my organization is . . .
- I think this is because . . .
- Of all the jobs I have had, I think the most stressful to be because . . .
- The sort of person who copes best with stress is . . .
- The sort of person who copes worst with stress is . . .
- What my colleagues find stressful in their work is . . .
- What I find most stressful in my private life is . . .
- The single thing an individual(s) could do in my private life that would most reduce my stress is . . .
- The single thing my manager could do that would most reduce my stress is . . .
- The single thing my organization could do that would most reduce my stress is . . .
- The single thing the government could do that would most reduce my stress is . . .

The answers that you have given provide a picture of how you, as an individual, see stress in your own life and work. It is a brief and over-simplified picture. It does not intend to provide any indication of *how much* stress you might be under.

You may find it helpful to compare your responses with the multiple-cause diagram provided in Figure 8.3.

Charles Handy (1985) has listed a number of factors associated with the *job* that contribute to stress:

- Responsibility for the work of others.
- Responsibility for innovation.
- Co-ordination/liaison roles.
- Relationship problems with colleagues.
- Career uncertainty.

Cooper *et al.* (1988) further suggests the following sources of work related stress:

- Factors associated with the job.
- Aspects of the individual's work role.
- Work-based relationships.
- Career issues.
- The structure and climate of the organization.

EXERCISE

You may find it helpful at this point to review the answers you wrote to the earlier questions. Can you fit your answers into the categories that have been identified?

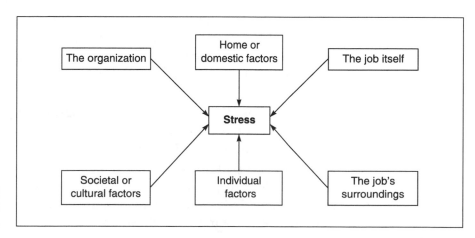

Figure 8.3
Factors associated with stress.

STRESS PERCEPTIONS

Stress as a cause

Stress can be seen as the *cause* of problems. On an individual level we associate stress with a wide range of illnesses such as heart disease, high blood pressure, migraine, asthma, ulcers, etc. Importantly, we also see stress as having an effect upon a person's behaviour. How often have you felt that a person's erratic or angry behaviour is down to *stress*?

Stress as the affect of a problem

Stress can also be viewed as the *result* of other problems. Therefore, the pressure of modern life, for instance, long working hours, the high rate of relationship break-up, etc., are all factors that can be seen as the causes of stress.

Stress as a problem in itself

Perhaps stress is a function of how we *react* to pressure. Some people can cope with incidences of stress better than others. Therefore you should look at the actual nature of the stress you and others feel before developing better coping mechanisms.

Stress can be seen, according to Looker and Gregson (1989), as *good*, *bad* or *ugly*. It is *good* in the sense that it can be associated with excitement, stimulation, creativity, success, achievement and increased productivity. It is *bad* when it is associated with boredom, frustration, distress, pressure, poor performance, unhappy and disharmonious relationships or failure. It is *ugly* when it is associated with specific health (and sometimes life-threatening) concerns such as ulcers, heart attacks, clinical depression and so on.

Stress is a word that has many meanings. It conjures up the notion of a *strain*; in the engineering industry, for instance, the word has a technical meaning associated with the amount of pressure a material can resist before deforming. The meaning of stress becomes enriched when applied to people because, unlike concrete, balanced people have some choice over reactions. Unlike the motorway bridge, they can engage in a range of behaviours.

Thus, when applied to human behaviour, stress is part of an inter-active system. Peoples' personalities vary, as do their experiences and motivation, and therefore the same amount of stress applied to different people is likely to have different results.

Stress as a process

Cooper *et al.* (1988) offer a way of looking at stress in terms of a process. They suggest that people generally aim for a steady-state in the way they relate to the world. This suggestion is based upon models used in a range of fields (biology, physics and social science), which seek to explain behaviour as aimed at correcting a disturbance. You can see this happening in the way your own body tries to adjust when the outside temperature rises or falls. If it is hot your body sweats in order to lose heat. If it is very cold then shivering is an adjustment process to enable the body to increase temperature. Both are *involuntary behaviours,* which you have little control over.

Cooper *et al.* further suggest that this model can apply to how we react to disturbance in our outside world. They see each person as having a stability range, within which they feel comfortable. When this stability is threatened by an outside force, the person tries to restore the position to one of comfort. Thus stress can be seen as a feedback cycle, as shown in Figure 8.4.

We could suggest that a certain part of everyone's life is stable, changing little over time; although a person's life may appear chaotic and constantly moving, the argument is that there are *zones of stability* which each person needs and guards jealously.

Figure 8.4
The adjustment /
coping cycle
(adapted from
Cooper *et al.,*
1988).

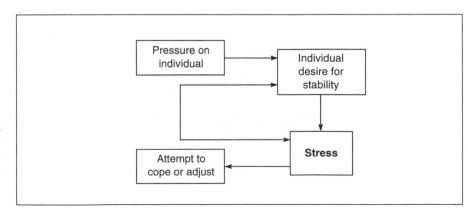

The physiology of pressure or threat

Pressure or threat has certain effects upon people in terms of their actual bodily reactions, some of which are quite noticeable to others. Some of the effects are hormonal; these are natural and in many ways functional. Our ancestors relied upon heightened awareness at times of danger in order to survive. Animals, even domesticated ones, still rely on this. The immediate physiological effects can include:

- Enlarging of pupils.
- Faster breathing.
- Faster heart rate.
- Paleness.
- Sweating.
- Trembling.
- Sickness/bowel effects.

Signs of stress at work

In the short term:

- *Fight instead of flight*—the short sharp row. The extreme of this would be taking it out on others.
- *Flight*—going sick, leaving, retiring.
- *Internal flight*—slow down, reduce commitment.

In the longer term:

- Illness or predisposition to illness.
- Absenteeism.
- Indecision.
- Arbitrary decisions.
- Excessive eating/drinking/smoking.
- Theft.
- Workaholism.
- Avoidance or over-reaction.

EXERCISE

How many of these signs do you recognize in yourself or others in you workplace?

Costs of stress at work

Stress obviously has a range of costs. An often-quoted figure is that in the UK £5 *billion* is lost each year as a result of stress affecting people at work. This figure was based upon sickness statistics where the sickness was diagnosed as anxiety or depression. Clearly that figure only represents a part of the stress related costs. There are other effects of stress that are harder to quantify, but it would be a useful exercise to consider those possible areas of cost.

There are in fact as many costs as your imagination can cope with. If you look at the costs simply in terms of the staff-related costs there are the costs of:

- Covering for people on sick leave as a result of stress.
- People leaving *before* they suffer stress related illness.
- Replacing people who leave as a result of stress (or before it becomes obvious).
- Training new people to do the job.
- Paying higher salaries and benefits to *compensate* people for stress-related activity.
- Costs for people who retire early for stress-related reasons.

In terms of the operations of the organization there are stress-related costs arising from:

- Mistakes being made leading to loss of business efficiency.
- Accidents leading to damage to persons, equipment and buildings.
- Fines imposed as a result of avoidable industrial accidents.
- Disciplining and cautioning staff.

In industrial relations terms there are stress-related costs arising from:

- The residue of ill-feeling harboured by stressed staff.
- Industrial disputes leading to loss of business.
- A lack of commitment to the organization's aims and values.

Indirectly we could attribute a stress-related cost to:

- Actual theft from the employer by staff who feel aggrieved because of the stress they are suffering.

- Deliberate negligence, at times verging on sabotage, by staff who feel aggrieved because of the stress they are suffering.

Arguably we could also apportion stress-related costs arising from:

- The cost to the Health Service (and thus the tax system) of treating work stress-related illness.
- The cost of non-contributory benefits paid as a result of work-related stress.
- The loss of tax receipts from people who cease work for stress-related reasons (though these may in part be compensated by the tax receipts from people who take their jobs).
- Increases in insurance premiums arising from compensation for stress-related incidents.

We should also not forget to add in the stress-related cost arising from:

- Staff absence that is stress-related but which is not recorded as such in official statistics.
- The cost of official investigations of accidents and incidents of theft or sabotage.

ORGANIZATIONAL STRESS-INDUCING FACTORS

Some organizations operate in a way that inevitably is stress-inducing. Where the organization is strongly sales-driven and a manager or employee is only as good as their last achievement, the stress factor can be quite high. You often may hear statements like 'It's a young person's company' to describe such a situation. Advertising agencies can be stressful settings and are characterized by a young staff profile.

The nature of the organization is often a direct result of the nature of its industrial environment. It is evident that the pressure of change and the need to work increasingly more *efficiently* and *effectively* (doing the right *things* and doing them *right*, respectively), if seen negatively and with little reward in return, can have an effect upon the level of organizational stress.

The situation of a local authority refuse collection service

Prior to the introduction of compulsory competitive tendering, the service had employed a proportion of mentally handicapped operatives. After the change, the dustcart crews and managers became aware of the implications of higher performance targets. Suddenly, the mentally handicapped operatives were no longer welcome on the crews. One manager explained: 'Contract tendering places the crew under great stress to meet targets. We don't feel it is right to put mentally handicapped people in that situation'.

Management and stress

Moving into management is likely to be associated with a move into a higher stress rating. There are occupations that rate higher than management, but management is above average for the stress it incurs.

Many people, perhaps you are one of them, moved into management from a background of technical expertise. If so, then it is possible that the move will involve a potentially considerable increase in occupational stress.

However, it should not be assumed that the occupation is sufficient to explain the existence of high levels of stress. As earlier models have shown, the sources of stress are numerous. It is not generally possible to put stress down to one particular cause.

Work-role factors

Stress is linked to uncertainty about what the job requires. Stress is also associated with conflicting job demands.

The potential for stress in these two areas is considerable and probably increasing. Why? The world of work and organizations are undergoing faster rates of change. Some organizations have recognized that job descriptions become out of date too quickly and updating them is seen as a fruitless and increasingly meaningless task. Therefore they are getting rid of job descriptions and introducing in their place a method of objective-setting and review. Where managers are used to job descriptions they are often inexperienced in managing people by objectives and targets.

In such organizations there is considerable potential for role uncertainty unless the targets and objectives are clearly set, and lines of accountability and authority can become easily blurred.

Both authors have worked in and with organizations where accountability has moved downwards (the terms *decentralization* or *devolution* are often used). A common dilemma in many such situations is that, although the transfer of responsibility has been clearly agreed and communicated, the *head office* perceives that the authority is retained centrally. The managers may then be treated as if they do not have the delegated authority. This can prove very frustrating, especially when key decisions are not acted upon.

There are particular phenomena that can cause uncertainty over job role:

- *Promotion* Alice was very happy about being promoted. She enjoyed working with her colleagues and saw them as friends. After moving into the supervisor's job she found that light conversation at the lunch table became harder. She didn't feel able to share confidences with her team in the way she had in the past. Her colleagues, on the other hand, seemed to regard her as still *one of the team*. They were quite taken aback when she commented on the need to improve timekeeping. The Alice they knew 'wouldn't say that . . .'
- *A new job* Leslie worked for a commercial manufacturing company. He was used to being set clear targets and was expected to meet them efficiently and without discussion. He moved to work for a voluntary organization and set about his new job in his accustomed fashion. He was surprised when colleagues upbraided him for failing to consult sufficiently and being insufficiently sensitive to the politics of the Management Committee.
- *A transfer within the company* Rahni welcomed the opportunity to work with the sales department. She felt that her experience in production had equipped her to move into a sales role. However, when she asked what time people finished work in sales she was surprised to get no clear answer.
- *A change in procedures* A local authority conducted an audit of the forms in current usage. They found that many of them were duplicating information held on other forms. The senior managers agreed to simplify and reduce the number of forms. The clerical staff found the new forms hard to

understand and began photocopying the older versions of the forms. The new forms piled up unused.

■ *A change in the law* The government increasingly requires local authorities to put services out to contract. In order to meet this legislation, local authorities had to set up separate purchasing and contracting departments. People who had worked together harmoniously suddenly began to develop *them and us* attitudes. Distrust and suspicion grew.

COPING STRATEGIES FOR STRESS

Some aspects of stress are more controllable than others. If your main source of stress is the nature of the occupation you find yourself in, and if you regard the stress as unacceptable, then you may need to consider an alternative and less-stressful occupation. For most people, however, stress is an amalgam of many factors. Occupation is but one of these factors, most of which can be positively influenced by the people concerned. Indeed, some of these factors can be controlled by the individual experiencing the problems, though they may not be aware that they can.

The way you respond to stress at work may be appropriate or inappropriate. Appropriate responses enable you to cope successfully.

Assertiveness

Assertive behaviour is about recognizing that, in any situation, you and others have *rights*. Let us see how this behaviour operates in a potentially stressful situation (see also Chapter 7).

Your line manager asks you to work late. You do not consider that the request is reasonable because, despite an unexpected backlog of work, you have promised your partner/spouse that you will be home at a specific time due to prior commitments.

You might respond by saying:

'I promised I'd be home by 7 o'clock, but I suppose I could stay on if I have to.'
'You must be joking—no way.'
'I appreciate there is a problem, but I can't stay on late tonight.'

The first response is passive. Even though you are indicating a pressure elsewhere, you are indicating that you are accepting that the right of the other person takes precedence. The second response is aggressive. It is not simply a statement of your own rights but also a denial of the rights of the other person to even suggest that you work late. The third response is assertive. You are acknowledging the other person's right to ask, but are clearly stating that you yourself have a right to your denial.

EXERCISE

Try it again, only this time apply it to something which you have felt uncomfortable about. Here are several suggestions in case you find it hard to think of a situation:

- You are asked to take on a new job responsibility but you feel that you have not had sufficient training or preparation.
- You are asked to clear up a mess that is not of your making.
- You feel that there is some part of your pay and benefits package that has fallen behind what you regard as the going-rate for your job.

Find a friend or colleague to assist you. If no-one is available then face a mirror as you say the words which you would use when expressing your concerns. Then review what you have said. You may find it helpful to write it down. Ask yourself (and your friend or colleague if appropriate) the following questions:

- What right(s) was I stating for myself?
- What right(s) was I accepting that the other person had?
- How did my tone of voice support or detract from what I said?
- How did my facial expression support or detract from what I said?
- How did my body posture support or detract from what I said?
- (If you had a friend or colleague helping) How was my message received?

Some experts suggest that it is worth keeping a diary in which you record stressful events, who was associated with them and how you handled them. The purpose of such a diary is not simply to have a factual record but rather to enable you to adopt appropriate (e.g. assertive) behaviour. It is an effective learning aid.

The ability to use assertive behaviour is probably the single most effective strategy available to you. It is something within *your control*. It gives you a means to deal with the various aspects of stress not only in your work but also in your life generally.

By using assertiveness techniques, you can then move on to apply it to implement such strategies as:

- Delegation—upwards, downwards and sideways.
- Participation—in establishing work objectives.
- Prioritization—of tasks.
- Control over your use of time.

Time management

Poor time management can lead to stress and poor performance as well as vice versa. You might be *crying out for help* by claiming that you never have enough time to complete your tasks and meet your objectives. However, situations invariably appear worse than they really are and a positive approach to managing your time can also go a long way to ensuring lower stress levels. (See below for a separate section on time management.)

It is a common mistake to believe it is only shy and quiet people who need to develop their assertiveness. However, this is relatively simple and straightforward to achieve compared to the defensive/offensive, aggressive individual. There is a fine line between assertiveness and aggression and it is not easy for this type of person to learn the differences between the two types of behaviour.

Group identification of stress and means of controlling it

Teams or groups of colleagues can work together to:

- Raise stress awareness.
- Identify and discuss various negative behaviours.
- Identify formal education/training needs.
- Regularly review priorities and workload (one-to-one and group).
- Use counselling as a preventative.

- Use counselling as a cure.
- Delegate upwards, downwards and sideways.
- Participate in establishing objectives.
- Exercise control over the use of time.
- Give and receive responsibility and authority fairly and appropriately.
- Encourage polite interchange and mutual respect—e.g. please, thank you, smile, etc.
- Empathize with others and understand needs.
- Encourage and be encouraged to meet challenges.
- Exchange ideas and understanding about stress and its causes.
- Say 'no' appropriately and encourage others to do the same.
- Promote participation and exchange of ideas.
- Create a culture of personal responsibility, independence and individual innovation, balanced with openness and safety in seeking and giving help.

See also Chapter 7 for assertiveness.

MANAGING YOUR TIME

Time is probably your most valuable, non-renewable resource. Unfortunately, it can also be the most abused! Time cannot be:

- Turned on or off.
- Replaced.
- Stored up.

There are only 24 hours in a day, so time is also a *limited* resource.

A key principle in time management can be associated with the Pareto principle, commonly known as the 80/20 rule. A 19th century Italian economist, Wilfredo Pareto, observed that the significant items in a group seemed to form the smallest proportion of that group:

20% of a workforce does 80% of the work.
20% of a document contains 80% of the relevant information.
20% of a company's sales accounts for 80% of its profit.

Applying this rule to time management, 20% of your tasks may produce 80% of your results.

Time management is a process by which you take control of your time and use it to do the things you want, or need, to do. Good time management will improve the quality of your life because you will:

- Achieve more goals.
- Become less stressed.
- Gain more personal and job satisfaction.
- Produce better results—quality rather than quantity.
- Have more time to think.
- Have more leisure time.

You can improve the way you manage your time if you understand how you use your time at the moment. You will then be able to pinpoint areas where your management of time can be improved and then take specific steps to increase your control over your time. You are therefore recommended to:

- Keep a daily time log.
- Complete time sheets.
- Make lists or notes of what you do, when, and for how long.

See Chapter 4 for more detail about the effects of the expensive resource of time.

EXERCISE

Plan and prepare ways of allocating your time and recording actual time spent that are appropriate to your situation.

When analysing how effectively you use your time, ask yourself:

Do I spend enough time on planning and scheduling my work?
Do I make 'to-do' lists and prioritize tasks?
Am I doing work that could be done by others? Am I *managing* or *doing* the work?
Do I need to allocate specific times to specific activities (e.g. Monday mornings for administration)? Are there regular activities that can be planned in?
Do I leave enough time between activities to allow myself to adjust my role?
Am I so busy getting low-priority work out of the way that I do not get time for high-priority activities?
Are there areas that I want to change? What are they? What changes do I want to make?

Personal peak performance time

It is also well known that people vary as to what time of the day they reach their *peak* in terms of performance. We have all heard people say that they are a 'night person' or 'I am at my best in the mornings'. It is useful for you to understand yourself when developing time management skills and maximizing your use of time:

- Think about and identify your energy cycle.
- Use your 'peak' time for concentrating on priority tasks.
- Use your 'trough' time for doing simple, routine tasks.
- For many people, maximum performance time is in the morning.
- Also for many, after lunch is a relatively relaxing time (watch people drowse during early afternoon meetings or training sessions!)
- There is often a secondary peak later in the day.

However, you can only improve your time management if you really want to. There are a number of techniques that you can adopt, but they will only work if you are genuinely committed to changing the way you approach your management of time.

SUMMARY OF ISSUES

In working through this chapter, you will have encountered a number of issues and perhaps some ideas that are new to you. The objectives of the chapter were to:

- Introduce the concept of self-management and identify ways to develop self-help techniques.
- Discuss stress, how it occurs, how to deal with it and how to prevent it.
- Present concepts and theories and how people learn and what enables personal change.
- Discuss the idea of continuous personal development (CPD) and the notion of personal commitment.

How well have the authors met these objectives?

More importantly, how have approached and used the material yourself, and how much have you developed since the beginning of your course of study, or working through the chapter? You are strongly recommended to extend your research and study to include as much as possible of the material identified in further reading and references, so that you can build on your expertise, incorporating more complex approaches and ideas as you develop further in your managerial role.

These objectives, if re-revisited over a period of time and put into practice in your job, will help you to achieve the personal competency of self-management, broken down into the elements identified in the table below at the end of this chapter.

PREPARING FOR ACTION PLANNING

In order for you to reflect on your own behaviour and that of others with whom you work, you might find it useful to use the self-assessment table at the end of this chapter (reproduce as many as you wish) to re-evaluate your skills and knowledge.

Remember to review the checklist of questions, as identified in the Introduction to this book, at Appendix 1.

Analyse your own behaviour in terms of strengths (positive outcomes) and weaknesses (negative effects), in dealing with actual work-based occurrences with regards to the various situations discussed in this chapter, and summarized above.

Decide how you might deal with them differently in the future and what are your immediate training requirements and future development needs.

Discuss them with appropriate others and negotiate how you might address them.

FURTHER READING AND REFERENCES

Blaxter, L, Hughes, C. and Tight, M. (2001) *How to Research* (2nd edition). Buckingham: Open University Press. ISBN: 0-335-20903-3

Boak, G. (1991) *Developing Managerial Competences: The Management Learning Contract Approach*. London: Pitman. ISBN: 0-273-03326-3

Capronia, P. (2001) *The Practical Coach: Management Skills for Everyday Life*. New Jersey: Prentice Hall (Chapters 2 and 5). ISBN: 0-13-849142-9

Cooper, C., Cooper, R., Eaker, L. (1988) *Living with Stress*. Harmondsworth: Penguin. ISBN: 0-14-009866-6

Davis, M.H. (1996) *Empathy: A Psychological Approach*. Colorado: Westview Press. ISBN: 0-8133-3001-7

Guirdham, M. (2002) *Interactive Behaviour at Work* (3rd edition). Harlow: Pearson Education (Chapters 4, 5, 6 and 12). ISBN: 0-273-65590-6

Harrison, R. (1992) *Employee Development*. London: CIPD. ISBN: 0-85292-487-9

Handy, C. (1985) *Understanding Organisations*. Harmondsworth: Penguin.

Honey, P. and Mumford, A. (1986) *The Manual of Learning Styles*. Maidenhead: Peter Honey. ISBN: 0-9508444-2-X

Honey, P. and Mumford, A. (1990a) *The Manual of Learning Opportunities*. Maidenhead: Peter Honey. ISBN: 0-9508444-4-6

Honey, P. and Mumford, A. (1990b) *The Opportunist Learner: A Learner's Guide to Using Learning Opportunities*. Maidenhead: Peter Honey. ISBN: 0-9508444-6-2

Hunsaker, P.L. (2001) *Training in Management Skills*. New Jersey: Prentice Hall (Chapters 2 and 6). ISBN: 0-13-955014-3

Mumford, A., editor (1994) *Handbook of Management Development* (4th edition). Vermont: Gower Publishing (Chapters 3, 4, 5 and 6). ISBN: 0-556-07445-1

Pedler, M., Burgoyne, J. and Boydell, T. (1986) *A Manager's Guide to Self-Development* (2nd edition). Maidenhead: McGraw-Hill. ISBN: 0-07-084924-2

Rylatt, A. (2001) Learning Unlimited: Transforming Learning in the Workplace. London: Kogan Page. ISBN: 0-7494-3544-5

Whetton, D., Cameron, K. and Woods, M. (2000) *Developing Management Skills for Europe* (2nd edition). Harlow: Pearson Education (Chapters 1 and 2). ISBN: 0-201-34276-6

Recommended journal articles

Karakowsky, L. and McBey, K. (1999) The lesson of work: towards an understanding of the implication of the workplace for adult learning and development. *Journal of Workplace Learning: Employee Counselling Today* 11 (6):192–201. Bradford: MCB University Press. ISSN: 1366-5626. Website: http://www.emerald-library.com

Leggett, B. Getting the sound to match the vision. *The Guardian* 12/08/2000

Longenecker, C.O. and Fink, L.S. (2001) Improving management performance in rapidly changing organizations. *Journal of Management Development* 20 (1): 7–18. Bradford: MCB University Press. ISSN: 1366-5626. Website: http://www.emerald-library.com

Martin, G. and Butler, M. (2000) Comparing managerial careers, management development and management education in the UK and the USA: some theoretical and practical considerations. *International Journal of Training and Development* 4 (3): 196–207. Bradford: MCB University Press. ISSN: 1360-3736. Website: http://www.emerald-library.com

Parsloe, E. (2001) Searching for standards: defining a professional framework. *Training Journal* December: 10–12. Bradford: MCB University Press. ISSN: 1465-6523. Website: http://www.emerald-library.com

The Times Newspaper (2001) How to be more effective in the office. *The Times* 19/12/2001

Competency element	Competency level: 1 (low)–5 (high)	Requires development	No direct experience	What can help? (identify opportunities)	Who can help?	When can it be achieved?	How can it be achieved?
Gives a consistent and stable performance							
Takes action to reduce the causes of stress							
Accepts personal comments or criticism without becoming defensive or offensive							
Remains calm in difficult or uncertain situations							
Handles others' emotions without becoming personally involved in them							
Takes responsibility for meeting her/his own learning and development needs							

Seeks feedback on performance to identify his/her own strengths and weaknesses	Learns from her/his own mistakes and those of others	Changes behaviour where needed as a result of feedback	Reflects systematically on own performance and modifies behaviour accordingly	Develops self to meet the competence demand of changing situations	Transfers learning from one situation to another

CHAPTER 9

The strategic perspective

Managers who act strategically, identify the way forward in a complex
environment, referring constantly to a longer term vision for the
organization.

LINKS TO THE CHARTERED MANAGEMENT INSTITUTE'S MODULE

This chapter aims to address the aims and learning outcomes as identified in the Introduction to this text under the heading *Links to the
Chartered Management Institute's Module 'Understanding Yourself'*.
However, this chapter, whilst supporting the module, stands in addition to the material covered within it.

INTRODUCING THE RELATIONSHIP BETWEEN THE PERSONAL COMPETENCY MODEL AND THE STRATEGIC PERSPECTIVE

The Personal Competency Model (PCM), as already discussed, identifies the behaviours and skills that are necessary for you to develop
before you are able to prove competence in any managerial function.
This chapter attempts to deal with the various behaviours and skills
necessary for you to apply across all managerial functions, transferring your learning to different occasions, at different times and under
varying circumstances (contexts), consistently.

The outcomes below, as identified within this section of the model, should be borne in mind while you work through this chapter.

Outcomes required for maintaining the strategic perspective

There is one set of behaviours highlighted in this chapter, concentrating on the importance of the individual manager *maintaining the strategic perspective*.

In order to maintain *the strategic perspective* the manager:

- Displays an understanding of how the different parts of the organization and its environment fit together.
- Works towards a clearly defined vision of the future.
- Clearly relates goals and actions to the strategic aims of the organization.
- Takes opportunities when they arise to achieve the longer-term aims or needs of the organization.

INTRODUCTION AND OBJECTIVES

The objectives of the chapter are to:

- Introduce *strategy* and the manager.
- Discuss ways to examine the environment.
- Introduce methods to assess the organization.
- Show how to implement decisions.

The aim of the chapter would therefore be to provide you, the manager (or potential manager), with an understanding of how you might adopt a strategic perspective in your activities. We would identify a strategic perspective as distinguished by a forward-looking orientation. The environment for organizations is increasingly complex and challenging. Managers can no longer assume that what is true today will hold true for any substantial future time. Management gurus provide new models and some management gurus are quite comfortable with the rapid obsolescence of these models. Indeed, one such guru told a manager attending his seminar that the advice in a book he (the guru) had written only a couple of years previously was useless.

Therefore, in this chapter we will not seek to offer 'the flavour of the month' approaches to strategic thinking. Rather, we will introduce you to approaches that we believe possess reasonable durability.

STRATEGY AND THE MANAGER

It is important at the outset to make a distinction between the kind of planning that is involved throughout an organization and the concept of strategy.

Strategic actions

We could take an organization for which one of the authors worked many years ago. It was a small factory that undertook a range of contract work, usually involving minor assembly-line work. The workforce was mostly local people who were hourly paid and who worked on shifts.

The manager of the factory saw her role as getting contracts for work and she left the organization of the work to two supervisors who managed the shifts. The factory employed local women and also took on some students (including the author) during the summer holidays.

Quite clearly the supervisors had to plan the workload and this had to be done with some care. The contracts varied in size and in importance. The supervisors were aware of this and also knew the staff. High-value and important contract work was given to the more experienced staff, low-value and less critical work to temporary staff.

The owner obviously needed to be informed about the progress of contract work. However; she was also trying to do more than simply 'fill the sausage machine'. She saw the importance of having a range of contracts and avoiding a dependence upon one source of business. In this way she was behaving strategically (though she would have probably called it plain common sense!). What was also interesting was the attitude of some of the workers at the factory. When there was a 'rush job' the workers would often be asked to work extra shifts in the evening. Some of the workers had children and this presented them with a child-care problem. With the tacit agreement of the supervisors some of these workers sought employment for their teenage children on these shifts. In fact, in a few cases the parents actually substituted their teenager for themselves on the extra shifts. Though this practice was questionable it could be argued that it represented 'strategic behaviour' on the part of the workforce. Strategic thinking is not necessarily the preserve of the manager.

Ways of perceiving strategy

For the manager, a key element of strategy is thinking. Indeed, we would argue that without thought a strategic decision becomes purely reactive. Johnson and Scholes (2002, pp. 5–10) comment that strategic decisions *in organizations* possess the following characteristics:

- They relate to the scope of an organization's activities.
- They involve matching the activities of the organization to the environment in which it operates.
- They involve matching activities to resources and in particular the resource capacity.
- Strategic decisions have major resource implications.
- They affect the operational decisions that the organization takes.
- The values and expectations of the stakeholders in the organization will have a significant effect.
- A strategic decision is likely to have longer-term implications.

Similarly, Johnson and Scholes suggest that strategy exists at a number of levels in an organization and we could indicate these as follows:

- *Corporate level*—here the decisions would focus upon what business to be in, how the organization should be structured and how it should be financed.
- *Business level*—the focus here being upon competing within a particular market or sector; what sort of products or services should be offered and to which customers.
- *Operational level*—here the strategy links the various functions (finance, personnel, IT, etc.) in order to enable them to ensure that the business and corporate strategy is achieved.

In this context we would add the level of the individual to the discussion; an individual can have a *strategic perspective* as well a number of people whose job it is to address organizational *strategy*. Indeed, many small stock market investors become large stock market investors because they have adopted a strategic perspective on investment which has proven to be more accurate than that held by the large financial institutions.

Perhaps you have decided to pursue a management qualification route independently of the view of your employer. If so, then your strategic perspective is individual and possibly at variance with that held by your organization.

What is strategy?

Henry Mintzberg (1994), a well-known writer and author, has had a key influence upon the development of thinking about how strategy is formulated. He suggests that strategic formulation does not take place evenly. Rather, there are different patterns of strategic change. The patterns can in some ways be compared to the behaviour of the surface of an ocean. The water in an ocean offers the following kinds of behaviour:

- There are the incremental adjustments represented by the rise and fall of the tide.
- There are aspects that offer continuity such as the deep ocean currents that change little over time.
- There are periods of flux and uncertainty, which could be typified by storms that agitate the surface of the sea.
- There are occasional major transformations such as a tidal wave caused by volcanic eruption.

If you apply this model to your own experience as a manager and as an individual you may find it useful to note down examples from your organizational and personal life to illustrate each of the ocean movements that have been referred to above. We have done this for one of the authors in Figure 9.1.

What is perhaps different between the conception of Mintzberg and the way we represent it is that Mintzberg, in talking about strategy, sees the patterns as mutually exclusive. If transformational strategic change is happening then incremental change is not. However, if we compare the individual and the organization, we can argue that it is quite possible for the individual to be undergoing a different kind of personal strategic change to that of his/her

Figure 9.1
Examples from
organizational and
personal life
compared to
oceanic
movements.

Oceanic movement	Organisational example	Personal example
• Tidal changes • Deep-ocean current • Storms • Tidal wave	• Annual workload negotiation • Move to contract staff • Major re-organization • Organizational closure/takeover	• Improving computer skills • Learning a foreign language • Changing job • Career change

organization. If you compare yourself to your organization, then are you similar or dissimilar in your experience of recent and current strategic change?

How strategy relates to behaviour: mission and values

If in the previous section you found that there was a difference between yourself and your organization, how might you account for that difference? Let us suppose that your organization is going through a period of flux (storm) and yet you personally are seeking continuity (deep ocean current). One clue might lie in the actual values or goals that are espoused both by you and your organization. Possibly the organization has had to make a major strategic change and this has been associated with a re-ordered set of values. In the public sector many organizations have to come to terms with 'the contract culture' and meeting performance targets. This has sometimes upset quite deeply held organizational values about public service and 'doing things in the right way'.

When a new set of values supersedes a previously accepted pattern of belief in an organization, it is sometimes linked with a change in mission. Strategic management textbooks talk of organizations having a 'mission statement'. Johnson and Scholes (2002, p.13) define this as 'an overriding premise in line with the values or expectations of the stakeholders' (of the organization).

Security with safety

One of the authors worked for a time for a major security company. At that time the company had a mission statement emblazoned on all its vehicles. The statement read 'for customers, co-workers and the common good'. The author was initially cynical about whether this statement was representative of a related value system. The company had, at the time, been the subject of press reporting which suggested that it was virtually a 'private army'. However, during the author's training period the message that came across was that the company valued the well-being of staff highly. Members of the security staff were told that their own safety was paramount and that the organization was not looking for 'have-a-go heroes'. At the time, the security industry had a very dubious reputation and the author subsequently wondered whether this company's very public espousal of a broad set of values was also an attempt to distinguish the company from its competitors.

Problems in behaving strategically

Mintzberg also looked at differences between intended strategies and actual outcomes. He suggested that there are pure forms of strategy, which can help us understand the way in which strategy is arrived at in organizations:

- *Deliberate strategy* is defined by three conditions:
  - There must have been precise intentions in the organization set out in some detail about what was intended.
  - These intentions must have been held in common by the members of the organization.
  - Events must have worked out exactly as intended without any surprises.
- *Emergent strategy* requires that there must have been no intention to achieve the actual consequence from the actions taken.

Obviously it is unlikely that many strategic situations would fit in either of these categories. Rather these two represent the two ends of a continuum. They illustrate the problem for the manager in behaving strategically. A former prime minister, Harold Macmillan, summed it up when he commented on what had influenced his actions. He said 'events, dear boy'. Managers do not operate in laboratory conditions. There are many factors that impact upon the likelihood of a deliberate strategy occurring. Many, if not most, of the factors are not within the direct control of the manager.

	Dominant theme	Main focus	Principal concepts and techniques	Organizational implications
1950s	Budgetary planning	Financial control	Budgeting and investment appraisal	Financial management as key
1960s	Corporate planning	Planning growth	Market forecasting	Planning department
1970s	Corporate strategy	Portfolio planning	Analyse strategic business units	Integrate strategic and financial control
Late 1970s and early 1980s	Industry and competitor analysis	Choice of industries and markets and positioning	Analysis of industry structure and competitor analysis	Divestment of unattractive business units
Late 1980s and early 1990s	Quest for competitive advantage	Sources of competitive advantage within firm	Resource analysis and organizational competence	Corporate restructuring and business process re-engineering

Figure 9.2
The evolution of strategic management (Grant, 1995).

Hence most managers have to be aware of the need to adapt to changing circumstances, and this may mean jettisoning a planned strategy to take advantage of a sudden opportunity. Figure 9.2 illustrates the range of strategic alternatives.

EXAMINING THE ENVIRONMENT

The term *environment* is much used. Some people associate it with a particular value system or moral code—e.g. *caring for the environment*. However; in strategic terms, *environment* as used here does not only refer to the *green environment*. Rather it is used to indicate the context within which the manager and the organization operate, which does of course include this concern for our environmental conditions. You may, however, hear business commentators speak of a *competitive environment*. It is perhaps ironic that, as politicians extol the value of competition, business leaders may complain that the competition is excessive and then seek government aid to enable them to compete or to impose restrictions and tariffs to keep out goods from overseas.

The environment, like the weather; is always there. No manager can ignore it. Rather, what is needed is some way to understand and evaluate its impact upon the organization and the individual manager.

The nature of environmental analysis

The way in which you approach your environment will depend upon a number of factors. The more senior you are in your organization, the more likely you will look beyond the immediate environment of the organization. The smaller your organization, the more likely it is to be affected by changes in the environment. The more concentrated and focused your organization is in terms of products or services, the more specific your environment is likely to be to those products or services.

Philip Kotler (1984), who takes a marketing focus, views the organizational environment as operating at four levels. First, there are the people or organizations within the environment who are crucial to the organization in carrying out its prime function. Thus, for a garage these would be the suppliers of petrol and oil, the customers and new car distributors. If the garage needs banking facilities then the bank would be included. If the garage became involved in supplying second-hand cars then the local car auction would also be a key part of what Kotler has called the *task environment*.

Then there are the other garages that compete with our garage. Nowadays this would include hypermarkets that also sell petrol. There are also other suppliers of new and second-hand cars. This constitutes the *competitive environment*.

Even in a free-enterprise system there are certain rules and regulations. The garage has to comply with these. As a business it has to file accounts and pay taxes. Therefore there is a *public environment*, which has an impact upon the garage.

Finally, there is what Kotler has called the *macro-environment*, which involves the more general influences that impact upon the organization. Is the country going through a boom or a recession? Is there a move away from car usage or is it becoming more popular? What about the population itself? Is it getting older/younger; etc.?

Two different techniques to analyse the wider environment

Strategic management courses generally offer managers the following two techniques of environmental appraisal. They are both simple and easy to apply and have much to commend them. These techniques were covered briefly in Chapter 7 to introduce the ideas under *keeping abreast of change,* where PESTEL was broadened to include the green environment.

PESTeL analysis

The first technique is usually referred to by an acronym (this is a word made up of the first letters of each part of the technique). The acronyms used are STEP, PEST or PESTeL. The letters mean (PESTeL):

- Political.
- Economic.
- Sociological.
- Technological.
- Legal.
- *Political* All organizations and managers are affected to some extent by the political environment. Between 1979 and 1997 there was a Conservative government in the UK; Tony Blair has headed a Labour government since then. Many changes have been experienced during these terms of office. The post-war consensus, which led one previous Conservative prime minister to observe 'We are all socialists now', has been broken. Yet the *free-enterprise* ethos of the Thatcher years was associated with an enormous amount of government legislation. You may wish to research the effects these changes had on your own particular industry and organization.
- *Economic* Most people who are buying their homes or who have borrowed large amounts of money from commercial institutions are keenly aware of the impact of interest rates. One of the authors originally trained as an economist and it is a matter of some distress to observe the relatively minor (and apparently diminishing) role of this subject on many management courses. Who do you know who can make the economic (as opposed to emotional) case for or against converting to the Euro from Sterling? What are fiscal and monetary policies and how do they impact upon you and your organization? As a manager—and as a voter—you should be able to appreciate these matters.
- *Sociological* Here most people feel more comfortable. They pick up a broadsheet newspaper or magazine and read about 'Generation X' and the growth of 'portfolio working'. Currently (2002) we are experiencing a shift to an ageing population and a commensurate *ageing workforce* based on two major societal changes: improved health and people living longer; lower birth rates since the early 1980s. These all

are aspects of societal trends. Some of these trends will almost certainly be highly significant for your organization. It is predicted, for example, that people are increasingly forming smaller households and that therefore there will be a demand for more housing of a more suitable type and size. If you work in an organization associated with construction then this trend is a vital determinant of planning decisions.

■ *Technological* The pace of technical advance is faster now than it has been at any time in our history. In computers it is suggested that the obsolescence of equipment means that the machine you buy today has a product life of some 6 months. This impacts differently upon organizations. Some organizations are in fact facing a pressure for less rather than more technology. In agriculture, for example, there is a growing demand for organic products that have been produced in a non-intensive way. However, look how the mobile phone has taken over our lives in recent years; it seems we cannot go anywhere or do anything without taking and receiving calls of both a business and social nature. How has this affected the way we work, live and behave? What other facilities does the mobile now offer us? It seems we are able to walk around with the Internet, our personal data as well as our video recorders now, all accessed through one very small electronic device!

■ *Legal* All organizations and managers confront the need to observe the law of the land. When organizations operate in different countries, then the legal complexity becomes greater. The de-layering of organizations has meant that increasingly managers are expected to know what their legal position is in the workplace.

A PESTeL analysis can become more useful to you as you become more practised in its application. This is a detailed analysis of the external environment looking nationally and internationally as necessary.

■ *Demography* Because people make up markets, organizations need to constantly monitor the changes in:
  ■ Birth rate—which continues to decline in the UK.
  ■ Population—which is ageing and organizations need to consider policies that address needs appropriately.

- Changes in the family—e.g. single parents; remarriage following divorce; increases in fostering and adoption, etc.
- Rises in non-family households—more couples are choosing not to have families.
- Geographical shifts in population—these are likely to prove more important in the UK as multinationals continue their move to rural districts.
- Better-educated population—increasing the need to address marketing in the service sectors.
- Changing ethnic and racial population—requiring different cultural needs to be addressed.

- *Economic environment* Requires the analysis of the total purchasing power, which includes four main trends:
  - Slow-down of the real-income growth.
  - Continued inflationary pressure.
  - Low savings and high debt—mortgages, bank loans, etc.
  - Changing consumer expenditure patterns.
- *Physical environment* Requires attention to causes of the erosion of the ozone layer; diminishing rain forests and the general diminution of the world's natural resources including:
  - Impending shortages of certain raw materials.
  - Increased cost of energy.
  - Increased levels of pollution.
  - Strong government intervention in natural-resource management.
- *Technological environment* As this is one of the most dramatic forces shaping people's destiny, organizations are required to address:
  - The accelerating pace of technological change.
  - Unlimited innovational opportunities.
  - Improving research and development.
  - Minor improvements rather than major discoveries.
  - Increasing regulation of technological change.
- *Political/legal environment* This comprises laws, government agencies and pressure groups, requiring organizations to consider the implications of:
  - Substantial legislation regulating British business.
  - Increases in government agencies and subcontracting.
  - Growth of public-interest groups.

- *Socio/cultural environment* This involves the combined effects of experiences shaping people's beliefs, values, attitudes, norms and behaviour. Organizations need to consider:
  - How persistent are core cultural values in the changing environment?
  - That each culture consists of subcultures.
  - That secondary cultural values undergo shifts through time.

The issues emerging from your environmental analyses will vary between organizations and between the circumstances confronting them, as well as across time and *space*. Many major organizational changes are made as a result of analysing PESTEL or PESTeL regularly and thoroughly. The secret to successful application of SWOT (as below and Chapter 7) and PESTel analyses is a manager's ability to communicate the messages effectively to senior management teams.

The authors sometimes superimpose the OT part of the SWOT analysis onto PESTel. It can be very enlightening and insightful to an innovative manager.

Five forces analysis

Michael Porter (1980) developed a framework for identifying the external environment by assessing the nature of competition within a particular industry or service sector. The five forces, which Porter sees as significant, are as follows:

- *The intensity of competition within the industry itself* Consider your own industry or employment sector and answer the following questions:
  - Are the various competitors roughly equal in size?
  - Are there a large number of competitors?
  - Is the market a mature one (i.e. growth prospects are limited)?
  - Are there high fixed costs?
  - Are there high barriers to leaving the industry?
  - Does increasing capacity involve making large investment or purchasing decisions?
  - Is there a lack of differentiation between your product or service and that of your competitors?
  - Do competitors lay great stress upon achieving success?

The more questions which you answer 'yes' to, the greater the intensity of competition within your industry or employment sector.

■ *The threat of new entrants* Ask yourself the following questions about your industry or employment sector:
  ▪ Are there significant advantages attached to being a large producer or player?
  ▪ Do you need a lot of money to enter your industry?
  ▪ Is it difficult to distribute your industry product or service?
  ▪ Do existing players have a major cost advantage?
  ▪ Are existing players likely to retaliate (e.g. by reducing prices) against a new entrant?
  ▪ Are the current players protected by a legal monopoly or regulatory system?
  ▪ Is the product or service one that is strongly differentiated (i.e. brand or company name is important)?

The more questions to which you answer 'yes', the greater are the barriers to new entrants within your industry or employment sector.

■ *The power of customers or buyers* Ask yourself the following questions about your industry or employment sector:
  ▪ Do your buyers tend to purchase in large quantities?
  ▪ Are there relatively few buyers?
  ▪ Are there alternatives for buyers to your product or service?
  ▪ Are the buyers' profit margins relatively low?
  ▪ Could the buyers consider making the product or producing the service themselves?
  ▪ Is the product or service fairly standard?

The more questions to which you answer 'yes', the greater the power buyers possess.

■ *The power of suppliers* Ask yourself the following questions about your industry or employment sector:
  ▪ Do you tend to purchase in small quantities?
  ▪ Are there relatively few suppliers?
  ▪ Are there few alternatives to the product or service supplied?

- Are you as a buyer not particularly important to the supplier?
- Could the suppliers consider selling on the product or service themselves (i.e. cutting out your part of the process)?
- Is the product or service supplied differentiated?

The more questions to which you answer 'yes', the greater the power suppliers possess.

- *The threat of substitutes* Ask yourself the following questions about your industry or employment sector:
  - Is there a substitute service or product that represents a real threat to your product or service?
  - Can a buyer switch to such a substitute relatively easily?
  - Would it be difficult to hold on to your buyers by offering product or service improvements?

The more questions to which you answer 'yes', the greater the threat substitutes represent.

The development of a 'helicopter' approach

The previous two techniques are only of value if you use them thoughtfully. It is all too easy to only be aware of the immediate forces that impact upon the organization. One of the authors worked some years ago in a college that ran secretarial courses. The staff members teaching on these training courses were strongly averse to replacing their typewriters with word-processors. The reality of the office environment and the spread of IT have effectively rendered the typewriter redundant.

Part of a strategic perspective is developing a 'helicopter' approach to assessing the environment. You need to be able to rise above the trees and see the forest around you. Applying the above two techniques in a careful and wide-ranging fashion will help you do this. It certainly should help you identify the '*typewriters*' in your industry.

Using the information

Once you have carried out such an analysis then it is essential that you use the information you have obtained. Perhaps you also need to check that assumptions underlying your analysis are accurate. It is all too easy to over-rate skills that you have spent many years acquiring. Possibly new technology has rendered those skills redundant. Often your competitors are a better source of information than your own colleagues. Most managers who attend trade fairs or business exhibitions are open to sharing their opinions about what is happening in your industry.

ASSESSING THE ORGANIZATION

Once you have analysed the environment then the next logical step is to look at the organization. As with the previous example, it is quite feasible to conduct this analysis with you, the manager, as the subject. Indeed, these kinds of techniques would be familiar to careers and vocational advisors.

The first technique involves looking at the stakeholders. This analysis in some respect can easily bridge across into the environmental analysis depending upon how widely you cast the net. The public discussion about a *stakeholder society* is an example of casting the net quite widely. Thus, while the traditional view of stakeholders in an organization would only encompass owners, shareholders, managers and employees, a broader view would include the banks, the customers and the suppliers. A still wider view would include the community at large and even the organization's competitors. At that point the stakeholder analysis has become an environmental analysis!

In the context of this chapter we are using the stakeholder analysis in a narrower fashion.

The importance of key stakeholders

Previously we referred to the concept of a *mission* and *mission statement*. The key stakeholders are crucial to setting the values and purpose of the organization. Some organizations have only one such stakeholder (or stakeholder group). Some companies, for example, may regard the shareholders as the one crucial stakeholder group that determines the mission of the organization.

However, it is far more common for organizations to have a significant number of stakeholders. These may, on a simple listing, consist of the following groups:

- Owners/shareholders.
- Managers.
- Employees.
- Customers/clientele (internal and external to the organization).
- Suppliers.

The groups listed may indeed break down into further subcategories because of a diversity of views within the group itself. As an example we might break down the stakeholders of a large stock exchange listed company as follows:

- *Owners/shareholders*:
  - These would include large shareholders (pension funds and unit trusts), some of whom might hold the shares on behalf of others. They would be concerned with the company performance and *soundness* of the assets.
  - Also would be included small shareholders who have shares in their own right. They may be very interested in, for example, the chief executive's salary, which is probably many times their own income. They may be retired people who depend upon the share dividend for their income.
  - Stock market speculators would also be included in this category as they may hold the shares (or even simply hold a share option—a right to buy or sell the shares). Their interest would be largely around short-term share price fluctuations.
- *Managers*:
  - Top managers whose remuneration might be strongly linked to the share price because of options to purchase shares at a set price would be relevant here.
  - Managers whose pay is performance-related.
  - Managers whose job security is based upon the success of the company (e.g. contract managers, etc.).
- *Employees*:
  - Employees who have share options and who may be shareholders.
  - Employees who are strong trade unionists and who see pay rises as justified by company profits.
  - Employees who are on temporary or time-limited contracts would come into this category also.

- *Customers/clientele*:
  - Large customers upon whom the company depends for much of their business.
  - Small customers who rely upon the company terms of credit to stay in business.
  - *Clients* who need the company products (i.e. users of medicines, etc.).
- *Suppliers*:
  - Large suppliers who depend upon the company for much of their business.
  - Suppliers who are owed money by the company.
  - Banking and legal suppliers providing an *intangible* service.

EXERCISE

Use the table shown in Figure 9.3 as a template for your own analysis. This could relate to the industry within which you are working, your current organization, a previous one, or some other aspect of your life.

Simply listing out stakeholders is only part of the exercise. An employee is able to conduct a stakeholder analysis because she/he is, after all, a stakeholder!

The main value of the stakeholder analysis for developing a strategic perspective as a manager (or as a prospective manager) is the way in which you develop it further. One way to do this is to *map* out the stakeholders using further criteria. These criteria might be such factors as:

- How powerful the stakeholder is.
- How interested the stakeholder is in using that power.

We have set out in Figure 9.3 an example of such a stakeholder analysis using a university as an example. You will note that there is a significant difference in power possessed by students depending upon whether they are current or prospective students. Currently there is considerable discussion as to whether UK university students should be able to transfer more easily from one university to another (as they can in the USA). If this were to be introduced, then enrolled students would possess, as customers, more power to simply take their business elsewhere than they do at present.

Stakeholder	Strength	Importance	Main expectations
Current students	Voice opinions and influence of next intake Limited ability to leave	Limited power unless expressed collectively	To be educated To receive a degree To have a social life To have post-university prospects
Prospective students	Able to choose whether to come to university	Seen as vital and courted assiduosly	To be educated To receive a degree To have a social life To have post-university prospects
Parents of students	Able to influence student Often power to influence others (politicians, etc.)	Seen as important in influencing student decision	Quality of education Career prospect Reputation
Academic staff	Knowledge of subject Tenure (in some cases)	Dependant on individual academic	Research opportunity Professional development Job security Academic freedom
Non-academic staff	Knowledge of systems Trade union base	Limited impact on organization	Job security
University managers	Authority of position Control of budgets	Key in setting strategic direction	Career prospects Control of resources
Employers	Influence of managers Provision of endowments Careers for graduates Work placements	Depends on company (some very strong)	Usable graduates Useful research
Funding councils	Ability to award funds Require statistics Conduct audits	Vital to resourcing and academic standing	Accountability Efficiency Reports and figures

Figure 9.3
Stakeholder analysis of university (Blundell and Murdock, 1997).

USING THE SWOT STRATEGIC TECHNIQUE

SWOT (Strengths, Weaknesses, Opportunities, Threats) analysis is a standard technique that is familiar to all management students. It is a useful way to bring information together under some simple headings. As a technique it is not simply the preserve of a manager, you may indeed have unconsciously used it in considering a major change in your life. Let us consider the example of a decision on whether or not to sell your current property and buy another.

Few people move house in a careless and unthinking way. It represents a major life change and often involves one of the most significant financial commitments you will ever make. So when you consider doing it you would very probably go through a considerable amount of soul searching and analysis.

One key factor is what factor (or factors) is driving the situation. Perhaps your current accommodation is too small or you do not like the location. You may have had a pay increase or come into some money. These kinds of factors represent *strengths* and *weaknesses* in your current situation. Hopefully you will be in a position of *strength* but in this age of uncertainty it is also possible that you have to trade-down in property in order to reduce your mortgage or deal with a reduced income (or both).

As you weigh up your personal situation you will almost certainly also evaluate the options of alternative properties. A prospective property will present *opportunities*—perhaps to build an extension or to refurbish to your own taste. There may also be possible *threats*—what is the local authority planning to do with the disused factory down the street? Is the area likely to deteriorate?

In evaluating what to do you therefore may well have carried out, albeit subconsciously, a form of SWOT analysis. It should not be a matter of surprise to management educators that SWOT analysis is almost always the technique of choice that students reach for when they are given a free hand.

Obviously, strengths and weaknesses are relative.

Homeward bound

Some years ago Lada cars were regarded as relatively unattractive and had a very poor second-hand value. Then with the changes to the former Soviet Union a number of entrepreneurs began to export them back to the former Soviet Bloc countries. Soon advertisements appeared in the motoring sections of newspapers seeking Lada cars. A television programme showed how the cars were being loaded onto ships and taken back to Eastern Europe where there were eager customers for both the cars and spare parts. A car that was relatively unattractive to own in the UK suddenly had a good market in its area of origin.

A major responsibility for organizations is to monitor and search the environment for new opportunities. Sometimes motivation of those concerned may be low in times of recession. In fact, difficult times require even more thorough searches, because it is at these times that opportunities are more easily missed. It can also be said that the lack of opportunity searching can be one of the causes of recessions in particular industries or even whole economies.

> A company's marketing environment consists of the actors and forces external to the marketing management function of the firm that impinge on the marketing managements ability to develop and maintain successful transactions with its target customers. (Kotler, 1984)

The actors referred to by Kotler in his definition of an organization's marketing environment include those operating in the micro-environment and those in the macro-environment.

There are two basic tools used by managers to analyse and understand the environment in which their organizations operate:

- Strengths, Weaknesses, Opportunities and Threats (or SWOT) analysis for the micro-environment.
- Sociological, Technological, Economic and Political (STEP) analysis for the macro-environment.

SWOT analysis and the micro-environment

The strengths and weaknesses part of SWOT stresses the internal environment and past and present experiences, while the opportunities and threats focus on the external environment and potential future experiences. Remember, every threat to an organization also poses an opportunity, or a challenge, although they are not entirely mutually exclusive!

- *The organization*—requiring managers to constantly ask themselves questions such as:
  - What are we in business for?
  - Is the original mission still appropriate?
  - How often do we redefine our objectives?
  - Should we be changing direction (e.g. markets, products/services)?
  - What are the major strengths and weaknesses of the organization in the past and the present in providing appropriate goods or services?
- *The organization's suppliers*—requiring a constant review of:
  - Relevance of suppliers used.
  - Whether the organization is 'supplier-led'; what are the choices for alternatives?
  - Whether they continue to supply effectively and efficiently.
  - Whether their supplies are and will continue to be appropriate.
  - Whether delivery continues to be reliable and timely.
  - Would vertical integration (taking them over) be more beneficial to the organization?
- *Marketing intermediaries*, including:
  - Agents, brokers, wholesalers, etc.:
    Are they necessary?
    Are they cost-effective and a value to the organization?
    Are there alternative ways of reselling goods/services?
  - Physical distribution firms—requiring constant review of:
    Whether customers continue to be reached through their channels.
    Whether their selling pitch is appropriate and accurate.
    Their ability/inclination to promote the organization's products or services.
    Whether they need training/development in promoting the organization's products or services.
    Whether they continue to be needed at all.
    Would vertical integration be appropriate here?
  - Marketing service agencies (e.g. marketing research firms, consulting firms, advertising agencies, etc.):
    How often are their services reviewed?

Are they cost-effective?

Do they reach the relevant markets and so on?

- Financial intermediaries (e.g. banks, credit companies, insurance companies, etc.):

    Does the organization continue to get good deals?

    When were their services last reviewed?

    What are the alternatives, etc.?

- *Customers*—how does the organization determine:
  - Who they are?
  - Where they are?
  - What their needs are?
  - Does the organization address their needs?
  - Does the organization fulfil their needs? and so on.
- *Competitors*—does the organization:
  - Carry out regular competitor analyses to determine:

      Who they are?

      Where they are?

      Their strengths and weaknesses?

      Their major threats to the organization's goods
      and service?

      Whether they also analyse the market thoroughly
      to determine where the opportunities are?

  - Determine what benefits the organization offers to customers that are specific and unique as compared to competitors?
- *Public institutions* (e.g. financial, media, government, education, citizen-action)—does the organization understand and address the influences these institutions have nationally in:
  - The ability of the organization to obtain funds?
  - The effects of publicity on the organization—good and bad?
  - What implications the impact of local government policies may have on organizational strategy?
  - The effects of any local initiatives in training and education policies.
  - Public opinion towards the organization's products, services, recruitment and retention, environmental policies and so on.

While not very easy the first time you try it, SWOT analysis is an excellent tool to help managers reflect objectively. The criteria used are largely up to you. You may wish to analyse the management function areas appropriate to your organization or the desired outcomes/impacts that are expected as a result of strategic decision-making, whatever you consider most appropriate to your particular area of work. Once you have made the attempt, you will find future exercises will become more sophisticated as you repeat the procedure, and you will become more discerning in the criteria you use and the judgements you make.

Johnson and Scholes indicate that strengths and weaknesses are also closely linked to core competences of an organization and they suggest asking four key questions to establish how important strategically such core competences might be:

1 Who owns these core competences? One argument offered by some organizations to defend a decision not to invest in training is that they will see their investment *walk out of the door* as their staff members are poached by competitors.

2 How long are the competences good for? Currently advertisements for secretarial staff still ask for shorthand skills. However, it can be argued that technology (and de-layering) is rendering such skills obsolete.

3 To what extent can the competencies be transferred? How much is Richard Branson's name worth without his involvement? The ability of a retailer in selling washing machines may not transfer to selling personal computers.

4 How easily can the competencies be copied or learnt by a competitor? In February 1997 the motoring organizations expressed concern that certain car manufacturers were producing vehicles which could not be repaired or maintained other than by regular dealers.

EXERCISE

Extend your results from the previous exercise to include a SWOT analysis using some or all of the ideas included here.

THE INVOLVEMENT OF COLLEAGUES

If you refer back to the home purchase example at the beginning of the previous section then ask yourself the following question. 'Would you consult members of your family about the factors involved in the decision?'

For example, if you were moving home because you felt that your children needed more space then would you check that the children shared your interpretation? Perhaps their conception of more space is not simply defined by having more bedrooms. They may prefer to have a *den* or workshop in the garden or a large loft space.

However, in organizations, just as in many families, the key people are often not involved in the discussion about strategic decisions. *Who* should be involved? *Why* should they be involved? *When* should they be involved? *How* should they be involved? are the key questions that any effective manager needs to answer.

Who to involve?

A trite and simple answer is to say 'everyone who constitutes a stakeholder' in the organization. However; you will get no thanks if you consult everyone in your organization about every single decision that has a strategic implication.

Why should they be involved?

If the decision affects their work, their behaviour, their views, attitudes, interpretations, perceptions, beliefs and values—almost for every reason imaginable—then the relevant people should be involved.

When to involve people?

Almost everyone reading this book will have a good example of when something described as *consultation about a change* was simply an information-giving exercise about a decision that had already been made and was not subject to any alteration. When you are seeking to *consult* people about a strategic issue then it is *only* a valid involvement in the process if you approach them before the decision has been made.

How should people be involved?

One of the authors recently supervised a research project that examined the way in which a major change was communicated to a blue-collar part-time workforce. The research identified a strong preference amongst this group of staff for face-to-face communication involving their own line managers. Official documents and 'paper-based forms of communication' were less popular.

In your own personal life, using the example of a housing move, how would you consult your 6-year-old child, your partner or spouse and your solicitor? Quite possibly you would involve them in different ways. The solicitor would prefer paper-based communication to ensure a clear record is kept. Your child would probably want to have his/her say based upon physically seeing the possible new home. As a manager you need to be sensitive about the communication preference of different people and groups of staff. (Refer back to Chapter 2 for more detail here.)

Some examples

Consider the following decisions (all of which could be arguably strategic in their implications):

- Whether to move from contract cleaners to resourcing your own cleaning department.
- Whether to make the office a no-smoking zone.
- How to invest the company pension fund.

The first decision obviously affects a number of people, but what is most important is obtaining the necessary information about the available options. It is certainly not the sort of thing that many organizations would *put to the vote*. Rather the decision would probably be based upon a cost–benefit analysis. However, without seeking the information from appropriate staff and managers it is unlikely that any sort of balanced decision could be made. Given contract notice periods it may be necessary to consult people well in advance of the actual decision date.

The second decision is one that affects all of the people who work in the organization. It also may impact upon people who visit—such as customers or suppliers. Therefore there would need to be a careful and thorough consultation. Even if it was agreed, there might need to be special arrangements made for people who are smokers.

The third decision also affects all the people who work in the organization. However, it would be impractical to consult all the staff about specialized and fairly complex investment decisions. The pension fund has trustees who are expected to monitor these on behalf of the staff. Nevertheless, the sad experience of the Mirror Group pensioners demonstrated the importance of the involvement of trustees who focus on the interests of the pension fund membership.

THE APPLICATION TO DECISION-MAKING

Strategic thinking is just that—thinking about strategy. Conan Doyle's famous detective, Sherlock Holmes, had a brother called Mycroft. Sherlock Holmes comments that Mycroft possesses the greater intellect but is indifferent to whether any action takes place. He would rather be considered wrong than to invest the energy in proving his case.

Henry Mintzberg (1994) reported a survey in *Fortune* magazine, which suggested that less than 10% of strategies are successfully implemented. Other management *gurus* see it as much less than this!

One of the authors spent some time in the early 1980s with a group of health service planners. The planners gave an account of how they conscientiously drew up strategic planning documents, which then were filed away in cupboards.

This can be contrasted with a more recent (1997) discussion with a colleague who had spent time consulting with a medium-sized company about strategic issues. After a couple of days of intense discussion the colleague produced a full and detailed report for the chief executive. The chief executive requested a much briefer document avoiding the detail. Within a day this had been transformed into succinct decisions that were communicated throughout the organization in terms of time constraints and measurable targets.

The point about taking a strategic perspective is that it has an impact upon the decisions that you take either as an individual or as part of an organization. Sometimes the conscious decision not to act (or react) is as important.

Allegedly when John Major took over from Margaret Thatcher as Prime Minister he was reported to have asked, when confronted with an issue, 'What if we do nothing?' This was a very significant change from his predecessor. To some this may be perceived as a weakness, yet we would argue that it is not necessarily the case. The history of his predecessor had the example of the poll tax change where she had determined upon a course of action despite major opposition from cabinet colleagues.

You can, as an individual, assess your career and likely prospects. As a result, you may conclude that your knowledge base is out of date and that your prospects in your current organization are limited and precarious. This should lead you to take decisions over what to do about it. The option of 'What if I do nothing?' has a clear (and presumably undesired) consequence in this case? (Refer to Chapter 10 for the *consideration of decision options* where it is addressed in some detail.)

THE IMPLEMENTATION OF DECISIONS

A key element of the strategic perspective is actually carrying out decisions, which emerge through the process of strategic analysis and reflection. As we mentioned previously, many strategies fail in their implementation.

Chapter 4, which is concerned with *focusing upon results*, is relevant to your understanding and development of implementing strategic decisions. Managers are rarely able to achieve change on their own, so winning the active involvement of staff and colleagues is critical.

Often, however, it is very useful to demonstrate that a decision is being implemented through personal example.

Doing the easiest first

When Heather Rabbetts was appointed chief executive of the London Borough of Lambeth, she took on what had been described as the worst job in local government. Previous chief executives had left in frustration and many saw the organization as almost beyond help. There was no lack of advice about what was wrong—the problem lay in implementing change. Ms Rabbetts identified some areas where it was possible to visibly implement change. One was in ensuring that the broken light bulbs in the public areas of housing estates were replaced. Two staff members were given this specific task to complete. It was, on the face of it, a relatively simple and minor task. However, the fact that the chief executive ensured that it was implemented sent out a powerful message both within and outside the organization.

THE ALLOCATION OF RESOURCES

In many organizations there is a natural inertia. It is demonstrated by the stock answer to the question 'Why are we doing this the way that we do?' The stock answer is 'Because we have always done it this way'.

When a strategic change occurs in an organization—or in an individual—it is often accompanied by a change in the way that resources are allocated. If you are undertaking some kind of management qualification, then it is quite likely that you will have had to decide to reallocate your own personal resources. If you have to meet the financial cost yourself—at least in part—then you may have had to change your spending or saving pattern. This would be a re-allocation of financial resources. You will have had to make a commitment of personal time to the course. This commitment may well involve reducing the time that you spend on other activities—hobbies and sports, for example. You may have had to reschedule work activities or obtain resources such as a computer in order to complete your planned course.

In short, your strategic decision has a resource implication mostly for you but also for your organization. It is a source of interest to us that organizations (particularly in the public sector) are sometimes prepared to give a manager a day off a week for a management course but regard the cost of the course as not within their resources.

The commitment and use of resources represents one of the most important managerial responsibilities. It sends a powerful message to organizational stakeholders. A strategic decision that is accompanied by a resource decision has a much greater probability of being implemented. Sir John Harvey-Jones, when he visited a major hospital trust during the *Troubleshooter* series on TV, stressed the importance of keeping resourcing promises. Hospital managers had encouraged senior hospital doctors to put forward initiatives to improve services. However, these initiatives had not been resourced in the budget. John Harvey-Jones commented to the new hospital chief executive that when a manager had made a promise then it was essential to deliver upon it.

THE USE OF PLANNING

We have covered the issues of practical planning activities in Chapter 4. Strategic planning in the sense of a highly structured exercise has been criticized by Henry Mintzberg, who suggests that there are a number of possible uses for planning in terms of adopting a strategic perspective.

First, planning represents *thinking about the future*. In this respect it is arguable that all managers engage in this, so Mintzberg suggests that this does not distinguish planning for the everyday managerial role.

Second, planning can be seen as *controlling the future*. This, to some extent, is also synonymous with management activity since much of a manager's time is spent on trying to forestall or head off undesirable future possibilities and encourage or enable desirable ones. In short, a good manager engages in *fire prevention* as opposed to simply fighting fires as they flare.

Third, planning can be viewed as *decision-making*. Mintzberg argues that planning as decision-making is akin to future thinking because decision-making is always undertaken with some view to the future. The more cynical reader may, however; observe that decision-making is sometimes undertaken simply to avoid the consequences of the past!

Fourth, planning could be regarded as *integrated decision-making*. This is a more sophisticated view of the manager's role that encompasses making commitments and realizing that individual decisions impact upon each other.

Finally, planning can be described as a formalized procedure to produce an articulated result in the form of an integrated system of decisions. Here the concept of planning is akin to the ideal model of planning envisaged by writers in the 1960s and 1970s. Stages are set out and the parts all fit together like a complex engineering diagram.

Which of these views of strategic planning is best? Arguably it all depends upon the nature of your organization and its environment. There is little point in engaging in long-drawn-out and sophisticated planning procedures where you have a dramatically and rapidly changing environment. Many miners thought that the government's planning document *A Plan for Coal* offered an assurance of the survival of their industry. They were sadly mistaken. On the other hand, there are some aspects of the economy where change is more predictable and longer-term plans can be made. The major utilities such as water are able to plan with a high degree of confidence that the consumer will still desire their product.

MONITORING PROGRESS

Some years ago a television documentary followed a number of young managers in various industries. One of the managers was responsible for an *up-market* fast-food restaurant. He was asked in the programme what was the secret of successful management. He responded that there were three keys to success, and they were, 'Follow-up, follow-up and follow-up'.

There are some organizations where employees do the right thing and can be simply left alone to get on with the job. Arguably, such an organization should be disposing of most, if not all, its managers.

In the public sector the advent of compulsory competitive tendering was seen by some as meaning that staff supervision was no longer needed since the requirements were all set out in the contract. The supervisor no longer had to make sure that the workers were digging holes since the *hole-digging* was contracted out.

However, the old saying 'What gets measured gets done' can be rewritten as 'What gets monitored gets done'. Some activities are more easily monitored than others. One of the authors worked, while a student, for an organization that delivered leaflets. Some of the leaflet deliverers knew that the organization only checked certain streets to ensure that the leaflets had been delivered. High-rise flats and less desirable areas were not checked. So these deliverers would only deliver leaflets to the areas that they knew would be checked and simply dropped the leaflets intended for the other areas into skips. This was at odds with the strategy (and contract) of the leafleting company and its corporate customers. However, because the monitoring was inadequate the delivery workers cut corners.

EXERCISE

Take this opportunity to plan, implement and monitor the progress of a change strategy for your own organization (or personal 'strategy') as appropriate.

LEADERSHIP AND STRATEGY

Chapter 2 looks at leadership in some detail, but to bring it round to leading strategic change it might be helpful to discuss some particular skills required of the *strategic leader*.

Where strategy is concerned, often a particular kind of leadership is required.

Square pegs in square holes?

A famous army general once commented that he saw his officers along two dimensions: the degree of energy and the degree of intelligence they possessed. The intelligent and energetic he made into commanders of brigades (large parts of the army) since they would not only carry out orders but would also exercise initiative in how they implemented them. The intelligent and the lazy he kept as staff officers in his headquarters since they could be relied upon to find shortcuts to avoid the expenditure of unnecessary energy. The less intelligent but energetic he entrusted with smaller roles in the field of battle since they could be relied upon to carry out their orders. Finally, the least intelligent and most lazy he sought to get rid of.

The example illustrates the point that leadership involves making judgements. These judgements may in some cases be wrong. Good leaders will recognize this and be honest about their mistakes.

There are two aspects of leadership that are key to success in leading strategic change. First, a manager who has won no respect from the workforce is likely to find it almost impossible to achieve major change. Respect is not the same as being liked. Respect is not something that can be conferred like a company car or a new office desk. It has to be earned by the manager. A significant factor in whether respect is earned is whether the manager behaves ethically. Unscrupulous, devious and deceitful behaviour may have a short-term pay-off. However, in the longer term, it is likely to rebound on the manager. Even in the Mafia the term 'a man of respect' had an implication other than that of a propensity to violence.

Second, a manager must provide an example to others. If the factory has been flooded by a burst-pipe, then the manager must be willing literally to wade in and lend a hand. In strategic terms, this means that, where a major change is being sought, then the manager must take the initiative and demonstrate the ability to *change* also to gain credibility. This can rebound, as a top water company manager found when he advocated, by personal example, being frugal in water usage. Unfortunately, the press found that he was going to a relative's house and using their bath.

Working through this material will not turn you into a company strategic manager. Hopefully, it will encourage you to think more strategically and where your job involves a strategic perspective you will find useful guidance. At various points we have referred you to other chapters in this book. This chapter should not be read in isolation. The suggested *further reading* at the end of the chapter is especially important if you wish to explore the techniques further or seek alternative methods.

It is important to stress that *a strategic perspective* can be held irrespective of position within an organization. The examples we have sought to use have, at times, been independent of whether you hold a management role.

However, if you are a manager, then do remember that, if your role influences the strategic direction of your organization, you have a particular responsibility to exercise that role as skilfully and conscientiously as you can.

SUMMARY OF ISSUES

In working through this chapter, you will have encountered a number of issues and perhaps some ideas that are new to you. The objectives of the chapter were to:

- Introduce strategy and the manager.
- Discuss ways to examine the environment.
- Introduce methods to assess the organization.
- Show how to implement decisions.

How well have the authors met these objectives?

More importantly, how have you approached and used the material yourself, and how much have you developed since the beginning of your course of study, or working through the chapter? You are strongly recommended to extend your research and study to include as much as possible of the material identified in further reading and references below, so that you can build on your expertise, incorporating more complex approaches and ideas as you develop further in your managerial role.

These objectives, if re-revisited over a period of time and put into practice in your job, should help you to achieve the personal competency of maintaining a strategic perspective, broken down into the elements identified in the table at the end of this chapter.

PREPARING FOR ACTION PLANNING

In order for you to reflect on your own behaviour and that of others with whom you work, you might find it useful to use the self-assessment check at the end of this chapter (reproduce as many as you wish) to re-evaluate your skills and knowledge.

Remember to review the checklist of questions, as identified in the Introduction to this book, at Appendix 1.

Analyse your own behaviour in terms of strengths (positive outcomes) and weaknesses (negative effects), in dealing with actual work-based occurrences with regards to the various situations discussed in this chapter and summarized above.

Decide how you might deal with them differently in the future and what are your immediate training requirements and future development needs.

Discuss them with appropriate others and negotiate how you might address them.

FURTHER READING AND REFERENCES

Blaxter, L, Hughes, C. and Tight, M. (2001) *How to Research* (2nd edition). Buckingham: Open University Press. ISBN: 0-335-20903-3

Blundell, B. and Murdock, A. (1997) *Managing in the Public Sector.* Oxford: Butterworth Heinemann. ISBN: 0-75062-195-8

Drucker, P.F. (1987) *The Frontiers of Management: Where Tomorrow's Decisions are Being Shaped Today.* London: Heinemann Professional Publishing. ISBN: 0-434-90392-2

Drucker, P.F. (1992) *Managing for the Future.* Oxford: Butterworth Heinemann. ISBN: 0-7506-0492-1

Grant, R. (1995) *Contemporary Strategic Analysis*, 2/e. Oxford: Blackwell. ISBN: 0-63126-780-5

Johnson, G. and Scholes, K. (2002) *Exploring Corporate Strategy: Text and Cases* (3rd edition). Hemel Hempstead: Prentice Hall. ISBN: 0-273-65117-X

Joyce, P. and Woods, A. (2001) *Strategic Management: A Fresh Approach to Developing Skills, Knowledge and Creativity.* London: Kogan Page. ISBN: 0-7494-3583-6

Kanter, R.M. (1990) *The Change Masters: Corporate Entrepreneurs at Work*. London: Unwin. ISBN: 0-04-658244-4

Kitchen, N. (2002) *Leading your People to Success*. Maidenhead: McGraw-Hill. ISBN: 0-07-709869-2

Kotler, P. (1984) *Marketing Management: Analysis, Planning and Control* (5th edition). Englewood Cliffs: Prentice Hall. ISBN: 0-13-558024-2

Mintzberg, H. (1994) *The Rise and Fall of Strategic Planning*. Hemel Hempstead: Prentice Hall. ISBN: 0-13781824-6

Perkins, S.J. (1999) *Globalization the People Dimension: Human Resource Strategies for Global Expansion*. London: Kogan Page. ISBN: 0-7494-3124-5

Slack, N. and Lewis, M. (2002) *Operations Strategy*. Harlow: Pearson Education. ISBN: 0-273-63781-9

Recommended journal articles

Leggett, B. (2000) Getting the sound to match the vision. *The Guardian* 12/08/2000

Longenecker, C.O. and Fink, L.S. (2001) Improving management performance in rapidly changing organisations. *Journal of Management Development* 20 (1): 7–18. Bradford: MCB University Press. ISSN: 1366-5626. Website: http://www.emerald-library.com

Parsloe, E. (2001) Searching for standards: defining a professional framework. *Training Journal* December: 10–12. Bradford: MCB University Press. ISSN: 1465-6523. Website: http://www.emerald-library.com

Competency element	Competency level: 1 (low)– 5 (high)	Requires development	No direct experience	What can help? (identify oppor- tunities)	Who can help?	When can it be achieved?	How can it be achieved?
Displays an understanding of how the different parts of the organization and its environment fit together							
Works towards a clearly defined vision of the future							
Clearly relates goals and actions to the strategic aims of the organization							
Takes opportunities when they arise to achieve the longer term aims or needs of the organization							

Thinking and decision-taking

Managers displaying thinking and decision-making skills analyse and make deductions from information in order to form judgements and take decisions.

LINKS TO THE CHARTERED MANAGEMENT INSTITUTE'S MODULE

This chapter aims to address the aims and learning outcomes as identified in the Introduction to this text under the heading *Links to the Chartered Management Institute's Module 'Understanding Yourself'*. However, this chapter, whilst supporting the module, stands in addition to the material covered within it.

INTRODUCING THE RELATIONSHIP BETWEEN THE PERSONAL COMPETENCY MODEL AND THINKING AND DECISION

The Personal Competency Model (PCM), as already discussed, identifies the behaviours and skills that are necessary for you to develop before you are able to prove competence in any managerial function.

This chapter attempts to deal with the various behaviours and skills that are necessary for you to apply across all managerial functions, transferring your learning to different occasions, at different times and under varying circumstances (contexts), consistently.

The outcomes below, as identified within this section of the model, should be borne in mind while you work through this chapter.

Outcomes required in thinking and decision-making

There are three major sets of behaviour to this chapter. The first is the manager's ability in *analysing*. When analysing, the manager:

■ Breaks situations down into simple tasks and activities.
■ Identifies a range of elements in and perspectives on a situation.
■ Identifies implications, consequences or causal relationships in a situation.
■ Uses a range of ideas to explain the actions, needs and motives of others.

The second behavioural set focuses on the manager's need for *conceptualizing* in order to make decisions. In this process, the manager:

■ Uses her/his own experience and evidence from others to identify problems and understand situations.
■ Identifies patterns or meaning from events and data that are not obviously related.
■ Builds a total and valid picture (or concept) from restricted or incomplete data (which happens to be most of the time).

The third set of behaviours addresses a manager's *judgement and decision-making* abilities. When forming judgements and making decisions, the manager:

■ Produces a variety of solutions before taking a decision.
■ Balances intuition with logic in decision-making.
■ Reconciles and makes use of a variety of perspectives when making sense of a situation.
■ Produces his/her own ideas from experience and practice.
■ Takes the experience and practice of others into account.
■ Takes decisions that are realistic for the situation.

- Focuses on facts, problems and solutions when handling an emotional situation (not personalities).
- Takes decisions in uncertain situations, or based on restricted information when necessary.

INTRODUCTION AND OBJECTIVES

The objectives are to:

- Present an overview of the problem-solving notion.
- Discuss ways to generate *creative* thought.
- Define vertical and lateral thinking and discuss their uses and value.
- Present some convergent and divergent problem-solving strategies.
- Discuss the value of participate decision-making.

Thinking, or communicating with oneself, is something we naturally do more unconsciously than consciously. It is such an automatic process that, unless we have become aware and educate ourselves accordingly, much of our thinking can be wasted. It is the purest form of *communicating* and does not necessarily involve language. If we are thinking in a structured way, we undoubtedly use our mother language in order to proceed logically in our thinking. When unstructured thoughts come to us, they can be in the form of pictures, symbols, even quite complicated conundrums at times. We frequently ignore or dismiss them as irrelevant to our present need.

There are times when our random, unstructured thinking is of extreme value; hence the increasing use of brainstorming exercises. It is not so easy to *brainstorm* as some people may believe. We are all concerned, in one way or another, about our individual abilities to do what is right, our credibility in the eyes of others, fear of looking stupid and so on.

We should learn to trust our own thinking more and share random thoughts with others in the workplace. It is a wonderful way of gaining trust and support, because this is a way of refining and developing ideas and issues—allowing the contribution of others to influence our values, beliefs and behaviour. Our own self-guilt often prevents our development of good thinking and communicating with ourselves.

This chapter will introduce you to problem-solving and decision-making. You may have considerable experience in solving problems and making decisions. Managers are expected to do this. However, the problem-solving and decision-making methods used may be ineffectual or otherwise inappropriate.

Management writers argue about the relationship between problem-solving and decision-making. Some claim that problem-solving is part of decision-making. Others feel the reverse is true and argue that decision-making is part of problem-solving. There are those who feel that problem-solving and decision-making should be seen as *similar terms* to describe the same process.

Here the view adopted is to see them both as part of a process. The focus of the most of this chapter is on the concept of a problem that has to be identified, understood and solved. The end of the chapter draws together the *analysis*, *conceptualization* and *thinking* undergone in the process of solving problems, allowing the manager to then *make decisions* about what to do, who to involve and how to effectively communicate for action.

AN OVERVIEW OF PROBLEM-SOLVING

One problem after another

Consider a day in the life of Sandy Jones, a manager, in terms of a succession of problems encountered. As you read the problems confronting Sandy, consider what your reaction might be.

- Sandy learns from the news that the train services are delayed, creating a problem in getting to work for an 8.30 a.m. meeting.
- On arriving at work, Sandy has to cover for the absence of a senior colleague who has been taken ill.
- Sandy receives a letter from an aggrieved customer complaining about poor service.
- Sandy's boss discovers that all the managers wish to take holidays in August and asks Sandy to come up with some ideas in response to this.
- The telephone bills run up by Sandy's section are twice as high as for the same time last year. The finance manager calls Sandy about it.

Before reading any further take a sheet of paper and write down your reactions. If you have a colleague or friend available, share the problems with them then compare your reactions with theirs.

Some of Sandy's problems might require an immediate solution. Others might be satisfactorily resolved with investigation. Some may not have any obvious solution. Some, on reflection and investigation, may not be problems at all!

It is not the nature of the solutions themselves that you propose, which is of interest as much as whether you actually propose any at all.

Sandy's reaction to the first problem almost certainly would be based upon personal knowledge and experience. Perhaps Sandy has an alternative to using the train. A telephone message could be passed to the person chairing the meeting. Possibly the meeting may be postponed. After all, other people attending the meeting may also be affected by the travel delays.

The second problem would require Sandy to establish what the colleague had scheduled for the day; Sandy would need to find this out from the colleague or those familiar with his/her schedule. Perhaps some of the responsibility could be delegated. If the colleague had a tight schedule then Sandy may well have to rearrange priorities and postpone meetings. Sandy may be quite familiar with her sick colleague's work and work contacts, or she may not be.

The letter of complaint could require urgent investigation. Much would depend upon the context and the expectations of the organization. If the organization was well used to receiving complaints it may be almost a routine response. On the other hand, the company may be concerned about any complaint because of the quality standards or the nature of the product. In such an organization complaints may have the highest priority and be handled at quite a senior level.

The situation of holiday leave is one where there is likely to be different priorities in operation. The managers' interests may differ from that of the organization.

The use of the telephone may not in fact represent a problem. However, in order to establish this Sandy would need to provide information to explain why the bill had gone up. Possibly Sandy's organization does a lot of telephone selling and the usage is a sign of an active sales-force. Alternatively, it could represent a lack of control over resources, or even deliberate abuse of resources by staff making many personal calls.

How did you respond to Sandy's problems? Did you see them in terms of your own particular experience, work-setting or work habits. If so, then your response could probably have led you to propose

solutions. This would not be an uncommon reaction in managers who are *hands-on* and proactive. This could be said to be more characteristic of an *activist* or *pragmatist learning style* as identified by Honey and Mumford (see Chapter 8).

On the other hand, if your reaction was to ask questions to elicit more information, then you were possibly reacting in a way less dependent upon your work-setting, experience or habits. The reluctance to *rush to judgement* associated with the desire to acquire more (and more) information can be associated with the r*eflector* or *theorist learning styles*.

You may have realized that some of the problems Sandy confronts are more amenable to team discussion than others. Similarly, some have tight time constraints. The first problem, for example, requires Sandy to react quite quickly or accept the consequences of *non-action*. Apologizing after the meeting for failing to attend is less appropriate than communicating reasons for non-attendance in advance.

Some of the problems may not be problems at all. The higher telephone usage may be an inevitable result of staff doing their work effectively. The absent colleague may have had no commitments scheduled for that day.

Some of the problems may not have any obvious solutions. There may not be any possibility of building a consensus to accept a solution because those involved have incompatible and opposing priorities. The intention of all managers to take leave at the same time may fall into this category; however, most people, given encouragement and support, are more likely to sort out these issues for themselves. Committed and dedicated staff members are themselves unlikely to be satisfied with everyone taking leave at the same time.

Some of the problems could be extremely serious. If the company made very high-value products where failure was seen as having life-threatening and/or high-cost implications, then a complaint would be taken very seriously. An aircraft manufacturer, for example, would take extremely seriously a complaint that vital parts of the airplane were failing.

How to categorize problems

There is a wide range of ways to categorize problems. Here are several ways that you may find helpful in thinking about problems you encounter in your work and home life.

Tudor Rickards (1990) uses the following set of categories:

- *'One right answer' problems* We are all familiar with these. What is 15% of 100 invites the answer '15'. You would justifiably argue with someone proposing a different solution. There is often a considerable element of creativity involved in finding the answer to such problems. The livelihood of crossword puzzle compilers relies on this.
- *Insight problems* Here the answer comes from a new perspective. This involves an element of creative thinking. We have all been there at some time. Anyone who has locked themselves out of their car or house has probably tried to think creatively about how to get in without the key. The account of Archimedes arriving at an insight in his bath is an example. He was trying to work out how much gold was in a crown. He knew the weight of the crown but was unable to work out the volume. It was necessary to have both the weight and volume of the crown in order to know whether it was pure gold. As he sat down in his bath he realized the water level rose and he could use the displaced water to measure the volume of an object.
- *Wicked problems* The success of the solution requires that it be tried out. Is the reason the light will not work a defective bulb, a blown fuse, or the lack of a power supply? One way to find out is to test for each possible cause in turn. It may well be a combination rather than one single cause. More commonly it occurs in organizations when a solution has to be tried out in order to see if it will solve the problem. Restructuring and re-organization are examples of this.

The introduction of water metering on the Isle of Wight some years ago was an attempt to try out a possible solution to the various problems of water supply and rationing. The concept of paying for the amount of water you use is seen as something that has to be tried out in practice. The views of experts or the results of consumer surveys would not be regarded as sufficient to support the massive cost implications of changing over a substantial part of the country. There is also the consumer reaction to be considered. A number of water supply companies have since introduced metering across the UK.

■ *Vicious problems* A problem may seem to have a straightforward answer but the human element adds a complication. The presence of outmoded and costly work practices in both the newspaper industry and in the car industry challenged managers for many years. The solutions might have seemed obvious but the industrial relations implications were enormous. There is scope for what Tudor Rickards calls 'lose:lose' behaviours in which those affected by the problems all end up worse off.

> The UK coal dispute in the 1980s offers an example where there was, from the management perspective, a clear need to rationalize the coal industry and make it more competitive. However, the perspective of many of the miners was of a threat to whole communities and a way of life. In hindsight we may well look back and wonder how it got to the stage of such entrenched positions. Surely there must be a more positive way of settling disputes and bringing about necessary change without so much suffering and ill-feeling?

■ *Fuzzy problems* Here the problem is difficult to solve because straightforward logic cannot be easily applied. An example is the attempt to computerize mail services by using computers to *read* addresses on envelopes. It works reasonably well with typed envelopes but handwritten addresses pose a major challenge. The machine can process the envelopes far more quickly than the human operator can. Yet the human operator is able to categorize the handwritten addresses.

■ The way the Post Office resolved this problem was to install a video camera facility, which took a picture of each address the machine could not read. The letters were fed through the machine in batches and the human operator fed in the correct code for the letters whose addresses were highlighted on a video screen. The computer remembered the order of the letters in the batch. So the batch of letters could be passed through the machine a second time for the handwritten addresses to be machine-coded using the information keyed in by the human operator. While the human operator was keying in the correct information, the machine could be processing other batches of letters.

It is worth noting that a problem can occupy more than one category. A fuzzy problem may also be a wicked one for example.

Problems can also be seen as existing along dimensions rather than in separate categories. Here are some examples of such dimensions:

Straightforward——————————————— Complex

A straightforward problem usually can be identified because there is sufficient knowledge as to what would constitute a solution and the problem has clear boundaries. Concerns about the risks of early electrically operated car windows to small children would be an example. Although manufacturers have since installed the necessary safeguards, government legislation to require all manufacturers to do it would have constituted a solution had it been necessary.

A complex problem often has no obvious solution and may be unbounded (*soft*—involving wide ranges of thinking and involvement of others, as opposed to bounded or *hard*—mostly factual and logical with clear and obvious routes to take). An example of an unbounded problem would be the congestion of road traffic in large inner-city areas. It is argued that building more roads just leads to more cars followed by more congestion. Improving public transport on the other hand has been seen as requiring enormous investment, and although many authorities are now developing better infrastructures for public transport, including *park and ride* facilities, many people still prefer to bring their cars into the cities.

Traffic congestion problems are further complicated by the wide range of reasons for travel, including the need to move goods and freight, known these days as *logistics*. The way the problem is *defined* can create the complexity. Transport is related to how and where people work. It is hard to put a precise boundary around *transport* without looking at patterns of change in work generally.

Not technical———————————————Highly technical

A non-technical problem is one that is readily understood and solvable by a 'lay person'—i.e. someone who has no particular technical or professional training. We handle such problems all the time in our everyday lives: where to go shopping, when to take a holiday, who to invite to your office leaving party and so on.

Technical problems, on the other hand, require a level of technical or professional training or experience in order to arrive at a solution.

When your dentist inspects a cavity in a tooth, she/he makes a judgement about whether a filling is suitable or whether a more radical solution is indicated. Similarly, the experienced plumber might know from listening to that worrying groan in your central heating system whether your boiler requires a part to be replaced or simply a routine service. When you pay for technical advice you are often paying a premium for the training or experience that enables the person to diagnose the problem.

Hence, the oft-quoted account of the service engineer who fixes a domestic appliance by tapping it with a hammer. The customer queries the bill of £30, so the engineer divides the bill into two parts:

- £1 for tapping the appliance with a hammer.
- £29 for the 10 years' knowledge and experience which enabled me to know how hard to tap and where to tap.

Some problems have a high emotional content. They arouse strong feelings in those involved and sometimes in those not directly involved. Charities involved in famine relief are well aware of the powerful images created by pictures of starving children. The issues associated with adoption of Romanian babies were both complex and highly emotional, as is the more recent issue of refugees illegally entering the country. Managers often use a shorthand phrase to describe *emotionally charged* problems. They call them *people problems*. What is important is to be aware of the limitations of strict logic in the resolution of such problems.

Emotionally charged————Not emotionally charged

There are some problems that have little emotional content. They sometimes involve little personal involvement. The selection of your lunchtime sandwich might be an example. Others may require enormous effort and commitment to resolve, such as the various ethnic food options and individual dietary needs to be considered when planning a staff canteen. The conduct of scientific research would be another example.

Sometimes it can be helpful to use two dimensions to create a box or graph in which to locate problems. This may show, for example, that, of a range of technical problems, some are highly emotionally charged and thus need to be handled differently. The diagram in Figure 10.1 represents examples of how four typical office problems could fit into the categories.

Technical	Repair of office equipment	Introduction of new technology
Non-technical	Agreement on lunch rota	Staff re-organization
	Not emotionally charged	**Emotionally charged**

Figure 10.1 Using boxes to categorize problems.

The use of simple devices such as this to define and present problems can be of great value to the manager in trying to understand the nature of a problem. They also can serve as a useful communication tool in consulting with staff about workplace problems. The box diagram in Figure 10.1 could be used to show staff that uncertainty and unease over re-organization is in a different category from the lunch rota or getting equipment repaired. All problems can become emotionally charged if badly handled. Thus the agreement over the lunch rota could become an emotional one if, for instance, it was not being dealt with openly and honestly and that an ulterior motive was being pursued.

EXERCISE

Take a current or recent situation from your own working environment, or one with which you are familiar, where a problem emerged and analyse into which category or categories it fitted. Did you ask enough questions before making judgements? How might you deal with such a situation in the future?

CREATIVE THINKING

Creative thinking is the relating of things or ideas that were previously unrelated. People often feel that a problem has a *single correct answer*. This viewpoint leads to a narrowing down of options. Narrowing down does not promote creativity.

John Rawlinson (1981) distinguishes between analytical and creative thought:

- *Analytical thought*:
  - Relies on logic.
  - Aims to come up with only a few answers (or only one answer).
  - Is convergent in that it aims to narrow down the range of possibilities.

- Is vertical (see below).
- Uses various techniques to close down the range of options (see below).

You will see this exemplified in the problem-solving approach of Kepner and Tregoe (1981) later in this chapter.

- *Creative thought*:
  - Uses imagination.
  - Seeks many possible answers or ideas.
  - Is divergent in that it aims to open up the range of possibilities.
  - Is lateral (see below).
  - Uses various techniques to open up the range of options. One of these techniques is brainstorming described later in this chapter.

In practice, a combination of both analytical and creative thought is usually required.

What is associated with creativity?

Henry Mintzberg (1973) and others have noted that an understanding of how the brain functions is important to understanding why people seem able to cope with some mental activities but not others. In particular, Mintzberg wonders why it is that top managers often seem impervious to the sophisticated techniques of planning that they have available to them.

The brain is divided into two distinct hemispheres. Over-simplified you can think of it as an orange split into two halves. Each hemisphere controls movement on the opposite side of the body (left-brain, right-body; right-brain, left-body). The left side of the brain controls such mental processes as speech; therefore, stroke victims can suffer major speech impairment as a result of a stroke affecting the left hemisphere of the brain.

Research suggests that because there is specialization between the two halves of the brain in respect of thought processes it can be determined that the left side of the brain thinks in a logical fashion, and because speech is a logical ordering of sound it is a left-brain activity. The right side of the brain, on the other hand, tends to think more in visual images, is more creative and can *challenge* the logic of the left-brain. Here the way information is handled is more in terms of relationships and the broader picture rather than in terms of a logical sequence.

Therefore certain types of intellectual activity, such as understanding mathematical logic, are of a left-brain focus. Other activities such as the creation of a picture or design of an advertising logo are primarily right-brain activities.

Formal planning activities in management using scientific or logical techniques are left-brain-oriented. When you follow the bakery problem later in the chapter, using the Kempner–Tregoe (1981) technique, you will be using the left side of your brain. However, practising managers often operate intuitively. This usually comes from experience. They recognize that problems are rarely amenable to strict logic and that we live in an imperfect world; hence, the need to use the right brain in managerial activity.

Mintzberg (1973) illustrates the 'right-brain tendencies' of managers from the following findings of his research:

Managers tend to favour verbal over written communication. This is because it enables a whole picture to be formed. The tone of voice and type of expression adds to the image.

Much of the analysis managers undertake is not of hard numerical data but rather of fuzzy and more opinionated information. The organization grapevine is a source that managers are prone to use as much, if not more, than anyone else.

Managers often find it hard to pass information down to people. Yet in order to delegate work this has to be done. A possible explanation is that managers rely on the right side of the brain but the source of the information is logical and held on the left side.

Managers work in short bursts of activity encompassing considerable variety. Longer-paced orderly and logically planned activities tend to be the exception.

There are a number of managerial roles Mintzberg identifies. He regards the most important as being 'leader', 'liaison' and 'disturbance handler'. These roles are often based upon experience and intuition rather than the application of logically based research findings.

When managers engage in decision-making there are parts of the process that often involve the use of intuition. The manager uses the right side of the brain in the diagnosis of what is going wrong and in designing customized solutions.

There are aspects of the decision process where unpredictable factors have an impact. Issues such as the timing of a decision and the 'right atmosphere' for a change are often subject to intuitive feelings rather than logical thought processes.

When managers come to make a choice between options, the method most used is judgement. The application of rational analysis is less frequently used. The implication is that intuition and 'right-brain thinking' play a significant role.

Managers confront not the stable and predictable world that planning would wish to cater for, but rather they have to deal with an unpredictable and turbulent environment. The strict application of logical thought is in itself not sufficient for a manager to survive.

Mintzberg suggests that strategic vision in organizations is often located within one person.

Barriers to creative thought

The potential value in creative thinking in managers can be stifled because of obstacles, which are often self-imposed. We have limits to our thinking, which arise from constraints we consciously or unconsciously impose upon ourselves.

This is the kind of person who searches for a lost object in the knowledge that they are looking in the wrong place but are hopelessly tied to a different kind of logic. Hence the classic story of the person looking for a dropped key under a street-light when he or she has dropped the key in the shadows. The reason for looking under the street-light is that 'It is easier to see what you are looking for'.

This has been observed in managers who have found particular solutions that have worked in previous situations and cling to them even when they are less appropriate to the problems at hand. The effect is to limit the managers' search to particular areas.

As an example consider the following:

$$1 + 0 =$$

Most people would react immediately with '1'. However, when thinking creatively the option of '10' is also possible. If the inclination to view 1 and 0 as numbers, in the logical traditionally accepted sense, is resisted and + is viewed creatively, the possibility of 'in and out' occurs.

If 1 and 0 are simply seen as geometric shapes, then a wide variety of ways to combine them becomes apparent, making a range of both familiar and unfamiliar shapes (tree, child's top, eye with eyelid, etc.).

Patterns

We often use particular patterns as a way of forming our thought process. Although useful, these patterns can impede creativity.

As an example consider the following:

1, 4, 7, 11, 14, 17 ...

Which is next in the sequence: 21 or 41? Many people opt for '21' by seeing the sequence as a mathematical progression. However, if the pattern is seen in terms of numbers made up only of straight lines, then the next number in the sequence is 41 (only straight lines).

Consider the next letter in this sequence:

F, G, H ...
I or J?

Conformity

A large proportion of people have a natural tendency to avoid *standing out from the crowd*. This can be an obstruction to creativity.

A famous industrial manager, Alfred Sloan, had convened a meeting of his managers to review some proposals that had been made. He asked if any of the managers had any problems about the proposals and received a reply that none had. Whereupon he adjourned the meeting until such time as the managers had found some problems with the proposals.

Not challenging the obvious

The perception of a problem is often based upon an assumption that has to be challenged in order for a creative solution to emerge. During World War II, Barnes Wallis invented a number of new and highly effective bombs. One assumption made by many people that he challenged was that one had to hit the target in order to destroy it. Some of the fortifications in question were believed impregnable to direct hits. Wallis conceived of destroying them by near misses, which would undermine the foundations.

Jump to judgement

There is often a willingness to rush to a solution before the various dimensions of the problem have been fully explored. This involves *closing off* the options at too early a stage.

> The concern about meeting the needs of elderly people, for example, led to the rapid expansion of facilities such as residential homes, nursing homes and day centres. It was assumed that such provision would be the answer to the problem. Experience has shown that the needs of elderly people must be met by a range of resources and that it is often the families of elderly people who need the resource as much as the elderly themselves.

Looking a fool

It is only natural to avoid potential embarrassment. The fear of seeming foolish often stifles creativity. The technique of classic brainstorming outlined later relies upon the suspension of judgement as to the wisdom or foolishness of the generated ideas.

EXERCISE

Based on the discussion above, how might you endeavour to introduce a more creative way of thinking when faced with problems requiring resolution in the future? Take existing or previous examples to help you in this.

VERTICAL AND LATERAL THINKING

Edward de Bono developed the concept of *lateral thinking*. He contrasted it with *vertical thinking*. He maintains that traditional education focuses upon the development of vertical thought processes. It is important to note that although they are two different and distinct types of thought process it does not necessarily follow that they always lead to different outcomes. He views both as important in problem-solving. He distinguishes between *lateral* and *vertical* thinking as shown in Figure 10.2.

An example from de Bono's own younger days was when on an initiative exercise he was in a team of people tasked with using ropes and bits of wood to get across a water-filled hole where de Bono is reported to have suggested that the problem be solved by moving the hole! Lateral and vertical thought are extremely important concepts to understand in problem-solving. Let us consider some examples.

You are going on holiday with your caravan and you arrive at Dover Harbour late at night to catch the early morning ferry. You have no alarm clock and know that you need to sleep. How will you wake up in time to catch the ferry?

A logical (vertical) approach would probably focus upon the possibility of obtaining an alarm clock or securing the help of someone to wake you up in time. The steps would be considered in logical sequence. Try local shops and supermarkets, service stations, etc. Failing that you could see if a local hotel might agree to wake you up for a fee.

Lateral thinking would open up a range of other possibilities. One solution might be to scatter bread on the caravan roof so that birds would come and feed in the early morning. Why not park illegally so that the 'authorities' would make you move?

Lateral thinking	Vertical thinking
Seeks changes	Seeks judgement
Looks for differences	Looks for yes/no answers
Uses information to provoke new ideas	Uses information to analyse what works or does not
Uses intuitive leaps	
Welcomes distraction	Proceeds in logical steps
Follows unlikely avenues	Focuses on what is relevant
Open-ended: no promise of a result	Follows the most likely avenue
	Closed: promises at least a minimal outcome

Figure 10.2 Lateral versus vertical thinking (de Bono, 1996).

> Perhaps you could make an alarm clock by using what you have. A canister dripping water onto another which, when it becomes just so full, will fall over making a noise. What businesses are likely to open up early and generate sufficient noise to awaken you ... perhaps the local dairy? Why park near the docks anyway? Why not drive out and park near a farm so that the farm animals will wake you up?

Special techniques to promote lateral thinking

Awareness

This is awareness of current ideas and what characterizes them. De Bono suggests that the following aspects of current ideas are useful in gaining this understanding.

Dominant ideas

These can determine how the problem or issue is viewed. Different people may hold different dominant ideas about the same issue. Attitude to trade union recognition may vary but is often shaped by dominant ideas about the role of trade unions in society, etc.

Assumptions or tethering factors

Here people often have operating assumptions about the problem. De Bono uses the example that people assume that the longer you park your car the less it should cost per hour. However, if traffic congestion is caused by parked rather than moving traffic then perhaps the rate per hour should increase the longer you park your car.

CONVERGENT AND DIVERGENT PROBLEM-SOLVING STRATEGIES

Problems can generally be divided into two categories. On the one hand, there is the problem that shows itself because something that was expected to occur has not occurred the way in which it was anticipated. Another way of expressing this is as a *deviation* from some standard or expected result. The nature of the problem can be described in terms of this deviation.

Then there are problems where something prevents what you want to happen from taking place. There is an obstacle in the way that has to be overcome. Typically it is associated with a desire to make some kind of change. Here the need is often to generate ideas and options.

The Customer Charter for London Underground (July 1992) states:

'We aim to run 460 trains each peak period. Our target is to run not less than 97.5% of them at the busiest times. Last year we averaged 96.4%. We will show our performance line by line on a poster at every station.'

From this we can infer the following expected results:

- There is a target of 460 trains each peak period.
- There is a target of 449 trains during the busiest part of the peak period (97.5% of 460).
- There is a target of showing the performance of each tube line on a poster at every underground station.

These targets may represent desired changes (if they are targets which are not currently being met). If they are not currently capable of being met then they represent a *second kind of problem*. There may be obstacles such as insufficient trains, staffing problems or lack of space for posters at some stations.

Given the targets are currently being met, if one or more of these results fails to occur then it could be regarded as a *deviation* from the expected. As such it will be amenable to a structured problem solving approach.

There are a variety of models to guide a manager on how to solve both kinds of problems. John Adair has run courses on managerial decision-making and problem-solving. On these courses he asked managers what they actually did. From this John Adair suggests the following five stages which managers follow in problem-solving or in making a decision:

1 *Define the objective* This involves recognizing that a problem exists which requires some kind of solution or decision.
2 *Collect information* Here the manager gathers facts, opinions, etc. Some may need to be checked. It may also involve establishing what are the cause or causes of a problem. Time available and other resource constraints will be noted.

3 *Develop options* The manager uses a range of devices to identify possible solutions. This may be as simple as just listing out the options. Colleagues and people affected may need to be consulted.

4 *Evaluate and decide* The manager uses various devices to decide upon the most appropriate option. This will involve some kind of selection criteria.

5 *Implement* The chosen option is then acted upon. The progress of the solution is monitored and reviewed.

There is a sixth stage that should always take place, but is frequently omitted.

6 *Learning and feedback* A post mortem may be conducted to ascertain whether the option was worth doing. This can be a source of learning for the future.

Adair suggests that this five-point plan can serve as a general model of how managers behave. It has strong validity and the virtue of simplicity.

Let's see how it might operate in everyday life. Most of us will have to move home at some stage. If we live with other people then it is a problem that affects more than just the individual. The way the process might operate is as follows:

First of all you recognize that there is a problem over your current accommodation. Let us assume that you feel that it has become too small for your needs. You are aware that there is simply not enough space for your family and its possessions. Cupboards bulge and spill their contents. The bicycles rust outside because there is insufficient space indoors. The children need separate bedrooms.

You realize that there is a problem and that you need to make a decision to resolve it.

The next stage is (in most households) to consult with partners to confirm the nature of the problem. Perhaps the cupboards are bulging because they are full of junk and a big *clear-out* is all that is needed. The bikes may not be used at all. Do the children really need separate bedrooms? You also consider the implications of when you might wish to move. How urgent is the problem? Can you wait 6 months or even longer? The sensitive matter of money also rears up. Can you afford a higher mortgage or higher rent for a larger property? If you can, how much more can you afford? To where might you be able to relocate? Moving away from your current area may not be easy.

After gathering information you then consider what options are available. The option of moving to a larger property may be available. Alternatively, you may consider it is possible to extend your current property. If the issue is lack of storage for what you have, you may consider building a shed or moving the car out of the garage. On a more radical note you might consider having a major clear-out of everything not essential to your current needs. Perhaps the children could move into the large bedroom and the bedroom could be partitioned to give separate living space for each child.

The options might then be considered more closely. Some may immediately appear as impractical. The garden may be so small that a shed would overwhelm it. Perhaps the large bedroom is impractical for a partition. Here something will almost certainly become apparent. Moving may be favoured but not outside the area. The reasons why particular options are favoured or discounted have as much to do with subjective (emotional) reasons as objective (factual) ones. The partitioning of the bedroom may be feasible in practical terms but it does not resolve the emotional desire for the children to each have a *separate* bedroom. The wish to move locally may seem irrational given that other areas have more facilities, but you like the local shops and feel comfortable. Eventually you will realize and that decision will bring implementation issues.

Assuming you have decided to move then there is the selling of your current property. If it is rented you negotiate with the landlord about leaving dates and return of any damages deposit. You have to locate a new property and secure it. Then you have to make arrangements to move and have gas, electricity and telephone connected. Probably you will end up with a checklist of tasks and dates by which things need to be done.

Does this seem familiar to you? Problem-solving and decision-making can and do affect people in their everyday life. The principles are not so very different when it comes to putting them into practice in management.

Convergent problem-solving

Kepner and Tregoe (1981) divide problem-solving and decision-making into two separate phases. They developed a technique for structured problem-solving which has been very widely taught around the world. Kepner and Tregoe have a profitable consultancy operating in many countries based upon this problem-solving process.

Kepner and Tregoe's approach involves separating problem-solving and decision-making into two cycles. Each cycle has seven stages. The essence of the technique is that it is based upon a rational approach to problem-solving. A problem is seen as a deviation from an expected outcome. The stages for the problem-solving cycle are as follows:

1 A description of the *deviation* from the expected.
2 An *is/is not* series of statements.
3 *Distinctive* features which characterize the 'is' statements.
4 Whether each distinctive feature represents a *change*.
5 Once all distinctions and changes have been identified to look for possible *causes*.
6 Each cause is then *tested* to see if it explains the deviation in terms of the distinctions and is/is not statements.
7 Finally, the most probable cause is *verified* by testing it out in the work environment where possible.

These stages can be remembered by the phrase: DiD Close Circuit TV (DIDCCTV)

Lets see how this technique can operate in practice. We'll use an example from a large bakery.

The bakery problem

The bakery bought-in the raw ingredients to manufacture bread; the dough was mixed on site by machine from the ingredients. The loaves were then formed by machine and placed on large trays to be baked in several ovens. After they had been baked in the oven the loaves were removed and the trays placed upon trolleys and left to cool. Once the loaves had cooled they were then taken to slicing and wrapping machines where they were sliced and wrapped according to customer requirements. The loaves were then put back on trolleys and wheeled through to the van loading bays. They were then loaded onto the company's vans. The vans delivered the loaves to a wide range of customers. Most of the customers were supermarkets and small shops who sold the bread directly to the individual customer.

The bakery ran on well-established lines. There were clear demarcation lines between management and bakery operatives. The operatives ran the machinery, handled the bread and loaded the vans. There was overall supervision by charge-hands in the bakehouse and in the slice/wrap and loading areas. The charge-hands adopted a free and easy attitude to supervision since the work was routine. More senior managers made occasional visits to the factory floor and, when this happened, operatives made a show of working hard.

However, management became concerned about quality issues. Customers would bring back loaves of bread because they had found cigarette ends embedded in the loaf between two slices of bread. In each case a manager saw the customer and an offer of compensation was made. Some customers were angry, others simply amazed at their find.

The company was understandably very concerned about these incidents. Quite aside from the customer-relations impact there was the food hygiene concern. There were obvious Health and Safety implications.

The problem is one amenable to structured problem-solving using a schema such as the Kepner–Tregoe approach. The way it would be handled would be as follows.

Stage one: the deviation statement

Kepner and Tregoe see the problem as falling into several categories each of which needs to be explored:

- *Identity*: what we are trying to explain.
- *Location*: where the problem is observed.
- *Timing*: when the problem occurs.
- *Magnitude*: how serious the problem is.

The principle is to ask questions based upon the maxim taught to new journalists.

- *Why?* questions: i.e. Why is it a problem?
- *What?* questions: i.e. What is the nature of the problem?
- *Where?* questions: i.e. Where does the problem occur?

- *When?* questions: i.e. When does the problem occur?
- *How?* questions: i.e. How often does it occur?

The result of applying this to the bakery problem would be as follows:

- *Identity:* some loaves are contaminated by foreign matter—namely, cigarette ends.
- *Location:* the problem is observed by customers when unwrapping sliced bread.
- *Timing:* it is an infrequent occurrence that has only recently been noticed.
- *Magnitude:* the problem is potentially very serious for a food manufacturer.

Stage two: specification of what the problem IS and IS NOT

Here the concept is one of comparison. The aim is to compare where the problem IS to where the problem could be but IS NOT. Hence, the application of the Kepner and Tregoe approach to the bakery problem might look as in Figure 10.3.

Stage three: what is distinctive about the IS data

With the availability of *is not* information, comparisons can be made to furnish clues as to what distinguishes the *is* data as seen in Figure 10.4.

Stage four: study distinctions to determine if a change has occurred

Here the aim is to ascertain whether anything has been altered or changed in respect of any of the distinctions that have been identified.

	IS	Could be but IS NOT
Identify	Sliced bread Wrapped bread Cigarette ends	Unsliced bread or rolls Unwrapped bread Other items (e.g. coins)
Location	Customer observed	Noticed by retailers or own staff
Timing	Infrequent Irregular Recent origin	Frequent Regular Long standing
Magnitude	Serious Only few loaves	Minor More loaves

Figure 10.3
The bakery problem (1).

	IS	What is distinctive
Identify	Sliced bread Wrapped bread Cigarette ends	Goes through a slicing machine Goes through a wrapping machine Implies a human cause
Location	Customer observed	Disturbed wrapping paper or disfigured bread would be noticed on despatch or delivery to retailers
Timing	Infrequent Irregular Recent origin	Likely to be a chance happening rather than deliberate sabotage The slicing machines are due for major servicing
Magnitude	Serious Only a few loaves	Smoking while working is a dismissable offence but many staff members are heavy smokers Chance happening

Figure 10.4
The bakery problem (2).

Where there is such a change, then it can give a clue to the possible cause as shown in Figure 10.5.

Stage five: generate possible causes

Here the list of distinctions and changes are used to generate possible explanations for the cause. It is important to recognize that it may be more than one cause that may explain the problem.

- The problem clearly can be seen to affect only certain types of bread. That is the bread that has passed through one of the slicing and wrapping machines. This implies that the cause should be sought there rather than in the dough preparation or oven stages. To introduce cigarette ends into the bread after it has been wrapped would involve a high probability of disturbing the wrapper so that the loader, delivery driver or

	What is distinctive	Changes
Identify	Goes through a slicing machine Goes through a wrapping machine Implies a human cause	No change in machines
Location	Disturbed wrapping paper or disfigured bread would be noticed on despatch or delivery to retailers	No delivery changes
Timing	Likely to be a chance happening rather than deliberate sabotage The slicing machines are due for major servicing	Frequent machine stoppages
Magnitude	Smoking while working is a dismissable offence but many staff members are heavy smokers Chance happening	Smokers recruited

Figure 10.5
The bakery problem (3).

retailer would notice. Therefore, this also suggests that the cause should be sought in an earlier stage of the production process.

- The problem clearly has a human agency since cigarette ends are not part of the production process! Given the employment of smokers, it is probable that a number of the machine operators smoke. It is also possible that the cigarette ends could have been placed in the bread by the customers who complained, so that they could secure compensation.

- The strong stricture against smoking while working—especially while working machinery—would mean that anyone doing so would be careful not to get caught. Dropping cigarette ends on the floor would amount to self-incrimination.

- Perhaps one or more of the machine operators has been smoking adjacent to the machine and has discarded the cigarette end into the machine where it would not be noticed by a passing supervisor.

- The most likely machine for this to apply to is the one overdue for a major service. The frequent stoppages may mean that one operative has been smoking while the other has been trying to fix the fault.

Stage six: test each possible cause against the specification

- The location of the problem with the slicing and wrapping machines matches the specification.

- The recent recruitment of heavy smokers onto the staff would account for the recency.

- The overdue maintenance of one of the machines might also account for idle staff smoking near the machine.

- The possibility of customers putting the cigarette ends into the bread themselves would not explain why it only happened to bread that had gone through the slicing and wrapping machines.

Stage seven: verification of the most probable cause

In this case the company could transfer non-smokers onto the slicing and wrapping machines for a trial period to see if the incidents ceased. They could also affect the major service on the one machine so that people were not tempted to stand idle by it.

> ### Authors' note
>
> In the actual case from which this was drawn, the approach taken was to issue a further warning to staff about smoking on the factory floor. Further incidents of spoiled loaves did occur. The supervisor then endeavoured to track down the guilty party by asking for cigarettes from each of the machine operators and comparing them with those found in the loaves. The *guilty operative*, quite aware of the supervisor's intent, changed his brand of cigarettes.

Divergent problem-solving techniques

Here the objective is to *open up the possibilities*. The methods for being woken up for the Dover ferry could be putting bird seed on the roof, parking illegally or across a factory gate. There are some general principles that usefully apply to such techniques:

- Suspend judgement—get the ideas out *before* evaluating them.
- Get as many ideas as possible.
- Risky ideas are OK—after all, thought is not a crime.
- Seek to join ideas together to build new ones.
- Creative thinking is hard mental exercise—take break and do not try to push yourself or others into long stints at it.

The first question is whether you are *alone* or working in a team. If you are alone it is still possible to think creatively. A lot of artists work that way. Let us briefly outline a couple of techniques to enhance creativity when *on your own*. It should be stressed that these techniques are quite capable of being used in teams as well.

Checklists

Here you use a list of items that might help to clarify aspects of the problem or generate a range of possible solutions. It is often used to inventing new products or services. The four ' Ps' in marketing (Product, Price, Place and Promotion) is a basic checklist that can be used to generate ideas.

Another list was that developed by Eberle (1990) under the acronym of SCAMPER:

Substitute
Combine
Adapt
Magnify (or minimize)
Put to other uses
Eliminate
Reverse

The use of checklists has the advantage of simplicity but the disadvantage that they generate ideas in the particular direction associated with the item on the checklist. Would a checklist have given rise to the invention of a product like Polo mints where the key product characteristic is a hole in the middle?

Problem division

It may be that the problem can be divided into two or more dimensions and that each of these can be divided into categories that can be compared. As an example consider problems in communication within an organization. Figure 10.6 shows how this might be considered along two dimensions. The 3 × 3 matrix gives nine possible areas to generate improvements in communication within the organization. Obviously, further dimensions could also be added (seniority, department, location are all possibilities). These would give rise to far more possible areas to consider.

The use of analogies

An analogy is an observation which links one item to another in some kind of compared relationship. So you may be concerned with the

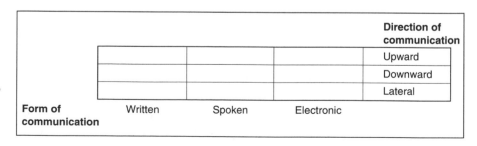

Figure 10.6
Communication problem in an organization.

quality of recruitment in your organization. You would generate analogies drawing on the concept of quality. A list of analogies might be the following:

- Finish of product.
- Attention to detail.
- Amount of thought.
- Checked carefully.
- Assurance that it has been produced to best of one's ability.
- Won't let me down.
- Don't mind paying extra for it.
- Five star hotel.
- Reliability.
- Focus on design.
- Time spent in conceptual stage.
- Conscientious about work and standards.
- Caring for customer.

The analogies are then considered, and ones that seem applicable can be, in turn, developed further. Perhaps the analogy of caring for the customer seems useful. Maybe that can be developed into the conception of regarding potential staff as customers. This could give rise such ideas as:

- Personalized letters.
- Better reception arrangements.
- Interviews arranged at their convenience.
- Providing lunch to interviewees.
- Demonstrating the companies products to interviewees.
- A senior manager greeting potential recruits.

Brainstorming

If you are working with a team then you may find it helpful to use brainstorming as an ideas-generating device. This is a technique developed over 50 years ago by Alex Osbourne. It is widely practised and has taken on a number of forms. The principles that underlie the concept have already been identified above as applying to divergent problem-solving techniques. The avoidance of early judgement and aiming for as many ideas as possible are central to it.

PERSONAL EFFECTIVENESS

The general form taken in a brainstorming sessions is as follows:

- Identify the problem and have it written down in question form. *How can we ensure quality recruitment?* It is important to have the problem couched as a *How?* style question
- Bring together a team of the right size and composition (ideally between 5 and 12 people). They should have been given the problem statement beforehand.
- Outline the format of the session (sequence of events and timeframe).
- Outline the rules of brainstorming:
  - No criticism of other people's ideas.
  - All ideas are OK—the wilder the better.
  - The aim is maximum numbers of ideas.
  - *Hitch-hiking* onto, or amending, other people's ideas is great way to approach it.
- Sometimes (especially with a new team) it helps to conduct a warm up. One of the members takes off a shoe and asks the team to think of uses for just one shoe. This warm up need only take 5–10 minutes.
- Display the problem statement for all to see.
- When the brainstorming session starts, one person writes down all the ideas as they are offered. The session should aim at about 25–40 minutes duration. A subteam of an odd number (say 5) then evaluates the ideas generated and picks the best.
- The selected ideas are reported back to the main team.

It is important to remember that brainstorming itself is about producing ideas *not* evaluating them. The leader must be careful to facilitate the production of as many ideas as possible.

Brainstorming promotes 'wild and offbeat' ideas. When people of different seniority are involved this can inhibit free-ranging ideas. The more junior staff members are often reluctant to suggest things that more senior people may disparage. More senior people may feel suggesting apparently foolish things might cause them to 'lose face'. Brainstorming is best used when:

- The problem in question can be stated in fairly simple terms.
- The leader (manager) feels comfortable about using it.
- Those involved are of a similar seniority (or seniority is not an issue).

Card writing

Where the team is not comfortable or suitable for brainstorming, then a writing technique to generate ideas can be used. People write ideas on cards (which can be anonymous). The cards are circulated or displayed and other team members then develop further ideas from them or seek to improve on the ideas.

The principle of having a clear and simple problem statement applies here as it does with brainstorming. It is also important to brief the team and give time for discussion of the statement to ensure it is understood. The process thus involves the following stages:

- Problem statement.
- Team briefing and discussion.
- Idea generation.
- Ideas evaluation (often by seeking to *team* ideas in some logical way by moving cards around on a table or pin-board).

USING TECHNIQUES TO DEAL WITH COMPLEX DATA

A high level of numeracy is not usually needed to resolve managerial problems, but what is often required is an ability to deal with a large amount of information.

There are several considerations to bear in mind when dealing with large amounts of data. First, it is worth considering the value to be gained by summarizing the information in order to get a general picture. Thus when the newspapers report that inflation has been 5% in the past year, they are giving an overall picture based upon the average rise in prices of a range of items. You accept this and recognize that it does not mean that a specific item (the newspaper, for example) has gone up in price by 5%. Think of the difficulty you would have getting an overall picture of inflation if the newspaper instead just listed the individual price rise of every item you might buy and left it to you to get a picture.

Second, it is useful to bear in mind that in a large set of data usually a relatively small number of the items of information account for a large part of the total amount of information. Therefore, returning to the inflation example, you would perhaps be less troubled by a price rise in caviar than you would by a rise in the mortgage interest rate. The reason for this is that (for the vast majority of people) far more of their income is spent on mortgage repayments than on caviar. An economist called Pareto noted this effect and coined what he described as the 80:20 rule. According to this rule, about 80% of the problem can be accounted for by about 20% of the possible causes.

Let us consider a fairly typical problem confronting a manager. Figure 10.7 provides a list of 40 members of staff and beside each person is the number of days that they have been absent from work in the past year.

Name	Days absent in past year
Adams	0
Akran	0
Ahmed	2
Bolt	9
Boston	65
Buck	1
Carson	5
Chung	10
Churchill	180
Comfort	1
Crawford	1
Crosby	2
Cummings	7
Davis	10
Duncker	50
Dunnett	2
Fallon	50
Field	2
Fulmer	4
Gesch	6
Gordon	45
Hamilton	7
Hicks	55
Jenson	9
Kempner	5
Khalid	5
Maguire	2
McIlroy	4
Miller	4
Osborne	10
Prince	25
Simons	5
Summers	8
Taylor	120
Timpson	2
Torvill	4
Van Oss	6
Vickers	6
Williams	9
Wilson	12

Figure 10.7
A staff sickness problem (1).

Let us assume that the manager is concerned about absence from work and wishes to quantify the problem. One way would be simply to start at the top of the list with Adams and ascertain reasons for Adams' absences. Then you proceed alphabetically down the list to Wilson, identifying in each case what reasons for absence exist and whether they can be tackled.

There is an advantage that there is certainly a clear methodology behind it and if you had to break off from the task you could return to where you left off. It also is *easy* in the sense that you are not setting yourself the task of rearranging the data. Can you think of any reasons why this strategy may not be the most appropriate?

Summarize the data

Another method may be to endeavour to summarize the data in order to get an idea of what the *average* amount of absence was. The total of days absent for the 40 staff is 750 days. If you divide 627 by 40 you get an average of nearly 19 days absence per member of staff. You could then pick out those members of staff who had more than the average amount of absence and look into the reasons for it.

This method has an advantage in that it enables you to focus initially upon the staff who account for most of the absence. If necessary you could then go on to look at the absence of the rest of the staff.

However, the average is affected by a small number of staff with very high absenteeism. You do not get a picture of the absence pattern for the rest of the staff.

Use the 80/20 rule

However, it is also possible to analyse the problem in more detail and look at the proportion of absence accounted for by the *worst 10% or 20%* of staff. As you can see from the breakdown in Figure 10.8, the *top 20%* of the staff account for *80% of the absence*. This illustrates Pareto's 80/20 rule.

It may possibly be one of the most simple and effective rules for a manager in the effective analysis of data. The best way to illustrate it for yourself is to try it out. You can try it out on a number of everyday matters. What about looking at your monthly household expenses. Keep the supermarket till receipts and look at your monthly outgoings (mortgage, loan repayments, utilities, etc.) See what proportion of your total outgoings is taken up by the most expensive items. It

Name	Days absent	Subtotal	% of absence
Adams	0		
Akran	0		
Buck	1		
Comfort	1	2	0.3
Crawford	1		
Crosby	2		
Dunnett	2		
Timpson	2	7	0.9
Maguire	2		
Ahmed	2		
Field	2		
McIlroy	4	10	1.3
Miller	4		
Torvill	4		
Fulmer	4		
Kempner	5	17	2.3
Carson	5		
Khalid	5		
Simons	5		
Van Oss	6	21	2.8
Vickers	6		
Gesch	6		
Cummings	7		
Hamilton	7	26	3.5
Summers	8		
Williams	9		
Jenson	9		
Bolt	9	35	4.7
Chung	10		
Davis	10		
Osborne	10		
Wilson	12	42	5.6
Prince	25		
Gordon	45		
Duncker	50		
Fallon	50	170	22.7
Hicks	55		
Boston	65		
Taylor	120		
Churchill	180	420	56.0
Total days absent		**750**	
Average days absent		**18.8**	

Figure 10.8
A staff sickness problem (2).

probably will not work out to be exactly 80% of the bill that is found in only 20% of the items, but you may be surprised how close it is.

Experienced managers use the Pareto 80/20 rule even though they may never have heard his name. When the board (or the director) says that 10% cuts are required, the responsible manager knows that it is the larger budgets that are the ones most likely to give the basis for meeting it. Hence, in the Health or Education sectors, expenditure cuts of any consequence will involve looking at staff, since staff salaries constitute such a high proportion of the budget. When a 10% increase in sales is required, the sales manager knows most of it is likely to be secured from focusing sales efforts at the top 20% of customers.

There is the old management dictum that 80% of the work is done by 20% of the employees. If you are one of those 20% perhaps you can understand why it is that your manager keeps coming to you for that little bit extra.

Use a diagram to illustrate possible causes

Diagrams can be extremely useful in understanding the nature of a problem. If we consider the *staff sickness* example then we might identify a range of possible causes or factors associated with it. These could be simply listed out. However, they could also be shown on a diagram such as in Figure 10.9. This sort of causal diagram is often known as a 'fishbone diagram' for obvious reasons. The advantage of using this form of representation is that it enables you to add and amend information in a way that is not so easy when you have a conventional form of notes.

Another form of analysis that is often of considerable value in understanding why something has happened (or has failed to happen) is through the use of a 'force field diagram'. This depicts the opposing pressures involved in a given situation. Returning again to the *staff sickness* problem, Figure 10.10 shows the various forces likely to be involved.

There are examples of the use of diagrams to facilitate presentation of information in Chapter 3.

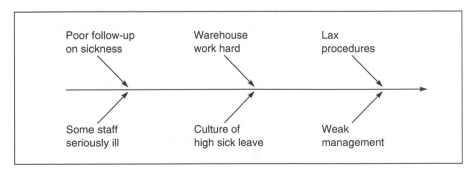

Figure 10.9
A staff sickness problem (3).

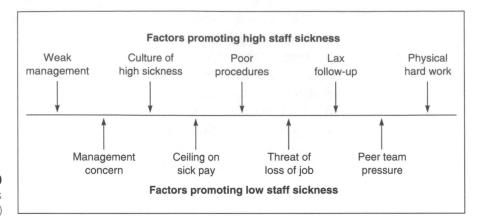

Figure 10.10
A staff sickness problem (4)

EXERCISE

Making use of linear and lateral thinking, as well as convergent and divergent problem-solving, analyse the environment within which you currently work to determine how you and your colleagues may be able to apply these techniques and improve your approaches to problem-solving and decision-making.

PARTICIPATIVE DECISION-MAKING

You will have noticed that problem-solving (and decision-making) is often a team activity. To function effectively in teams, a manager needs to understand something about the process and life of teams. You can refer to Chapter 1 to remind yourself of team development processes and team roles, but for *participative decision-making* a simple approach could be to think in terms of the difference between task and maintenance roles. In most teams both these roles appear. Without a task focus the team often fails to achieve its purpose. If there is no maintenance focus then the team may prove to be a fraught and unpleasant experience for those involved.

- Task roles:
  - Concern with content.
  - Get the job done.
  - Appearance of being *tough*.
  - Related to rationale for team.

- *Maintenance roles*:
    - Give cohesion.
    - Awareness of individual emotional needs.
    - Related to the emotional life of the team.

These two roles complement each other. Task roles are necessary to get the job done. Maintenance roles promote communication and co-operation.

Team process

When bringing a team together to run a project or for other decision-making purposes, it would be helpful to remember the processes involved; they are likely to occur every time a new team comes together, even where some of the members have worked together before. Remember then that the general process is:

Forming→Storming→Norming→Performing→Ending

- *Forming* Anxiety, dependence on leader, search for *code of conduct*, testing out behaviour ('What shall we do?').
- *Storming* Conflict, rebel against leader, resist task ('It's impossible!'), test out leadership, work out implications of task.
- *Norming* Team cohesion emerges, resistance reduces, mutual support emerges, resolve to complete task ('We can do it').
- *Performing* Performance of task, flexible and functional roles, energy high, solutions emerge ('We're getting there').
- *Ending* Discussion moves away from task, members disengage, but they often desire to continue and not stop.

A failure to recognize the need to go through these stages can impede the successful operation of a decision-making team. Frequently the manager (team leader) displays impatience and tries to 'press on' to the performing part of the process. However, the team needs to go through the earlier stages in order to successfully engage in the performing stage.

Ending is also an issue sometimes for project teams. Having dealt with the particular problem that brought them together, the team is often reluctant to disband. Effective problem-solving teams usually have a definite and limited life cycle.

Roles in teams

It is helpful for you as a manager to be aware of different roles that people might play in teams. There is not the scope here to go into a great deal of detail. However, the following role descriptions are useful.

Belbin's nine roles were discussed in Chapter 1, but it should be borne in mind that very often the role, or roles, each individual fulfils will vary depending upon the nature of the decision to be made, or the project being undertaken. Expertise, experience and self-confidence of the team members concerned will change according the task at hand. This is healthy and should be promoted in the light of the discussions above. In general, the following responsibilities will need to undertaken as appropriate to each team, the purpose for its being, and the decisions to be made.

- *Initiator* The initiator starts things off; this usually falls to person who brought the team together. This person is important in changing team direction—giving new impetus.
- *Clarifier* Draws out the precise meaning of individual contributions in relation to the team task. Encourages people to be specific and puts generalizations in more concrete terms.
- *Information provider* May have the information to hand or offers to locate it. May be technical or 'understanding' information. May be superficial or profound but is always relevant to the team task.
- *Questioner* Asks the fundamental questions about team task. These help define nature of task and challenges assumptions being made. Questioner helps team take a step back.
- *Summarizer* Pulls the contributions together. Does not add further information but allows a check on progress. Sometimes formalized (minute-taker) but may be informal. Provides breathing space and allows for reflection, thus separating out stages of the team's work.
- *Supporter* Demonstrates warmth between individuals by supporting contributions or by later including them. Support may be non-verbal.
- *Joker* Obvious—provides light relief and allows team to let off steam—can be destructive to individual or team but can also be positive and creative.
- *Experience sharer* Makes personal statements about general issues relating to the team task. Allows team to move to deeper level. Prevents 'over-professionalism' of team.

■ *Process observer* Appears when team is stuck. Reflects on reason for blockage—'Why are we going around in circles?'

Sometimes as a manager you are able to select the team you would like to assist you if the project is a special or *non-programmed* situation. By this we mean that there are no previous skills, knowledge or understanding available to the team when it needs to make such decisions—they are unique. There are other times (e.g. staff restructuring) when the team you need to work with is already there and the problem is perhaps less unique—it is *programmed* and familiar in terms of the issues to be dealt with.

Returning to the issues discussed at the beginning of the chapter, the more an issue is soft, unbounded and affecting people and their relationships, the more you will be best advised to involve all, or representatives of all, who will be affected by the decisions you are making and their anticipated outcomes.

EXERCISE

You may have a new 'project' to undertake at work, or at least there will be something non-programmed emerging with which you will need to apply participative decision-making techniques. Try applying the various roles and approaches (combining concepts from Chapter 1) to team collaboration in order to plan how you will determine and then implement the necessary decisions.

EXAMPLES OF PROBLEM-SOLVING DRAWN FROM MANAGERS IN VARIOUS ORGANIZATIONS

The workshop approach

At the start of a project we set up a controls workshop. We get together a representative from each area. We have a brainstorming session. We think about all the things that could go wrong.

We then team like-minded comments together under Key Risk Areas. We then have a benchmark for where controls should be placed. We've found it to be quick and effective.

In all the workshops which we have had the majority of people have been complimentary that areas were identified that they had never considered. That it gave them an opportunity to see the system from a different perspective. It has shown people from branches that if they did not do certain things correctly then there would be problems.

Flowcharts are helpful as a way of sequencing events and you can use them to establish control points. You write a report over a number of pages and people sometimes have problems following the sequence of events. Whereas if you put things down in a flow chart then people can follow the logic of what's happening.

David Tait, Manager, Woolwich Building Society

Face to face

We've just gone through a merger with Town & Country Building Society. We had a fairly major exercise in systems conversions and coordination. It went extremely well through meticulous planning. We had a problem on a part of the system of day two of the merger. It was a part of the system that enabled us to get account numbers. The system went down. It took us three days to get it resolved.

In the end someone came up with something that wasn't obvious but enabled us to get around it.

There were a number of interested parties in the problem. What happened was that we were in communication with the interested parties. But when I said 'Have you got the people around a table?' the answer was 'No'. There had been some one-to-one meetings but otherwise it had all been telephone conversations. They needed to look at the paper reports and see why there was a problem with the account numbers. They had spent two-and-a-half days trying unsuccessfully to sort it out. There had been misunderstandings. We got the people together and the problem was solved in half an hour. The solution was to use a slightly different system environment, which would produce the information.

The lesson is common sense—some problems you can solve at arms length but some you can't especially when they are multi-disciplinary and there is no collective responsibility.

Nigel Wright, Manager, Woolwich Building Society

Brainstorming

I find brainstorming is pretty endemic. The other day at a meeting about joint assessment for community care, it was suggested that we did brainstorming and everyone seemed to know how to do it. I was quite surprised how widespread it is.

It depends on whether you are working in a team or on your own. A lot of what I do is working in teams. So chairing skills become important. It's about shutting up noisy people and bringing out quiet people. It's more the manager as a facilitator of a team, which means sometimes taking a dilemma to a team without any real idea of how things might turn out. It's different when you're taking something to a team where the solution is quite clear and you're trying to sell something to them.

If a team is not coming up with a solution the first question is will I notice it. Maybe someone else will and point it out. So I'd bring whatever process is going on to a halt. I'd look for a way out—maybe summarizing or asking other people for a way out.

As an example there was a project-implementation team where we were at a stage where we knew what we were aiming for and we were trying to work out a critical path. We were looking at setting up National Vocational Qualifications. We got as far as describing what kind of assessor training we might need. But then we had some real blocks and we got lost. We were trying to sort out the difference between what we were as a project team and as a team trying to implement it. I felt that I had lost the chair of the meeting a few times. It was like a free for all. I was getting confused over my chairing.

Richard Hooper, Training Manager, London Borough of Enfield Social Services Department.

SUMMARY OF ISSUES

In working through this chapter, you will have encountered a number of issues and perhaps some ideas that are new to you. The objectives of the chapter were to:

- Present an overview of the problem-solving notion.
- Discuss ways to generate *creative* thought.

- Define vertical and lateral thinking and discuss their uses and value.
- Present some convergent and divergent problem-solving strategies.
- Discuss the value of participate decision-making.

How well have the authors met these objectives?

More importantly, how have you approached and used the material yourself, and how much have you developed since the beginning of your course of study, or working through the chapter? You are strongly recommended to extend your research and study to include as much as possible of the material identified in further reading and references below, so that you can build on your expertise, incorporating more complex approaches and ideas as you develop further in your managerial role.

These objectives, if re-revisited over a period of time and put into practice in your job, should help you to achieve the personal competency of thinking and decision-taking, broken down into the elements identified in the table at the end of the chapter. In order for you to reflect on your own behaviour and that of others with whom you work, you might find it useful to use the table as a self-assessment check (reproduce as many as you wish) to re-evaluate your skills and knowledge.

PREPARING FOR ACTION PLANNING

Remember to review the checklist of questions, as identified in the Introduction to this book, at Appendix 1.

Analyse your own behaviour in terms of strengths (positive outcomes) and weaknesses (negative effects), in dealing with actual work-based occurrences with regards to the various situations discussed in this chapter, and summarized above.

Decide how you might deal with them differently in the future and what are your immediate training requirements and future development needs.

Discuss them with appropriate others and negotiate how you might address them.

FURTHER READING AND REFERENCES

Berne, E. (1987) *The Games People Play: The Psychology of Human Relationships*. London: Penguin. ISBN: 0-14-002768-8

Cooke, S. and Slack, S. (1991) *Making Management Decisions*. New Jersey: Prentice Hall. ISBN: 0-13543406-8

de Bono, E. (1996) *Textbook of Wisdom*. London: Penguin. ISBN: 0-670-87011-0

Eberle, R. (1981) *Scamper, Games for Imagination Development*. Buffalo: D.O.K. Publishers

Eberle, R. (1981) *Scamper On*. Buffalo: D.O.K. Publishers

Fletcher, W. (1990) *Creative People*. Hutchinson Business Books. ISBN: 0-09174043-6

Goleman, D. (1996) *Emotional Intelligence: Why It Can Matter more than IQ*. London: Bloomsbury Publishing. ISBN: 0-7475-2830-6

Huczynski, A. and Buchanan, D. (2001) *Organizational Behaviour: An Introductory Text* (4th edition). Harlow: Pearson Education (Chapter 22). ISBN: 0-273-65102-1

Kepner, C. and Tregoe B. (1981) *The New Rational Manager*. Princeton: Princeton University Press

Krishnamurti, J. and Bohm, D. (1999) *The Limits of Thought: Discussions*. London: Routledge. ISBN: 0-415-19398-2

Margerison, C.J. (1974) *Managerial Problem Solving*. New York: McGraw-Hill. ISBN: 0070844453

Mintzberg, H. (1973) *The Nature of Managerial Work*. New York: Harper & Row. ISBN: 0060445564

Rawlinson, J.G. (1981) *Creative Thinking and Brainstorming*. Aldershot: Gower Publishing. ISBN: 0566022478

Rickards, T. (1990) *Creativity and Problem Solving at Work*. Aldershot: Gower Publishing. ISBN: 0566028913

Competency element	Competency level: 1 (low)– 5 (high)	Requires development	No direct experience	What can help? (identify oppor- tunities)	Who can help?	When can it be achieved?	How can it be achieved?
Breaks situations down into simple tasks and activities							
Identifies a range of elements in and perspectives on a situation							
Identifies implications, consequences or causal relationships in a situation							
Uses a range of ideas to explain the actions, needs and motives of others							

Uses her/his own experience and evidence from others to identify problems and understand situations	Identifies patterns or meaning from events and data that are not obviously related	Builds a total and valid picture (or concept) from restricted or incomplete data (which happens to be most of the time)	Produces a variety of solutions before taking a decision	Balances intuition with logic in decision-making

Reconciles and makes use of a variety of perspectives when making sense of a situation	Produces her/his own ideas from experience and practice	Takes the experience and practice of others into account	Takes decision that are realistic for the situation	Focuses on facts, problems and solutions when handling an emotional situation (not personalities)	Takes decisions in uncertain situations, or based on restricted information when necessary

Appendixes

This checklist is provided to help your *action planning*. It will give you an overall idea of the kinds of issues that might occur throughout your personal management development, and will provide you with those questions that can be most effectively adapted to the situations under discussion.

- Who/where are your largest customer bases (customers may be internal or external to the organization)?
- How do you find out about your customers needs?
- How do you make customers aware that your products/services are available?
- How effective are the communication mechanisms that you use?
- What would you do if there was a low take-up of the products/services you provide?
- How do you currently co-ordinate your activities in order to develop your product/service provision?
- How are organizational performance standards determined and by whom?
- How do you ensure that these performance standards are being met?
- How do you measure these standards?
- How do you deal with any customer complaints?

- How do you handle health and safety issues at your work-place?
- How appropriate is your location for the product/service you provide?
- Which outside agencies do you currently liaise with?
- Are there any joint working arrangements in your product/service provision (this may apply across teams, or between organizations)?
- Who are these and for what purposes do the arrangements exist?
- What actions would you/have you taken with others at times of particular difficulty or change?
- Which methods do you use to analyse facts and figures for your job purposes?
- How do you present these facts and figures to others for decision-making purposes?
- How effective are your analytical and mathematical skills in convincing others?
- Were the outcomes of these presentations appropriate for the decision-making purposes?
- How might you improve your analytical and mathematical skills?
- How do you liaise with others at off-site locations?
- How is information fed back into the decision-making process?
- What, if any, interdepartmental group activities do you participate in?
- What are the main purposes of these groups?
- How would you identify your own development needs within the job role?
- How would you meet the needs you have identified?
- How do you evaluate your progress?
- What are the main working relationships you maintain?
- How do you/would you maximize productive relationships and networks?
- How do you/would you promote equal opportunities within and between those with whom you relate?
- What are the key elements, in your opinion, in promoting effective working relationships?
- What do you see as your strengths in establishing good working relationships and which aspects would you want to develop further?

- How would you/do you go about establishing and developing working relationships with others, both internal and external to the organization?
- How easy/difficult do you find asking support of or taking problems to others?
- How might this be improved?
- How easy/difficult do you think others find asking you for support or in bringing their problems to you?
- How could it be improved?
- What support would you/do you give to others in their relations with others outside the organization (or department)?
- How could these relationships be improved?
- What formal and informal actions would you/have you taken to actively promote effective working relationships and prevent their breakdown?
- How do you/would you deal with conflict in your relationships or in the relationships of others arising from:
  - Differences of opinion on courses of action?
  - Personal animosity?
  - Moral dilemmas (between individuals or individuals and the organization)?
  - Racism?
  - Sexism?
  - Other discriminatory behaviour?
  - Non-compliance with organizational rules, norms or values?
- What do you see as *counselling* in the workplace?
- What is the purpose and what are the limitations of workplace counselling?
- What is your role as counsellor—both formally and informally?
- What are the key elements of effective workplace counselling?
- Who are the parties involved in starting and inducting those for whom you will be responsible?
- How effective is this process, the people involved, and how might you improve it?
- How do you determine the training and development needs of yourself and others?
- What activities do you use for the development of others (formal and informal)?
- How do you plan these activities?

- How do you review progress and evaluate the outcomes of training and development?
- Have you taken any steps to improve equality of opportunity in the development of others?
- What were the outcomes?
- Have there been any specific incidences which have caused you concern for the equality of opportunities in the development of all?
- How do you set work objectives (or participate in setting them) for yourself and others?
- How do you review and update these objectives?
- Identify an objective you have had to meet and specify how you planned the work activities to meet this objective.
- How did you decide which method would work best?
- How do you decide how to allocate work to others?
- What would you say is your leadership style?
- What are the effects of your style on others? For example, are you/do you think you are making the most use of the skills available to you (yours and others)?
- How does this tie in with the overall work objectives set?
- How do you evaluate your own performance against your work objectives?
- How do you evaluate the performance of others against their objectives?
- What methods do you use to give feedback to others about their performance?
- Can you pin-point anything which you consider particularly important when giving feedback?
- How do you address equal opportunities issues in this aspect of your work?
- What information do you need to do your job and for what purposes?
- Do you have any problems obtaining this information?
- To whom do you supply information?
- How much time do you spend in:
  - Gathering information?
  - Analysing information?
  - Providing information?
- How do you go about gathering, analysing and providing information?
- Can these methods be improved?
- How do you currently store and receive information?

- How often do you hold meetings (formal and informal), briefings and group discussions?
- For what purposes do you hold meetings, etc.?
- Do your meetings always (often, sometimes, rarely):
  - Start on time?
  - Finish on time?
  - Achieve their objectives?
- Do you always have the necessary information in advance of the meetings?
- Do you always supply the necessary information in advance of the meetings?
- Are you confident about:
  - Chairing meetings?
  - Contributing to the purpose of meetings?
  - Taking minutes?
- Would you say your meetings are always:
  - Well prepared?
  - Well administered?
  - Well controlled?
- Are the people at your meetings there because they:
  - Have a part to play?
  - Have an interest?
  - Have been sent?
- What are the meeting's follow-up processes?
- Do your meetings result in positive action? Have you attended committees in your current role and prepared reports for these committees?

Questions devised by, and adapted from, the Crediting Competence Team at South Bank University (reproduced with permission).

APPENDIX 2: EXAMPLES OF UNITS OF COMPETENCE

Those who are either relatively new to management, or are aspiring to become managers, should aim to achieve competence in all of the following units. This book aims to help you to develop your *behavioural* skills, as identified in the *Personal Competency Model*, as discussed earlier in this Introduction, and which are required for you to be *competent* in all of the managerial *functions* as identified in the following summary. It does not specify which units would be appropriate to any particular qualification. Qualifications are likely to present students and candidates with the need to address a core of competences and to select some options from a specific group of units.

The units have been numbered sequentially for ease of reference and bear no relation to the *actual* unit numbers as they appear in the MCI (Management Charter Initiative) integrated structure.

Unit number and title	Element title
A3 Manage activities to meet customer requirements	A3.1 Implement plans to meet customer requirements
	A3.2 Maintain healthy, safe and productive work conditions
	A3.3 Ensure activities meet customer requirements
A4 Contribute to improvements at work	A4.1 Support improvements in activities
	A4.2 Recommend improvements to organizational plans
F4 Implement quality assurance systems	F4.1 Establish quality assurance systems
	F4.2 Maintain quality assurance systems
	F4.3 Recommend improvements to quality assurance systems
B2 Manage the use of physical resources	B2.1 Secure resources for activities
	B2.2 Use resources effectively for activities
B3 Manage the use of financial resources	B3.1 Make recommendations for expenditure
	B3.2 Control expenditure against budgets
C2 Develop own resources	C2.1 Develop oneself to improve performance
	C2.2 Manage own time and resources to meet objectives
C5 Develop productive working relationships	C5.1 Develop the trust and support of colleagues and team members
	C5.2 Develop the trust and support of one's immediate manager
	C5.3 Minimize interpersonal conflict

C8 Select personnel for activities	C8.1 Establish personnel requirements for activities
	C8.2 Select personnel against team and organizational requirements
C10 Develop teams and individuals to enhance performance	C10.1 Identify training and development needs for teams and individuals
	C10.2 Plan the training and development needs for teams and individuals
	C10.3 Develop teams to improve performance
	C10.4 Support individual learning and development
	C10.5 Assess teams and individuals against training and development objectives
	C10.6 Improve development activities
C12 Lead the work of teams and individuals to achieve objectives	C12.1 Allocate work to teams and individuals
	C12.2 Agree objectives and work plans for teams and individuals
	C12.3 Evaluate the performance of teams and individuals
	C12.4 Provide feedback on performance to teams and individuals
D2 Facilitate meetings	D2.1 Participate in group discussions or meetings
	D2.2 Lead group discussions or meetings
D4 Provide information to support decision-making	D4.1 Obtain information for decision-making
	D4.2 Record and store information for decision-making
	D4.3 Analyse information to support decision-making
	D4.4 Advise and inform others

APPENDIX 3: THE PERSONAL COMPETENCY MODEL

The PCM identifies the behaviours and skills that are necessary for managers to develop before they are able to prove competence in the functions of management. Although each unit attempts to identify key behaviours and skills for ease of learning, development and assessment, it must be understood that all these behaviours and skills are necessary for managers to apply across all the units of competence, at different times and under varying circumstances.

Competency	Behavioural indicators
Act assertively	
Managers who act assertively show resilience and determination to succeed in the face of pressure and difficulties; they:	Take a leading role in initiating action and making decisions Take personal responsibility for making things happen Take control of situations and events
	Show integrity and fairness in decision-making Act in an assured and unhesitating manner when faced with a challenge Say no to unreasonable requests State own position and views clearly in conflict situations Maintain beliefs, commitment and effort in spite of set-backs or opposition
Act strategically	
Managers who act strategically identify the way forward in a complex environment, referring constantly to a longer-term vision for the organization; they:	Display an understanding of how the different parts of the organization and its environment fit together. Work towards a clearly defined vision of the future. Clearly relate goals and actions to the strategic aims of the organization. Take opportunities when they arise to achieve the longer-term aims or needs of the organization

Behave ethically	
Managers who behave ethically identify concerns and resolve complex dilemmas in an open, reasoned manner; they:	Comply with legislation, industry regulation, professional and organizational codes Set objectives and create cultures that are ethical Identify the interests of stakeholders and their implications for the organization and individuals Clearly identify and raise ethical concerns relevant to the organization Work towards the resolution of ethical dilemmas based on reasoned approaches Understand and resist personal pressures that encourage non-ethical behaviour Understand and resist apparent pressures from organizational systems to achieve results by any means
Build teams	
Managers who build effective teams encourage team effort, build cohesion and maintain motivation; they:	*Manage others:* Actively build relationships with others Make time available to support others Encourage and stimulate others to make the best use of their abilities Evaluate and enhance people's capability to do their jobs Provide feedback designed to improve people's future performance Show respect for the views and actions of others
	Show sensitivity to the needs and feelings of others Use power and authority in a fair and equitable manner
	Relate to others: Keep others informed about plans and progress Clearly identify what is required of others Invite others to contribute to planning and organizing work Set objectives that are both achievable and challenging Check individuals' commitment to a specific course of action Use a variety of techniques to promote morale and productivity

	Protect the work of others against negative impacts Identify the work of others against negative impacts Identify and resolve causes of conflict or resistance Communicate a vision that generates excitement, enthusiasm and commitment
Communicate	
Managers who communicate effectively are able to share information, ideas and arguments with a variety of audiences; they:	Listen actively, ask questions, clarify points and rephrase others' statements to check mutual understanding Identify the information needs of listeners Adopt communication styles appropriate to listeners and situations, including selecting an appropriate time and place Use a variety of media and communication aids to reinforce points and maintain interest Present difficult ideas and problems in ways that promote understanding Confirm listeners' understanding through questioning and interpretation of non-verbal signals Encourage listeners to ask questions or rephrase statements to clarify their understanding Modify communication in response to feedback from listeners
Focus on results	
Managers who focus on results are proactive and take responsibility for getting things done; they:	*Plan and prioritize:* Maintain a focus on objectives
	Tackle problems and take advantage of opportunities as they arise Prioritize objectives and schedule work to make best use of time and resources Set objectives in uncertain and complex situations Focus personal attention on specific details that are critical to the success of a key event

	Strive for excellence: Actively seek to do things better Use change as an opportunity for improvement Establish and communicate high expectations of performance, including setting an example to others Set goals that are demanding of self and others Monitor quality of work and progress against plans Continually strive to identify and minimise barriers to excellence
Influence others	
Managers who influence the behaviour of others plan their approaches and communicate clearly using a variety of techniques; they:	Develop and use contacts to trade information, and obtain support and resources Present themselves positively to others Create and prepare strategies for influencing others Understand the culture of the organization and act to work within it or influence it
Manage self	
Managers skilled in managing themselves show adaptability to the changing world, taking advantage of new ways of doing things; they:	*Control emotions and stress:* Give a consistent and stable performance Take action to reduce the causes of stress Accept personal comments or criticism without becoming defensive Remain calm in difficult or uncertain situations Handle others' emotions without becoming personally involved in them
	Manage personal learning and development: Take responsibility for meeting own learning and development needs Seek feedback on performance to identify strengths and weaknesses Learn from own mistakes and those of others Change behaviour where needed as a result of feedback Reflect systematically on own performance and modify behaviour accordingly
	Develop self to meet the demands of changing situations Transfer learning from one situation to another

Search for information	
Managers with information-search skills gather many different kinds of information by a variety of means; they:	Establish information networks to search for and gather relevant information Actively encourage the free exchange of information Make best use of existing sources of information Seek information from multiple sources Challenge the validity and reliability of sources of information Push for concrete information in an ambiguous situation
Think and take decisions	
Managers displaying thinking and decision-making skills analyse and make deductions from information in order to form judgements and take decisions; they:	*Analyse*: Break processes down into tasks and activities Identify a range of elements in and perspectives on a situation Identify implications, consequences or causal relationships in a situation Use a range of ideas to explain the actions, needs and motives of others
	Conceptualize: Use own experience and evidence from others to identify problems and understand situations Identify patterns or meaning from events and data that are not obviously related Build a total and valid picture from restricted or incomplete data
	Take decisions: Produce a variety of solutions before taking a decision Balance intuition with logic in decision-making Reconcile and make use of a variety of perspectives when making sense of a situation Produce own ideas from experience and practice Take decisions that are realistic for the situation Focus on facts, problems and solutions when handling an emotional situation Take decisions in uncertain situations or based on restricted information when necessary

PCM (Crown Copyright, 1997).

Index

Page references in italic indicate figures